Learner-Centered Assessment on College Campuses

Related Titles of Interest

For more information or to purchase a book, please call 1-800-278-3525.

Learner-Centered Assessment on College Campuses

Shifting the Focus from Teaching to Learning

Mary E. Huba
Iowa State University

Jann E. Freed
Central College

Allyn and Bacon

Boston • London • Toronto • Sydney • Tokyo • Singapore

Executive Editor: Stephen D. Dragin
Series Editorial Assistant: Bridget McSweeney
Marketing Manager: Brad Parkins

Copyright © 2000 by Allyn & Bacon
A Pearson Education Company
Needham Heights, MA 02494

Internet www.abacon.com

Library of Congress Cataloging-in-Publication Data

Huba, Mary E.
    Learner-centered assessment on college campuses / shifting the
focus from teaching to learning / Mary E. Huba, Jann E. Freed.
        p.   cm.
    Includes bibliographical references and index.
    ISBN 0-205-28738-7
    1. College teaching. 2. College students—Rating of.
3. Learning—Evaluation. 4. Educational tests and measurements.
I. Freed, Jann E.   II. Title
LB2331.H83   2000
378.1′25—dc21   99-38525
                                                   CIP

Printed in the United States of America
10

To George, Sarah, and Laura
Eleanor, Ed, and Chris
For encouragement, love, and support

To Eloise and Dick for consistently placing a high
value on education and learning
To Brenda for her appreciation of creative energy and activities
To John for supporting my professional development
To MacLean, Austin, and Marshall for understanding my
commitment to this project

Contents

Foreword

My own involvement in outcomes assessment dates from 1979, when the Tennessee Higher Education Commission announced that henceforth a portion of the state appropriation for public institutions would be based on campus performance on such measures as tests of students' general and disciplinary knowledge and alumni surveys. As a faculty intern in the Office of the Chancellor, I offered to use my background in program evaluation to help the University of Tennessee, Knoxville (UTK) respond to the state's performance funding initiative. I spent the next dozen years there encouraging faculty and administrators to use the best measurement tools available—and these were often created by the UTK faculty themselves—to assess student learning and to use the results to improve teaching, curriculum, and student services.

In the mid-1980s a half-dozen other states adopted their own versions of performance funding and several of the regional accrediting associations began to require outcomes assessment of member colleges and universities. By 1992 I thought it was time to ask the question, "Are we making a difference with assessment?" I assembled a team of some 60 coauthors and we developed the book *Making a Difference: Outcomes of a Decade of Assessment in Higher Education* (Jossey-Bass, 1993).

Specifically, I was interested in the answers to three questions. As a result of all of our activity in assessing outcomes: (1) Had instruction improved?, (2) Were students learning more?, and (3) Were institutions more effective? Then, as indeed is still the case, there was only scant evidence that students were learning more or that institutions were becoming more effective. There are no national standards or measures of college student learning and no widely accepted patterns of evidence for judging institutional effectiveness.

But I do believe that the powerful influences of the last two decades that have led so many academics to think about assessing the outcomes of college have produced improvements in instruction. And now Mary Huba and Jann Freed document and teach many of these improved instructional approaches in their wonderful new book, *Learner-Centered Assessment on College Campuses*.

Assessing college outcomes requires that faculty come together to determine what curricular and course outcomes should be. Huba and Freed emphasize that teachers and students are part of an educational system in which each part affects the behaviors and properties of the whole. In coming together to contemplate their collective impact and how to assess it, large numbers of faculty have begun to discuss their TEACHING—something that most had previously taken for granted, carried out privately, and seen little reason to improve.

After exchanging anecdotes about instructional strategies that seem to work in individual instances, faculty have been drawn to the literature and have discovered that decades of research on human learning have produced findings that various groups have summarized in sets of "principles of good practice." Much college teaching has been improved as faculty have been guided by the knowledge that students learn more if we set high expectations for them; engage them actively in their learning; provide opportunities for them to interact in connection with their work with faculty and with other students; and assess their progress often, providing prompt feedback. Huba and Freed have drawn on the reservoir of knowledge about ways to enhance learning, basing *Learner-Centered Assessment on College Campuses* on the theory of constructivism, which holds that students learn by constructing, rather than receiving knowledge. Moreover, they have attempted to make active learners of their readers throughout the book by providing regular opportunities to (1) consider what one knows about a topic before learning more, (2) reflect on what has been learned, and (3) try out the new learning in one's own setting.

Huba and Freed identify the continuous quality improvement (CQI) movement as a factor in the paradigm shift from teaching to learning. I agree, and believe that faculty attention to assessment has also played a role in this movement. After all, the fundamental assessment question is, "What did the student learn?"

In addition to demonstrating how assessment has improved approaches to instruction in a broad sense, the Huba and Freed volume also provides information about specific assessment tools, including classroom assessment techniques, CQI approaches to providing feedback, scoring rubrics, tasks for assessing problem-solving and critical-thinking skills, and portfolios. This work speaks directly to faculty, in terms they will readily embrace, about a concept many have approached previously with some fear and loathing—outcomes assessment. Its basis in theory and its eminently readable explanations of emerging practices in assessment make it a valuable faculty development resource. Thus it will contribute significantly to the very concept it explicates so expertly: the improvement of instruction through learner-centered assessment.

Trudy W. Banta
Vice Chancellor for Planning and
   Institutional Improvement
Professor of Higher Education
Indiana University–Purdue University
Indianapolis

Preface

This book developed from a conversation about college teaching that took place on an airplane after the 1996 annual meeting of the Association for the Study of Higher Education (ASHE). Catching up on developments and interests in our professional lives over the past several years, we realized that the ideas that excited each of us—assessment for one and continuous quality improvement for the other—were different but highly compatible "takes" on the same topic. Although each of us had been attending different professional meetings and reading different literatures over the years, we had become passionate about the same topic—learner-centered teaching. Our excitement about building a conversational bridge across two disciplines led to the idea of joining these disciplines in a book for college faculty.

On the one hand, we reasoned, a learner-centered approach should feel like second nature to college professors. Most of us who are faculty members became professors because we love to learn and share what we've learned with others. In a learner-centered approach, professors and students learn together. As we professors learn more about the intriguingly different ways our students acquire knowledge, we learn how to teach more effectively. As a result, our students learn concepts and skills that will support them throughout life as effective citizens and as professionals in their fields. A book on this topic should be something that faculty would want to read.

On the other hand, we acknowledged, many faculty have been reluctant to jump on the "learner-centered" bandwagon. One reason for this is clear:

people practice what they know. What most of us know about teaching comes from our own experience as students in traditional teacher-centered classrooms. Few of us have been formally trained to be effective teachers. As ironic as it sounds, mastery of a discipline does not translate into mastery of teaching the subject.

PRACTICING WHAT WE TEACH

We decided that any successful book about new approaches to teaching and assessing would have to consider its faculty readers to be learners and take into account current learning theory. New information about how people learn is the basis of constructivism, a contemporary learning theory that is forcing a paradigm shift in the education community. Even faculty who have formal educational backgrounds in pedagogy are finding that major changes in their approach to teaching are needed.

This is because researchers have discovered that students learn by constructing knowledge rather than by receiving knowledge from others. This apparently simple theory has profound implications for the way we teach. As professors, we must help students become actively involved in their learning and feel a sense of ownership for it. We need to help students review and examine what they already know about a topic and explore the ways in which it is compatible or incompatible with new information they encounter. Students need to talk about new ideas and practice new skills, and it helps to have a teacher who is willing to coach and guide them.

In developing this book, we have used the principles of constructivism as our guide. We begin each chapter with a reflection exercise entitled Making Connections that provides you with an opportunity to review what you already know about the topic of the chapter, getting you set, if you will, to think about new ideas so that you can examine them in terms of what you already know. At the end of each section in the chapter, there is a Reflections exercise in which we pose some questions for you to ask yourself as you attempt to create meaning or "make sense" of the ideas in the section. Finally, at the end of each chapter, there is an opportunity to Try Something New. Completing this section will help you apply some of the techniques presented in the chapter. Additional learning aids are found in the use of numerous examples, as well as in step-by-step guidelines for implementing the techniques discussed. Over 65 figures are included in the book.

In addition to constructivism, another factor that influenced the development of this book is the continuous quality improvement (CQI) movement. CQI principles, as they are applied to education, support the need for a transition to a learner-centered approach. Quality principles and practices suggest that education must become focused on the needs of learners rather than the needs of teachers. Data about teaching and learning should form the basis of instructional decision making, and both professors and students should be empowered to make those decisions. Every student and every course should be viewed as part of a system of interrelated and interdependent parts, and every part should be targeted for continuous improvement. All employees of the institution participate in the system, and the whole system is directed toward improved learning.

OVERVIEW OF THE BOOK

The first section of this book is devoted to the development of a learner-centered perspective. Chapter 1 discusses the role of assessment in facilitating a shift from a teacher-centered paradigm of teaching to one that is learner-centered. Chapter 2 describes the hallmarks of learner-centered teaching that derive from principles of constructivism and continuous quality improvement. Chapter 3 discusses principles of good practice in learner-centered assessment that have been developed for the field of higher education in recent years.

The second section of the book, Chapters 4 through 8, is devoted to practical techniques for strengthening our teaching by enhancing our approach to assessment. The techniques presented form a repertoire of strategies that can be used in assessment in courses, in an academic program, or at the institution. Chapter 9 concludes with a discussion of issues we must face at both the individual and organizational levels when shifting to a learner-centered approach.

INTENDED AUDIENCES

We envision this book as a resource for practicing or aspiring faculty individually or in many collective settings: new faculty orientations, informal groups of faculty seeking to improve their teaching, graduate teaching seminars in any discipline, and college teaching methods classes in higher education graduate programs. Consultants may also find the book useful when working with faculty in programs to improve teaching.

ACKNOWLEDGMENTS

We are grateful to our many colleagues and friends who influenced the development of the book. Brad Skaar planted the seed for such a volume several years ago when he visited one of us in desperation, asking for any extension-like handouts we had written on assessment. (At the time, we had none.) We are also deeply grateful to Linda Calvin and Sherry Dogruyusever, passionate teachers who lit a fire when they shared the excitement of learner-centered assessment in their lives.

We extend heartfelt thanks to Barbara Licklider whose insight into learning, dedication to learners, and ever-present willingness to share continually inspire and educate. We also thank the members of the Student Outcomes Assessment Committee at Iowa State University. Their wisdom about people and institutions enhanced our ability to apply theory in practice. Thank you to all those who allowed us to include their experiences in the book, as well as Sally Beisser, Ann Dieterich, Christopher Dzimadzi, Carol Fulton, John Littrell, Daniel Seymour, Marla Smith, Elizabeth Stanley, and members of the veteran LEA/RN group at Iowa State University, who either shared ideas, gathered information, or provided generous assistance in reviewing and reacting to drafts of the text.

We extend our gratitude to the following reviewers who were selected by Allyn and Bacon to review the manuscript: Donald Farmer, Kings College; Frances K. Stage, Indiana University–Bloomington; and Peter J. Gray, Syracuse University. Their reactions and suggestions were extremely helpful, and we appreciate the time they devoted to the reviews. We give our final thanks to Steve Dragin, our editor, who patiently guided us along as we learned to write a book.

AN INVITATION

In this book, we invite you to do what you love to do best—inquire. Explore the idea of learner-centered assessment and your role within it. Investigate new approaches to assessment that may challenge your basic beliefs about how learning takes place. Incorporate your current assessment strategies into a more expanded and varied repertoire. Focus on helping students use feedback to improve their learning. Learn how to improve your teaching by seeking feedback from students and critically reflecting on your practices. In whatever setting you use the book, we hope your investigations will be characterized by the excitement of learning—learning that relies on assessment for continual improvement.

▶ 1

Experiencing a Paradigm Shift Through Assessment

Definition of insanity: Doing the same thing, the same way, all the time—but expecting different results (Anonymous).

It is tradition. It was a part of my training, and seems like what I should be doing. I feel somehow guilty when I am not lecturing (Creed, 1986, p. 25).

Suddenly I *saw* things differently, and because I *saw* differently, I *thought* differently, I *felt* differently, and I *behaved* differently (Covey, 1989, p. 31).

Making Connections

As you begin to read the chapter, think about ideas and experiences you've already had that are related to experiencing a paradigm shift . . .

- What are your assumptions about how learners learn?
- What are your assumptions about the best way to teach?
- How do you know if your teaching has been successful?

- How have your ideas about teaching and learning changed over the years?
- How can you help your students improve what they learn and how they learn?
- What are your students learning that will help them be successful in the information age?

Continued

Making Connections   *Continued*

- In your role as a teacher, what is your relationship to the rest of your institution?
- What do you know about the assessment movement in higher education?
- How do assessment results help you understand what your stu-

dents know and don't know, what they can do and can't do?

What else do you know about experiencing a paradigm shift?

What questions do you have about experiencing a paradigm shift?

Tomorrow's citizens, tomorrow's leaders, tomorrow's experts are sitting in today's college classrooms. Are they learning what they need to know? Are faculty using teaching methods that prepare them for future roles?

Struggling to answer these questions, those of us who teach in higher education are looking at how we teach and trying to evaluate what we do. This is not an easy task. The many years we spent as students shaped our notions of what teaching is all about. These notions may be so deeply embedded in our world views that they are virtually invisible to us, eluding objective examination. On top of that, many of us have spent additional years teaching as we were taught—practicing the "old ways." Few of us have had opportunities to study teaching the way we study topics in our own disciplines. It is difficult to step back, analyze current approaches critically, make revisions, and move ahead, confident that the new direction is the right one.

TEACHER-CENTERED AND LEARNER-CENTERED PARADIGMS OF INSTRUCTION

Most of us learned to teach using the lecture method, and research has shown that traditional, teacher-centered methods are "not *in*effective . . . but the evidence is equally clear that these conventional methods are *not* as effective as some other, far less frequently used methods" (Terenzini & Pascarella, 1994, p. 29). In fact, the lecture method is clearly *less effective* than other methods in changing thoughts and attitudes (Bligh, 1972; Eison & Bonwell, 1988). These findings suggest that a change in the traditional method of college teaching is needed in order to enhance student learning (Kellogg Commission on the Future of State and Land-Grant Universities, 1997, 1999).

The primary learning environment for undergraduate students, the fairly passive lecture–discussion format where faculty talk and most students listen, is contrary to almost every principle of an optimal student learning setting . . . Intimate faculty-student contact that encourages feedback, that motivates students, that allows students to perform is the exception and not the norm (Guskin, 1997, pp. 6–7).

The current view in higher education is that we should focus on student learning rather than teaching in order to improve students' college experiences (e.g., Cross, 1998). The reason is not so much that our current approach is "broken" and in need of "fixing," but rather that we are underperforming (Engelkemeyer & Brown, 1998). We are failing to use existing knowledge about learning and our own institutional resources to produce graduates who leave the institution ready to succeed in the information age. "We have failed to realize the synergistic effect of designing, developing, and delivering curricula, programs, and services that collaboratively and collectively deepen, enhance, and enable higher levels of learning" (p. 10).

As shown in Figure 1–1, the shift from teaching to learning has been endorsed by many prominent leaders and theorists in higher education since the mid-1980s. In addition, in 1998, the Joint Task Force on Student Learning appointed by the American Association for Higher Education (AAHE), the American College Personnel Association (ACPA), and the National Association of Student Personnel Administrators (Joint Task Force, 1998a, 1998b) alerted us to the need for all segments of a college campus to work together to enhance and deepen student learning. The Task Force developed a set of propositions about learning that can be used by both faculty and student affairs professionals to guide future practice. These propositions are presented in Chapter 2.

The idea of focusing on learning rather than teaching requires that we rethink our role and the role of students in the learning process. To focus on learning rather than teaching, we must challenge our basic assumptions about how people learn and what the roles of a teacher should be. We must unlearn previously acquired teaching habits. We must grapple with fundamental questions about the roles of assessment and feedback in learning. We must change the culture we create in the courses we teach. In other words, we must experience a paradigm shift.

What is a paradigm? Paradigm means model, pattern, or example. A paradigm establishes rules, defines boundaries, and describes how things behave within those boundaries (Barker, 1992). A paradigm is like the rules of a game that define the playing field and the domain of possibilities on that field. A new paradigm changes the playing field by making it larger or smaller, or even moving it somewhere else, which in turn affects the domain

- Students learn by becoming involved . . . Student involvement refers to the amount of physical and psychological energy that the student devotes to the academic experience (Astin, 1985, pp. 133–134).

- The routine is always the same: Begin the unit, teach the unit, give the students a test, correct the test, return the test, review the "right" answers with the class, collect the test, and record the grades. Then move on to the next unit. If we continue this practice, how will students learn to use experiences from past units to improve the work they do on future units? (Bonstingl, 1996, p. 30)

- Learning is not a spectator sport. Students do not learn much just by sitting in class listening to teachers, memorizing prepackaged assignments, and spitting out answers. They must talk about what they are learning, write about it, relate it to past experiences, apply it to their daily lives. They must make what they learn part of themselves (Chickering & Gamson, 1987, p. 3).

- The ultimate criterion of good teaching is effective learning (Cross, 1993, p. 20).

- We also know, from research on cognition, that students who reflect on their learning are better learners than those who do not (Cross, 1996, p. 6).

- Learning is, after all, the goal of *all* education, and it is through a lens that focuses on learning that we must ultimately examine and judge our effectiveness as educators (Cross, 1996, p. 9).

- Students learn what they care about and remember what they understand (Erickson, 1984, p. 51).

- Our entire educational system is designed to teach people to do things the one right way as defined by the authority figure. We are taught to recite what we hear or read without critically interacting with the information as it moves in and out of short-term memory. In this exchange, the information leaves no tracks, and independent thinking skills are not developed (Lynch, 1991, p. 64).

- Classes in which students are expected to receive information passively rather than to participate actively will probably not be effective in encouraging students to think reflectively. Similarly, tests and assignments that emphasize only others' definitions of the issues or others' conclusions will not help students learn to define and conclude for themselves (King & Kitchener, 1994, p. 239).

FIGURE 1–1   Importance of Learner-Centered Teaching from the Viewpoint of Prominent Leaders in Higher Education

of possibilities. Those of us who shift our paradigm regarding teaching and learning have new rules, new boundaries, and new ways of behaving.

To develop new conceptualizations, we must analyze our old ways of thinking and make continuous changes. If our ways of thinking are not analyzed, they remain unchanged, existing patterns continue, and "structures of which we are unaware hold us prisoner" (Senge, 1990, p. 60). When people challenge present paradigms, paradigm structures loosen their hold and individuals begin to alter their behaviors to improve processes and systems. As expressed by Covey (1989) in the quote at the beginning of this chapter, to shift the paradigm, we must experience a personal change. To focus on student learning, we must shift from a traditional teaching paradigm to a learner-centered paradigm.

Changing the question from How will I teach this? *to* How will students learn this? *lays bare tacit assumptions about what should be learned and how it should be taught. Specifying what "this" is turns out to be a difficult problem. All too often what is learned turns out not to be what was intended, which often is different also from what was actually taught (Hakel, 1997, p. 19).*

Figure 1–2 is a comparison of the traditional teaching paradigm and the emerging learner-centered paradigm. Similar comparisons can be found in

Teacher-Centered Paradigm	Learner-Centered Paradigm
Knowledge is transmitted from professor to students.	Students construct knowledge through gathering and synthesizing information and integrating it with the general skills of inquiry, communication, critical thinking, problem solving, and so on.
Students passively receive information.	Students are actively involved.
Emphasis is on acquisition of knowledge outside the context in which it will be used.	Emphasis is on using and communicating knowledge effectively to address enduring and emerging issues and problems in real-life contexts.
Professor's role is to be primary information giver and primary evaluator.	Professor's role is to coach and facilitate. Professor and students evaluate learning together.
Teaching and assessing are separate.	Teaching and assessing are intertwined.
Assessment is used to monitor learning	Assessment is used to promote and diagnose learning.
Emphasis is on right answers.	Emphasis is on generating better questions and learning from errors.
Desired learning is assessed indirectly through the use of objectively scored tests.	Desired learning is assessed directly through papers, projects, performances, portfolios, and the like.
Focus is on a single discipline.	Approach is compatible with interdisciplinary investigation.
Culture is competitive and individualistic.	Culture is cooperative, collaborative, and supportive.
Only students are viewed as learners.	Professor and students learn together.

See also Barr and Tagg (1995); Bonstingl (1992); Boyatzis, Cowen, Kolb and Associates (1995); Duffy and Jones (1995); and Kleinsasser (1995).

FIGURE 1–2   Comparison of Teacher-Centered and Learner-Centered Paradigms

Barr and Tagg (1995); Bonstingl (1992); Boyatzis, Cowen, Kolb and Associates (1995); and Duffy and Jones (1995). When we examine this figure, we see that our thinking about teaching is based on assumptions about the role of students in learning, about our roles as teachers, and about the role of assessment. Our paradigm also includes assumptions about how people learn and about the type of environment or culture that supports learning. A thorough discussion of the differences between traditional and learner-centered paradigms is presented in Chapter 2, along with an opportunity to examine our own teaching practices and the assumptions that support them.

Reflections

As you create your own meaning from the ideas in this section, begin to think about . . .

- Which characteristics in Figure 1–2 best describe my beliefs and practice as a teacher?

- In what ways does my practice seem to fall within the traditional paradigm?
- In what ways does my practice seem to fall within the learner-centered paradigm?

A SYSTEMS PERSPECTIVE ON LEARNER-CENTERED TEACHING

In addition to examining our own teaching practices as we shift to a learner-centered approach, we must also consider our relationship to the institution in which we teach. This is because we and our students are part of an entire educational system that has developed at our institution from its teaching mission. In a system, each part affects the behaviors and properties of the whole system (Ackoff, 1995). Whenever there is a need for improvement, efforts should be targeted at the system as a whole as well as at the parts individually.

Thus, efforts to promote student-centered teaching and assessing should be made at the academic program and institutional levels, as well as at the level of the individual professor or course. According to Senge (1990), systems thinking is a conceptual "framework for seeing interrelationships rather than things, for seeing patterns of change rather than static snapshots" (p. 68). The outcome of a system is based on how each part is interacting with the rest of the parts, not on how each part is doing (Kofman & Senge, 1993).

Conceptualizing higher education as a system may make more sense to students than it does to professors. As professors, we tend to focus on preparing and delivering our own courses, whereas students enroll in and experience a program as a whole. Chapter 2 emphasizes that students are driven to make sense of their experiences and to actively construct their knowledge by integrating new information with current understanding. This means that, throughout their academic programs, students are developing their general skills and disciplinary expertise by making sense of the curriculum as they experience it. The knowledge, skills, and abilities that students achieve at the end of their programs are affected by how well courses and other experiences in the curriculum fit together and build on each other throughout the undergraduate years.

In this systems view of the curriculum, we must examine how the system fosters student learning. When and where are skills and content knowledge introduced? In which courses are they developed and reinforced? Is there unnecessary duplication of emphasis for some topics, but incomplete coverage for others? Are courses designed to be taken in an order that supports learning? Are the teaching styles and approaches of the faculty who deliver the curriculum compatible with each other and with the principles of student-centered learning? Are they effective?

When we begin to view our programs as systems, we think about our own courses differently. For example, we become aware that prerequisite courses are important inputs into our own courses and that our courses are the inputs for subsequent courses that students will take. The following story illustrates one professor's understanding that students' efforts to make sense of new information will be more effective when courses in a curriculum build on one another.

> *I taught the first-level theory course and I was asked to teach the second level. Since I did not know what the third level required, I enrolled in the third level course so that I would know how to teach the second level (Freed & Klugman, 1997, p. 35).*

In a systems framework, we work together to design and deliver a curriculum that is coherent to students rather than work separately to design individual courses that we find personally satisfying. We also seek partners in other academic departments, student affairs, the library, the computer center, and other segments of the institution that provide services to enhance learning. Systems thinking continually reminds us that our courses are components of an entire system to support learning.

This type of systems thinking has been encouraged by the assessment movement in higher education. Assessment is a learner-centered movement which encourages us to focus on the student learning component of our teaching as it takes place within the entire system of our institution and within the smaller systems of our academic programs and courses.

Reflections

As you create your own meaning from the ideas in this section, begin to think about . . .

- What kind of "system" am I a part of? How do my courses fit into the curriculum of my academic program?

- How can my faculty colleagues and I dialogue about the interrelationship of courses and experiences in our program?
- How can we involve appropriate colleagues from other parts of the institution?

DEFINITION OF ASSESSMENT

Learning is the focus and ultimate goal of the learner-centered paradigm. Because of this, assessment plays a key role in shifting to a learner-centered approach. When we assess our students' learning, we force the questions, "What have our students learned and how well have they learned it?" "How successful have we been at what we are trying to accomplish?" Because of this focus on learning, assessment in higher education is sometimes referred to as outcomes assessment or student outcomes assessment.

As shown in Figure 1–2, assessment in a learner-centered paradigm is also an integral part of teaching. In other words, through assessment, we not only monitor learning, but we also promote learning. As will be explained throughout this book, we can both encourage and shape the type of learning we desire through the types of assessment we use.

We define assessment as follows:

Assessment is the process of gathering and discussing information from multiple and diverse sources in order to develop a deep understanding of what students know, understand, and can do with their knowledge as a result of their educational experiences; the process culminates when assessment results are used to improve subsequent learning.

In a college or university at which the faculty take a learner-centered approach, the assessment process takes place at all levels—institutional, program, and course. The process is fundamentally the same at all levels, although the focus, methods, and interested parties may change somewhat from level to level.

Furthermore, the process at one level is related to the process at another. For example, the quality of student learning at the end of a program—the focus of program or institutional assessment—depends in part on how and how well we are assessing student learning in our courses. As individuals, are we focusing on developing the knowledge, skills, and abilities that the faculty as a whole have agreed are important? Are we using appropriate teaching and assessing strategies?

In turn, the quality of student learning in courses depends in part on the type of information yielded by program assessment data. Do the programmatic data reveal that we should focus more on student writing? Do they indicate that a particular concept is poorly understood by graduates and needs greater coverage? Do students report that some courses seem outdated or that a prerequisite is misplaced? Program assessment and classroom assessment interact to provide data to enhance student learning.

A practical sense of the many ways in which faculty have approached assessment at their institutions can be found in the 82 case examples provided by Banta, Lund, Black, and Oblander (1996). Illustrations of assessment in general education and various major disciplines are provided from a number of different institutions.

Reflections

As you create your own meaning from the ideas in this section, begin to think about . . .

- How is the definition of assessment presented in this section similar to my own view of assessment?
- How is it different?
- What do I know about assessment at my institution?

- What do I know about assessment in my academic program?
- How do I assess student learning in my courses?
- How does my approach to assessment support learning in my academic program?
- What changes have I made in my courses based on assessment results gathered in my academic program?

ELEMENTS OF THE ASSESSMENT PROCESS

There are four fundamental elements of learner-centered assessment. These are shown in Figure 1–3.

Formulating Statements of Intended Learning Outcomes

The first element of the assessment process is that, as faculty, we develop a set of intended learning outcomes, statements describing our intentions about

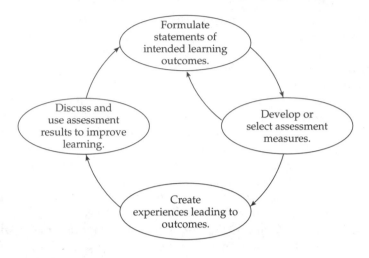

FIGURE 1–3   The Assessment Process

what students should know, understand, and be able to do with their knowledge when they graduate. Faculty at many institutions have formulated common learning outcomes for all students at the institution. Intended learning outcomes reflecting the discipline should also be developed for each academic program and for each course in the program.

Discussed at length in Chapter 4, these statements typically begin with the phrase, "Students will be able to . . ." The statements are obviously learner-centered, and developing them reflects a systems approach to teaching in the program. When we collectively decide what graduates of an institution or program should know, understand, and be able to do, we are working as a team, rather than as individuals. We are collectively confronting perhaps the most fundamental question in higher education, "What does the degree or certificate that we award mean and how can we prove it?" (Plater, 1998, p. 12)

When assessment takes place at the institutional or academic program level rather than the course level, only the most important goals of the institution or program are addressed in assessment. As will be discussed in Chapter 4, learning goals at the institutional level are likely to be more broadly stated than those at the program level, and those at the program level are likely to be more broadly stated than those at the course level. However, achieving the more specific learning goals that we develop for a course or even for a specific class period should help students make progress toward achieving program and/or institutional goals.

Reflections

As you create your own meaning from the ideas in this section, begin to think about . . .

- How successfully have faculty in my program worked together to formulate intended learning outcomes for our program?

- How could we work together to do this?
- What intended outcomes would I develop for my courses that would support program/institutional outcomes?

Developing or Selecting Assessment Measures

The second element of the assessment process is designing or selecting data gathering measures to assess whether or not our intended learning outcomes have been achieved. This element not only provides the foundation for data gathering, but it also brings to a culmination the previous step of determining learning outcomes. This is because the process of designing assessment measures forces us to come to a thorough understanding of what we really mean by our intended learning outcomes (Wiggins & McTighe, 1998). As we develop our assessment measures, we may find ourselves fine-tuning our learning outcomes.

Our assessment measures should include both direct and indirect assessments of student learning (Palomba & Banta, 1999). Direct assessments may take a variety of forms—projects, products, papers/theses, exhibitions, performances, case studies, clinical evaluations, portfolios, interviews, and oral exams (see Chapters 6, 7, and 8). In all of these assessments, we ask students to demonstrate what they know or can do with their knowledge. Most, if not all, of these forms of assessment can be incorporated into typical college courses, although a few (e.g., clinical evaluations) are likely to be used more in some disciplines than in others. At the program level, we can gather assessment data from assessments embedded in courses or design additional assessments that we administer outside of courses.

Indirect assessments of learning include self-report measures such as surveys distributed to students which can be used both in courses and at the program and institutional levels. (Designing measures for gathering feedback from students in courses is discussed in Chapter 5 of this book.) Other indirect measures used in program or institutional assessment, although not a focus of this book, include surveys of graduates or employers in which respondents share their perceptions about what graduates know or can do with their knowledge.

Both direct and indirect assessment measures should be chosen to provide accurate and useful information for making decisions about learning. In order to do so, they must evaluate the type of learning we desire in our students. For this reason, in this book there will be little discussion of tests comprised of objectively scored paper and pencil test items like multiple-choice and true–false. Many of us use these types of items heavily because they can be easily scored—even by machine—and we rely on the scores that result as the primary contributors to students' final grades. This type of evaluation is appealing because we can collect information efficiently and the results seem easy to interpret.

However, these items typically test only factual knowledge. It is possible to write multiple-choice and true–false items that go beyond checking recall of facts to measure higher-order thinking, and items that do so appear on standardized tests prepared by professional test developers at companies like the Educational Testing Service. However, when objectively scored items are written by individuals without professional training in test development, they tend to focus on factual knowledge.

Another criticism of objectively scored test items is that they assess knowledge bit by bit, item by item, typically with no reference to any eventual real-world application (Resnick & Resnick, 1992). They are only *indirect* indicators of more complex abilities such as reasoning about cutting-edge issues or using information to solve important problems in a particular field. Furthermore, objectively scored tests always have a right answer. For these reasons, when we use them, we send students the message that it is important to master isolated facts and skills and to always know the right answers.

However, the challenges faced by adults in general and by professionals in particular fields tend to be those that require the simultaneous coordination and integration of many aspects of knowledge and skill in situations with few right answers. As Howard Gardner (1991) points out, the ability to take objectively scored tests successfully is a useless skill as soon as one graduates from college. The rest of one's life, he says, is a series of projects.

The perspective of this book is that, in learner-centered teaching, we should design "assessments" to evaluate students' ability to think critically and use their knowledge to address enduring and emerging issues and problems in their disciplines. We define an assessment in the following way:

> *An assessment is an activity, assigned by the professor, that yields comprehensive information for analyzing, discussing, and judging a learner's performance of valued abilities and skills.*

This book discusses the development and use of assessments like projects, papers, performances, portfolios, or exhibitions that evaluate higher-order thinking and require students to *directly* reveal the very abilities that professors desire. Sometimes these are referred to as authentic assessments because of their intrinsic value (Wiggins, 1989); at other times, they are referred to as performance assessments because they require students to demonstrate their learning. At still other times, they are termed qualitative assessments because they allow us to evaluate the nature and quality of students' work. Further, our scoring is based on subjective judgment using criteria we develop, rather than on an answer key that permits us to objectively sum correct answers. Whatever they are called, these assessments are effective tools for assessing mastery of factual knowledge, but more importantly, for finding out if students can *use* their knowledge effectively to reason and solve problems.

For those of us who would like to continue using objectively scored tests, several excellent resources are available (e.g., Airasian, 1994; Brookhart, 1999; Gronlund & Linn, 1990; Payne, 1997; Stiggins, 1994; Thorndike, Cunningham, Thorndike, & Hagen, 1991). These books include guidelines for writing effective test items, and they give examples of items that measure more than recall of facts.

Reflections

As you create your own meaning from the ideas in this section, begin to think about . . .

- How successfully have faculty in my program worked together to develop and implement a plan for collecting assessment data focused on our learning outcomes? How could we work together to do this?
- Which of our measures are direct assessments of learning?

- Which of our measures are indirect assessments of learning?
- In what ways do I assess factual knowledge?
- How heavily do I use objectively scored test items that I select from publishers' testbanks or that I write myself?
- In what ways do I assess students' ability to use their knowledge as they reason and solve problems?

Creating Experiences Leading to Outcomes

The third element in the assessment process is ensuring that students have experiences both in and outside their courses that help them achieve the intended learning outcomes. If we expect students to achieve our intended outcomes, we must provide them with opportunities to learn what they need to learn. We should design the curriculum as a set of interrelated courses and experiences that will help students achieve the intended learning outcomes.

Students' learning will be affected by the way courses and other required experiences like independent studies, practica, and internships are organized in the curriculum and the order in which they are taken. The appropriateness of the prerequisite courses we designate will also influence how well students learn. Designing the curriculum by working backward from learning outcomes helps make the curriculum a coherent "story of learning" (Plater, 1998, p. 11).

Orchestrating stages in the skill development of students is also part of curriculum development. Where in the curriculum will students learn and practice skills like writing, speaking, teamwork, and problem solving? What teaching strategies will faculty use to help students develop these skills, and how will professors give feedback to students on their progress? Will all professors be responsible for these skills? Will the skills be addressed only in the general education component of the curriculum? Will some courses throughout the course of study be targeted as "intensives" (e.g., writing intensive, problem solving intensive, etc.)? All of these questions are curriculum questions that are central to an assessment program.

As we develop or revise the curriculum, we should include activities and experiences that will help students acquire the knowledge, skills, and understanding that *each* of our learning outcomes requires. Conversely, we should scrutinize each of the activities and experiences that we create in our courses and programs and ask ourselves, "How will this help students achieve the intended learning outcomes of the institution, program, or course?"

Reflections

As you create your own meaning from the ideas in this section, begin to think about . . .

- To what extent do my faculty colleagues and I design and revise curriculum with learning outcomes in mind?

- How could we change our approach to curricular design and revision so that we focus more on helping students achieve intended learning outcomes?
- How could we help students develop more effective skills?

Discussing and Using Assessment Results to Improve Learning

The fourth element is a process for discussing and using the assessment results to improve learning. Within courses, these discussions take place between us and our students, and the focus is on using the results to improve individual student performance. At the program or institutional level, discussions take place among the faculty as a whole.

Through our discussions of assessment results, we gain insights into the type of learning occurring in the program, and we are better able to make informed decisions about needed program changes. We understand what students can do well and in what areas they have not succeeded. We raise questions about the design of the curriculum or about the teaching strategies we use (Walvoord, Bardes, & Denton, 1998). We also develop a better understanding of how to assess learning in a useful manner.

In order to seek additional perspectives, we should share summaries of the process with key stakeholder groups (e.g., students, alumni, advisory groups) who may also provide insights about whether changes are needed in the program's intended learning outcomes, in the curriculum, in teaching strategies used by faculty, or in assessment techniques used. In this stage of the process, we reveal the nature and process of a college education to a broad audience, and we help build trust for institutions of higher education.

With information from the assessment itself as well as the perspectives of students, alumni, advisory groups and others, we can proceed to recommend and implement changes that will improve both the curriculum and the teaching taking place in the program. As discussed in Chapter 3, assessment data should also be used to inform processes like planning and resource allocation, catalog revision, and program review.

Reflections

As you create your own meaning from the ideas in this section, begin to think about . . .

- When and with whom have I discussed assessment findings

and their implications for learning?

- What stakeholder groups would be interested in knowing about learning in my courses and program?

A BRIEF HISTORY OF THE ASSESSMENT MOVEMENT IN HIGHER EDUCATION

Our role as faculty in assuming primary ownership for assessing academic programs is critical. We are responsible for developing the intended learning outcomes of our academic programs, for developing the curricula on which the programs are based, and for delivering the curricula through our teaching. It naturally follows that we should be responsible for building quality into the programs through evaluating the learning that takes place within them.

Assuming the responsibility for assessment provides us with several opportunities. One is the opportunity to ask important questions about the value and effectiveness of our instructional programs. Another is the opportunity to engage in conversations about student learning with each other. The final opportunity is to use data about student learning to strengthen the way decisions are made, leading to improvement in the curriculum and in instruction.

However, many faculty have been reluctant to engage in assessment because, in some states or regions of the country, assessment has been introduced as a requirement by external agencies such as legislatures or regional or specialized accreditation associations. The reasons for this can be traced historically.

Changing Resources and the Seeds of Reform

The post-war period of the 1950s and 1960s was a time of expansion in higher education (Brubacher & Rudy, 1976). "The enrollment [sic] of World War II veterans created the most rapid growth of colleges and universities in the history of higher education" (Henry, 1975, p. 55). Between 1955 and 1970, the number of students pursuing academic degrees tripled (Henry, 1975, p. 101). Generous support from federal and state governments helped institutions keep pace, culminating in the Johnson years, "golden ones for all of education and not the least for higher education" (Pusey, 1978, p. 109). During this time, the value of a college education was assumed, and universities functioned in a relatively autonomous fashion. There was little need to reveal to external audiences what was happening in college classrooms.

However, by the 1970s, higher education was in a grave financial crisis. Resources available to higher education could not keep pace with rising costs and inflation. Large private donations to institutions, common in the first half of the century, had declined sharply; inflation had reduced institutional income, and it had become increasingly difficult to raise tuition to offset costs and still maintain access to a college education (Brubacher & Rudy, 1976). Politicians were faced with the increasing need to fund welfare, hospitals, prisons (Erwin, 1991), schools, highways, and public utilities (Henry, 1975).

In addition, by the 1970s, the population of students attending college had become more diverse. As the goal of a college education for all became more widespread, college faculties were faced with challenges they had never experienced before. Concerns that college graduates did not have the skills and abilities needed in the workplace surfaced. The public and the politicians who represented them began to question the value of higher education. A movement to bring about reform in higher education—and education at all levels—began (Ewell, 1991).

As a result, in 1984 and 1985 alone, four reports were issued addressing the need for reform on the college campus (Ewell, 1991): *Access to Quality Undergraduate Education* (Southern Regional Education Board, 1985), *Integrity in the College Curriculum* (Association of American Colleges, 1985), *Involvement in Learning* (National Institute of Education, 1984), and *To Reclaim a Legacy* (Bennett, 1984). These reports received less attention than *A Nation at Risk*, the report that triggered the reform movement in elementary and secondary schools. However, according to Ewell, their messages were clear and strong: instruction in higher education must become learner-centered, and learners, faculty, and institutions all need feedback in order to improve.

Calls for Accountability

In some states, politicians assumed the responsibility for initiating reform. A number of legislatures (e.g., Arkansas, Colorado, Florida, Kentucky, Missouri, Ohio, Tennessee) have implemented performance funding programs, and although many such programs have floundered, additional states continue to consider this approach (Ewell, 1998; Serban, 1998). In performance funding, some portion of the public monies earmarked for higher education are allocated to institutions based on institutional ability to meet performance targets like retention rates, graduation rates, or demonstrations of student learning.

For example, the Tennessee legislature mandated that institutions pre- and post-test students, with incentive funding following, based on improvements (Astin, 1993). Florida instituted a "rising junior" test at its public institutions in order to ensure that students were prepared to enter the upper division or receive an associate in arts degree. However, the test was not sensitive to institutional differences and needs, but rather was a common instrument for use at all state-funded institutions and was developed by faculty members from across the state (Astin, 1993; McCabe, 1988).

In part to curtail the direct involvement of state legislatures in higher education, regional accreditation agencies—organizations comprised of institutions of higher education themselves—became involved. Accreditation agencies declared that they would require member institutions to conduct outcomes assessment in order to maintain their status as accredited institutions.

For example, in 1989, the Commission on Institutions of Higher Education of the North Central Association of Colleges and Schools introduced the requirement that every affiliated institution conduct outcomes assessment (Commission on Institutions of Higher Education, 1996). This was one of the few times in its 100-year history that the organization established a program and required every affiliated institution to give evidence within a period of time of making a good faith effort to implement it (S. Crow, personal communication, October 29, 1998). As time passed, specialized accrediting bodies—those that accredit professional programs rather than institutions (e.g., business, veterinary medicine, engineering, counseling, architecture)—also began to adopt an outcomes approach to program evaluation.

The Continuous Improvement Movement

Another factor influencing the assessment movement was the continuous improvement movement. Just as higher education was influenced by the business processes of long-range planning in the late 1970s and strategic planning in the mid-1980s, it was influenced in the late 1980s by the use of quality principles and practices. American businesses become involved in quality improvement because of the intense competition resulting from the introduction of better products from foreign countries. Likewise, colleges and universities pursued continuous improvement because of competition for students, the need to reduce costs and improve quality of services, and the desire to enhance learning. The introduction of quality improvement in higher education paralleled the development of the assessment movement, and the two initiatives have much in common.

W. E. Deming is recognized as one of the founders of the quality improvement movement. He believed that continuous improvement is the path to improved quality, greater productivity (less rework and more efficiency), and reduced cost (Deming, 1986). Deming's Fourteen Points (1986), the most cited set of principles for continuous improvement, have been reframed for other settings, one of which is education (Cornesky, 1993, 1994; Greenwood & Gaunt, 1994). Figure 1–4 outlines the original Fourteen Points according to Deming. Figure 1–5 presents one example of how Deming's interpretation of quality improvement has been adapted for education.

Gathering data for informed decision making is at the heart of Deming's philosophy of improvement. Deming advocated cross-functional teamwork and partnerships by stressing that barriers must be removed so that people can work together effectively and creatively. Deming believed that people need to have pride in what they do. Therefore, he encouraged education, professional development, and personal self-improvement for everyone (Deming, 1986).

At the end of the 1980s and the beginning of the 1990s, the quality movement in higher education was relatively new and existed only on the fringes of campus concerns. Research reveals that even though continuous improvement started and has made more progress on the administrative side of most

1. Create constancy of purpose toward improvement of product and service.
2. Adopt the new philosophy and take on leadership for change.
3. Cease dependence on inspection to achieve quality by building quality into the product in the first place.
4. Develop long-term relationships of loyalty and trust with suppliers.
5. Constantly improve systems and processes.
6. Institute training on the job.
7. Institute leadership—the aim of supervision should be to help people do a better job.
8. Drive out fear so that everyone may work effectively.
9. Break down barriers between departments—people must work as a team.
10. Eliminate zero-defect work targets and slogans. Recognize that the causes of low quality and productivity belong to the system, thus lying beyond the power of the workforce.
11. Eliminate numerical quotas and management by objective, substituting leadership instead.
12. Remove barriers to pride of workmanship.
13. Promote education and self-improvement.
14. Involve everyone in accomplishing the transformation.

(Reprinted from *Out of the Crisis* by W. Edwards Deming by permission of MIT and The W. Edwards Deming Institute. Published by MIT, Center for Advanced Educational Services, Cambridge, MA 02139. Copyright 1986 by The W. Edwards Deming Institute.)

FIGURE 1–4   Abbreviated Statement of W. Edwards Deming's Fourteen Points for Continuous Improvement

institutions, its principles are becoming increasingly used on the academic side to improve learning and teaching (Freed & Klingman, 1997; Schnell, 1996).

Improvement as Accountability

The preceding discussion illustrates the fact that assessment is a movement that began outside the academy in order to make institutions more accountable to external constituencies. However, it is becoming increasingly clear that the best way for institutions to be accountable to any audience is to incorporate the evaluation of student learning into the way they operate on a regular basis. When faculty collectively take charge of their educational programs, making visible their purpose and intent, and putting in place a data-based system of evaluation that focuses on improving student learning, the institution itself is the primary beneficiary while external audiences are satisfied as well.

1. Pursue continuous improvement of curriculum and learning diligently and constantly.
2. Adopt the system of profound knowledge in your classroom and [institution] as the prime management tool.
3. Build quality into teaching and learning and reduce the inspection of quality into work after the event.
4. Build a partnership relationship with colleagues, students, and . . . employers.
5. Constantly improve the system within which teaching/learning takes place.
6. Take every opportunity to train in new skills and to learn from your pupils.
7. Lead—do not drive or manipulate.
8. Drive out fear of punishment—create joy in learning.
9. Collaborate with colleagues from other departments and functions.
10. Communicate honestly, not through jargon and slogans.
11. So far as possible create a world without grades and rank order.
12. Encourage and celebrate to develop your students' pride in work.
13. Promote the development of the whole person in students and colleagues.
14. Wed your students to learning by the negotiation with them of a quality experience.

[From Greenwood & Gaunt, *Total Quality Management for Schools* (London: Cassell plc). Source: W. E. Deming, 'Out of Crisis,' 1982 (adapted to school rather than manufacturing context by L. Richelou and M. S. Greenwood).]

FIGURE 1–5   Deming's Fourteen Points Adapted for Education

Reflections

As you create your own meaning from the ideas in this section, begin to think about . . .

- How have the historical factors leading to the assessment movement influenced my environment?

- How have these factors affected faculty *knowledge* about assessment?

- How have these factors affected faculty *attitude* toward assessment?

ASSESSMENT AND THE IMPROVEMENT
OF UNDERGRADUATE EDUCATION

In its report, *Making Quality Count in Undergraduate Education*, the Education Commission of the States proposed twelve quality attributes of good practice in delivering an undergraduate education (1995). "Extensive research on American college students reveals . . . that when colleges and universities systematically engage in these good practices, student performance and satisfaction will improve" (Education Commission of the States, 1996, p. 5). Shown in Figure 1–6, these attributes address aspects of an institution's organizational culture and values, its curriculum, and the type of instruction that takes place within it (Education Commission of the States, 1996).

One of the attributes is "assessment and prompt feedback," and it is included in the list as an intrinsic element of quality instruction. However, we believe that learner-centered assessment, as discussed in this book, promotes or enhances all the attributes of quality that are listed in Figure 1–6. Assess-

---

Quality begins with an organizational culture that values:

1. High expectations
2. Respect for diverse talents and learning styles
3. Emphasis on the early years of study

A quality curriculum requires:

4. Coherence in learning
5. Synthesizing experiences
6. Ongoing practice of learned skills
7. Integrating education and experience

Quality instruction builds in:

8. Active learning
9. Assessment and prompt feedback
10. Collaboration
11. Adequate time on task
12. Out-of-class contact with faculty

(Education Commission of the States, 1995, 1996)

FIGURE 1–6   Attributes of Quality Undergraduate Education: What the Research Says

ment can thus be a powerful tool for improving—even transforming—undergraduate education (Angelo, 1999).

In the following sections, we briefly point out ways in which learner-centered assessment supports the attributes of a quality undergraduate education. Chapter 2 provides a more extended discussion in its review of the hallmarks of learner-centered teaching and assessment.

Learner-Centered Assessment Promotes High Expectations

"Students learn more effectively when expectations for learning are placed at high but attainable levels, and when these expectations are communicated clearly from the onset" (Education Commission of the States, 1996, p. 5). Learner-centered assessment clearly supports the principle of high expectations. In a learner-centered assessment environment, students are aware of the faculty's intended learning outcomes before instruction begins. They thus know what we expect them to know, understand, and be able to do with their knowledge. We give them challenging assessment tasks to evaluate their achievement, and using scoring rubrics, we describe for them the characteristics that are present in excellent work. These characteristics derive from the standards to which we hold educated people and practicing professionals in their disciplines.

Learner-Centered Assessment Respects Diverse Talents and Learning Styles

In learner-centered assessment, assessment tasks are designed so that students can complete them effectively in many different ways. There is not just one right answer, but rather students have the opportunity to do excellent work that reflects their own unique way of implementing their abilities and skills.

Learner-Centered Assessment Enhances the Early Years of Study

"A consensus is emerging that the first years of undergraduate study—particularly the freshman year—are critical to student success" (Education Commission of the States, 1996, p. 6). Learner-centered assessment enhances the first year of study by engaging students in meaningful intellectual work and helping them discover connections between what they learn in college and the ways in which they will use their knowledge in society or the professions after graduation. This is accomplished by designing assessment tasks that derive from challenging real-world problems and call upon students to use and extend their skills in critical thinking and problem solving.

Learner-Centered Assessment Promotes Coherence in Learning

Students should be presented with a set of learning experiences that consist of more than merely a required number of courses or credit hours. Instead, the curriculum should be structured in a way that sequences individual courses to reinforce specific outcomes and consciously directs instruction toward meeting those ends (Education Commission of the States, 1996, pp. 6–7).

Learner-centered assessment promotes a coherent curriculum by providing data to guide the curriculum development and revision process. If we want to know whether the curriculum as a whole or the experiences in individual courses are coherent to students, we can ask for their opinions directly. In learner-centered assessment, students give us feedback on their learning in a continual fashion, suggesting ways in which instruction and the curriculum can be improved to help achieve our intended learning outcomes. In addition, through assessment that takes place at the program level, as well as in courses, we can find out what students have learned well and in what areas they need to improve. The resulting information provides direction for curricular improvement.

Learner-Centered Assessment Synthesizes Experiences, Fosters Ongoing Practice of Learned Skills, and Integrates Education and Experience

Learner-centered assessment tasks frequently take the form of projects, papers, exhibitions, and so forth, in which students synthesize the knowledge, abilities, and skills they have learned in the general education curriculum, in their major field, and in their course experiences. These assessments also focus on *using* knowledge to address issues and problems that are important in students' chosen disciplines. Critical thinking, problem solving, and written and oral communication are the vehicles through which students employ their knowledge in the pursuit of important goals in the assessment tasks we give them.

Learner-Centered Assessment Actively Involves Students in Learning and Promotes Adequate Time on Task

All of the forms of learner-centered assessment we have discussed require active learning. Assessment tasks like projects, papers, and so on cannot be completed in a 50-minute time period. They actively involve students in learning over a period of several days or weeks. During this time, we can structure in-class activities to help students acquire the knowledge and skills they need to complete the assessment task. In this way, students are continually focused on achieving the intended learning outcomes of the course and program.

Learner-Centered Assessment Provides Prompt Feedback

When students are completing the assessments we have discussed in this chapter, we can assess their learning as it takes place and provide revelant feedback to guide the process. A major theme of this book is that learners cannot learn anything without feedback. Feedback is part and parcel of learner-centered assessment, whether students are giving feedback to us or we are giving feedback to them. Both types of feedback improve student learning, and this book emphasizes strategies to make feedback both timely and useful.

Learner-Centered Assessment Fosters Collaboration

"Students learn better when engaged in a team effort rather than working on their own . . . it is the way the world outside the academy works" (Education Commission of the States, 1996, p. 8). Unlike conventional tests which students complete silently and alone—and which are often graded on a competitive basis—learner-centered assessments provide opportunities for students to work together and develop their skills in teamwork and cooperation. As students talk about what they know and what they are learning, their knowledge and understanding deepen.

Learner-Centered Assessment Depends on Increased Student-Faculty Contact

In learner-centered assessment, we guide and coach students as they learn to do important things worth doing. We give students feedback on their learning, and we seek feedback from students about how to improve the learning environment. Through the use of portfolios and other self-evaluation activities, we and our students confer together about students' progress toward the intended learning outcomes of the program. This increases contact between us and our students both in and outside the classroom.

Reflections

As you create your own meaning from the ideas in this section, begin to think about . . .

• Which attributes of a quality un-

dergraduate education are present in my courses and my program?

• Which attributes would I most like to enhance?

LEARNER-CENTERED ASSESSMENT AND TIME

Using learner-centered assessment may be more time consuming than previous approaches, particularly in the beginning. We will need to take time to confer with our colleagues about fundamental issues like learning outcomes and the coherence of the curriculum. Initially, this will require an extra investment of time and energy as we attempt "to transcend the privacy of our own courses, syllabi, or student programs, let alone our departments, divisions, or schools" (Plater, 1998, p. 13). In our courses, when we try new techniques, we will undoubtedly spend more time analyzing and questioning our past approach to pedagogy and evaluating the new techniques we employ.

We will also discover that our institutions are structured to accommodate the traditional paradigm (Barr, 1998). It takes time and effort to implement a new approach when factors like schedules, room arrangements, reward systems—even the structures of our buildings—have been designed to make the traditional paradigm work efficiently.

Helping students change paradigms will take time as well (Warren, 1997). As we create new learning environments and use new teaching strategies, we will have to guide students to understand new ways of learning.

However, as we, our colleagues, and our students become more familiar and comfortable with learner-centered strategies, the overall time spent on teaching will probably decrease to former levels. We may have to learn to use time more efficiently and effectively at faculty meetings so that we can find the time we need to confer about issues related to learning and assessment on a continuing basis.

In our courses, as Figure 1–7 shows, we will learn to spend time *differently* than we have in the past. When we prepare to teach, we will continue to keep up-to-date in our disciplines. However, we will spend more time developing materials to facilitate learning and less time organizing presentations of information or constructing objectively scored tests.

Preparing to facilitate learning rather than lecture about what we know involves designing an approach to teaching that allows students to create their own understanding of the material. We will need to find time to develop materials like statements of intended learning outcomes, questions to guide student discussion of assigned readings, activities that involve students actively in their learning, criteria describing the characteristics of excellent work to use in grading, and assessments that promote enhanced learning.

Facilitating learning rather than imparting information may require the development of new teaching techniques as well. We may have to learn to ask questions that guide student thinking, to facilitate student discussion in ways that lead to increased understanding, to coach students as they work in pairs

	Teacher-Centered Paradigm	Learner-Centered Paradigm
Preparing to teach		
Keeping up-to-date	+++	+++
Developing materials to facilitate learning	—	+++
Preparing a presentation of information	++++	+
Developing objectively scored tests to monitor learning efficiently	+++	—
Teaching		
Facilitating learning	—	+++
Imparting information	++++	+
Giving feedback to improve learning	—	+++
Following up		
Examining grade distributions to monitor learning	+++	—
Using student input to improve the course	——	+++

FIGURE 1–7   Allocation of Professor's Time/Effort/Emphasis in Teacher-Centered and Learner-Centered Paradigms

or groups, and to coordinate in-class student activities. We will have to learn to share our learning outcomes with students and to devote time to periodic discussions of the progress students are making in achieving them. We should seek student input as we develop grading criteria, eliciting students' ideas about the characteristics of excellent work and sharing our ideas as well.

In a learner-centered environment, we will spend more time using these public criteria to discuss students' work with them and evaluate it at various stages of development. The need to monitor how well our students are doing by studying grade distributions will be replaced by more direct involvement in helping students improve their work.

Finally, in each course, we will need to seek and review student feedback about how well the course is helping students to learn and then spend the time to make adjustments that will enhance the learning environment. The payoff of better prepared students justifies the time it takes to make the transformation from teacher-centered to learner-centered practices.

Reflections

As you create your own meaning from the ideas in this section, begin to think about . . .

- On which of the practices in Figure 1–7 do I spend the most time?
- On which practices would I spend more time if I became more learner-centered?
- On which practices would I spend less time if I became more learner-centered?
- What characteristics of my institution would interfere with a learner-centered approach?

LOOKING AHEAD

In Chapter 2, we will discuss several hallmarks of learner-centered teaching and assessment. We will provide examples, as well as an opportunity to examine our own teaching practices in terms of the traditional vs. learner-centered paradigms. Chapter 3 examines several guidelines and practices that will foster the development of strong assessment programs on college campuses, thereby providing a foundation for refocusing the campus culture on learning rather than teaching.

Chapters 4 through 8 address several specific techniques for assessing student learning in a learner-centered environment: formulating intended learning outcomes (Chapter 4), gathering feedback from students to continually guide improvement in courses (Chapter 5), developing criteria for shaping and judging student work in the form of scoring rubrics (Chapter 6), designing assessments that promote and evaluate students' ability to think critically, solve problems, and use their discipline related knowledge (Chapter 7), and using portfolios to understand what and how students learn (Chapter 8). In Chapter 9, we discuss the implications for both us and our institutions of making the shift to a learner-centered paradigm.

TRY SOMETHING NEW

As authors, we have tried to design this book using current principles of learning. One of these principles is that individuals learn best when they have opportunities to examine what they already know about a topic before they encounter new information. This fosters deep learning by helping learners prepare to make connections between current and new knowledge. For this reason, we begin each chapter of this book with a series of questions entitled Making Connections.

We have also referred to the fact that adults learn best when they have opportunities to reflect upon their current knowledge and practice in the light of new information. Throughout this chapter, as well as the others in this book, we have provided opportunities for reflection in the several series of questions entitled Reflections.

A final aspect of the book is the opportunity at the end of each chapter to Try Something New. We suggest that you review your answers to the questions in the Making Connections and Reflections sections in this chapter. Then pursue one or more of the suggested activities below to begin shifting from teaching to learning.

1. Read an article from this chapter and identify three points that have implications for your teaching.
2. Invite a colleague to lunch and bring along a copy of Figure 1–2. Discuss together those features of your teaching that could be considered elements of the traditional paradigm and those that could be considered learner-centered.
3. Make a list of all the ways that you assess learning in your courses. Discuss your assessment approach with a colleague and seek his/her reactions.
4. Find out what your institution is doing to support the shift from teaching to learning, as well as to establish an assessment culture on campus.

REFERENCES

Ackoff, R. L. (1995, June). *The challenges of change and the need for systems thinking.* Paper presented at the AAHE Conference on Assessment and Quality, Boston, Massachusetts.

Airasian, P. W. (1994). *Classroom assessment* (2nd ed.). New York: McGraw-Hill, Inc.

Angelo, T. A. (1999, May). Doing assessment as if learning matters most. *AAHE Bulletin*, 3–6.

Association of American Colleges. (1985). *Integrity in the college curriculum: A report to the academic community.* Washington, DC: Association of American Colleges.

Astin, A. W. (1985). *Achieving educational excellence.* San Francisco: Jossey-Bass.

Astin, A. W. (1993). *Assessment for excellence.* Phoenix, AZ: Oryx Press.

Banta, T. W., Lund, J. P., Black, K. E., & Oblander, F. W. (1996). *Assessment in practice: Putting principles to work on college campuses.* San Francisco: Jossey-Bass.

Barker, J. A. (1992). *Paradigms: The business of discovering the future.* New York: Harper Business.

Barr, R. B. (1998, September-October). Obstacles to implementing the learning paradigm—What it takes to overcome them. *About Campus*, 18–25.

Barr, R. B., & Tagg, J. (1995, November/December). From teaching to learning: A new paradigm for undergraduate education. *Change*, 13–25.

Bennett, W. J. (1984). *To reclaim a legacy: A report on the humanities in higher education.* Washington, DC: National Endowment for the Humanities.

Bligh, D. A. (1972). *What's the use of lectures?* Baltimore: Penguin Books.

Bonstingl, J. J. (1992). The total quality classroom. *Educational Leadership, 49* (6), 66–70.

Bonstingl, J. J. (1996). *Schools of quality*. Alexandria, VA: Association for Supervision and Curriculum Development.

Boyatzis, Cowen, Kolb, & Associates. (1995). *Innovation in professional education*. San Francisco: Jossey-Bass.

Brookhart, S. M. (1999). *The art and science of classroom assessment: The missing part of pedagogy*. (ASHE-ERIC Higher Education Report: Vol. 27, No 1). Washington, DC: The George Washington University, Graduate School of Education and Human Development.

Brubacher, J. S., & Rudy, W. (1976). *Higher education in transition (3rd ed.)*. New York: Harper and Row.

Chickering, A. W., & Gamson, Z. F. (1987, March). Seven principles for good practice. *AAHE Bulletin,* 3–7.

Commission on Institutions of Higher Education of the North Central Association. (1996, February 22). *Commission statement on assessment of student academic achievement*. Chicago: North Central Association.

Cornesky, R. (1993). *The quality professor: Implementing TQM in the classroom*. Madison, WI: Magna Publications.

Cornesky, R. (1994). *Quality classroom practices for professors*. Port Orange, FL: Cornesky & Associates.

Covey, S. R. (1989). *The 7 habits of highly effective people*. New York: Simon & Schuster.

Creed, T. (Winter 1986). Why we lecture. *Symposium: A Saint John's Faculty Journal, 5,* 17–32.

Cross, K. P. (1993, February-March). Involving faculty in TQM. *AACC Journal,* 15–20.

Cross, K. P. (1996, March-April). New lenses on learning. *About Campus,* 4–9.

Cross, K. P. (1998, July-August). *Why* learning communities? *Why now? About Campus,* 4–11.

Deming, W. E. (1986). *Out of the crisis*. Cambridge, MA: Massachusetts Institute of Technology Center for Advanced Engineering Study.

Duffy, D. K., & Jones, J. W. (1995). *Teaching within the rhythms of the semester*. San Francisco: Jossey-Bass.

Education Commission of the States. (1995). *Making quality count in undergraduate education*. Denver, CO: Education Commission of the States.

Education Commission of the States. (1996, April). What research says about improving undergraduate education. *AAHE Bulletin,* 5–8.

Eison, J., & Bonwell, C. (1988, March). *Making real the promise of active learning*. Paper presented at the meeting of the American Association for Higher Education, Washington, DC.

Engelkemeyer, S. W., & Brown, S. C. (1998, October). Powerful partnerships: A shared responsibility for learning. *AAHE Bulletin,* 10–12.

Erickson, S. C. (1984). *The essence of good teaching*. San Francisco: Jossey-Bass.

Erwin, T. D. (1991). *Assessing student learning and development*. San Francisco: Jossey-Bass.

Ewell, P. T. (1991). To capture the ineffable: New forms of assessment in higher education. In G. Grant, (Ed.). *Review of Research in Education, 17,* 75–125. Washington, DC: American Educational Research Association.

Ewell, P. T. (1998, May-June). From the states—implementing performance funding in Washington state: Some new takes on an old problem. *Assessment Update, 10* (3), 7–8, 13.

Freed, J. E., & Klugman, M. R. (1997). *Quality principles and practices in higher education: Different questions for different times*. Phoenix, AZ: American Council on Education and The Oryx Press.

Gardner, H. (1991). *The unschooled mind: How children think and how schools should teach*. New York: Basic Books.

Greenwood, M. S., & Gaunt, H. J. (1994). *Total quality management for schools*. London: Cassell.

Gronlund, N. E., & Linn, R. L. (1990). *Measurement and evaluation in teaching* (6th ed.). New York: MacMillan Publishing Company.

Guskin, A. (1997, July-August). Learning more, spending less. *About Campus*, 4–9.

Hakel, M. D. (1997, July-August). What we must learn from Alverno. *About Campus*, 16–21.

Henry, D. D. (1975). *Challenges past, challenges present: An analysis of American higher education since 1930*. San Francisco: Jossey-Bass.

Joint Task Force on Student Learning. (1998a). *Learning principles and collaborative action*. Washington, DC: American Association for Higher Education.

Joint Task Force on Student Learning. (1998b). *Powerful partnerships: A shared responsibility for learning*. Washington, DC: American College Personnel Association. http://www.aahe.org, http://www.acpa.nche.edu, or http://www.naspa.org

Kellogg Commission on the Future of State and Land-Grant Universities. (1997). *Returning to our roots: The student experience*. Washington, DC: National Association of State Universities and Land-Grant Colleges. http://www.nasulgc.org

Kellogg Commission on the Future of State and Land-Grant Universities. (1999). *Returning to our roots: The engaged institution*. Washington, DC: National Association of State Universities and Land-Grant Colleges. http://www.nasulgc.org

King, P. M., & Kitchener, K. S. (1994). *Developing reflective judgment: Understanding and promoting intellectual growth and critical thinking in adolescents and adults*. San Francisco: Jossey-Bass.

Kleinsasser, A. M. (1995, March/April). Assessment culture and national testing. *The Clearing House*, 205–210.

Kofman, F., & Senge, P. M. (1993). Communities of commitment: The heart of learning organizations. *American Management Association*, 5–23.

Lynch, R. F. (1991, April). Shedding the shackles of George Patton, Henry Ford, and first-grade teachers. *Quality Progress*, 64.

McCabe, R. H. (1988). The assessment movement: What next? Who cares? In J. S. Stark & A. Thomas, (Eds.), *Assessment and program evaluation* (pp. 199–203). ASHE Reader Series. Needham Heights, MA: Simon & Schuster Custom Publishing.

National Institute of Education, Study Group on the Conditions of Excellence in American Higher Education. (1984). *Involvement in learning: Realizing the potential of American higher education*. Washington, DC: U. S. Government Printing Office.

Palomba, C. A., & Banta, T. W. (1999). *Assessment essentials*. San Francisco: Jossey-Bass.

Payne, D. A. (1997). *Applied educational assessment*. Belmont, CA: Wadsworth.

Plater, W. M. (1998, November-December). So . . . Why *aren't* we taking learning seriously? *About Campus*, 9–14.

Pusey, N. M. (1978). *American higher education: 1945–1970.* Cambridge, MA: Harvard University Press.

Resnick, L., & Resnick, D. (1992). Assessing the thinking curriculum: New tools for educational reform. In B. R. Gifford & M. C. O'Connor (Eds.), *Changing assessments: Alternative views of aptitude, achievement and instruction* (pp. 37–75). Boston: Kluwer Academic Publishers.

Schnell, M. S. (1996, April). Could collaboration be on the horizon? *AAHE Bulletin,* 15–17.

Senge, P. M. (1990). *The fifth discipline: The art and practice of the learning organization.* New York: Doubleday/Currency.

Serban, A. (1998, March-April). The performance funding wave: Views of state policymakers and campus leaders. *Assessment Update, 10* (2), 1–2, 10–11.

Southern Regional Education Board. (1985). *Access to quality undergraduate education: A report to the Southern Regional Education Board by its Commission for Educational Quality.* Atlanta: Southern Regional Education Board.

Stiggins, R. J. (1994). *Student-centered classroom assessment.* New York: Merrill.

Terenzini, P. T., & Pascarella, E. T. (1994, January/February). Living with myths: Undergraduate education in America. *Change,* 28–30.

Thorndike, R. M., Cunningham, G. K., Thorndike, R. L., & Hagen, E. P. (1991). *Measurement and evaluation in psychology and education* (5th ed.). New York: MacMillan.

Walvoord, B. E., Bardes, B., & Denton, J. (1998, September-October). Closing the feedback loop in classroom-based assessment. *Assessment Update, 10* (5), 1–2, 10–11.

Warren, R. G. (1997, March-April). Engaging students in active learning. *About Campus,* 16–20.

Wiggins, G. (1989, May). A true test: Toward more authentic and equitable assessment. *Phi Delta Kappan,* 703–713.

Wiggins, G., & McTighe, J. (1998). *Understanding by design.* Alexandria, VA: Association for Supervision and Curriculum Development.

▶ 2

Understanding Hallmarks of Learner-Centered Teaching and Assessment

There is a slow, but growing trend for practicing quality concepts in teaching . . . classes have become more learner-centered, classes are more focused on learning than teaching, and faculty members have found ways to involve students so that students take more ownership for their learning. In addition, faculty members are systematically collecting feedback from students so that they can make incremental improvement for the students during the course rather than waiting until the course is over (Freed & Klugman, 1997).

While teacher evaluation focuses on teachers and teaching, Classroom Assessment focuses on learners and learning (Angelo, 1994, p. 10).

Making Connections

As you begin to read the chapter, think about ideas and experiences you've already had that are related to learner-centered teaching and assessment . . .

- With what aspects of your *teaching* do you feel satisfied? Dissatisfied?

- With what aspects of *assessment* do you feel satisfied? Dissatisfied?
- How and to what extent do your students take ownership of their learning?

Continued

Making Connections   *Continued*

- What changes would you like to make in your teaching and assessing?
- How might these changes best be made?

What else do you know about learner-centered teaching and assessment?

What questions do you have about learner-centered teaching and assessment?

In this chapter, we will examine eight hallmarks of learner-centered teaching that derive from the field of continuous improvement and from the research of cognitive psychologists and educational researchers. We will see how they are related to some of the propositions for learning developed by the Joint Task Force on Student Learning appointed by the American Association for Higher Education (AAHE), the American College Personnel Association (ACPA), and the National Association of Student Personnel Administrators (Joint Task Force, 1998a, 1998b).

For each hallmark, we will review one or more examples, as well as some questions you can use to reflect on your own teaching. In the remainder of the book, the principles presented here will be translated into specific techniques to help make teaching more learner-centered.

Figure 2–1 summarizes the hallmarks of learner-centered teaching. Several hallmarks focus on learners, describing how they spend their time in ways that promote learning in a learner-centered environment. Other hallmarks focus on the professor, pointing out the viewpoints and activities that professors can employ in order to maximize student learning. The final hallmark indicates that, in learner-centered teaching, learning is viewed as an interpersonal activity. As theorists would put it, learning is "socially constructed." In learner-centered environments, all learners—students and professors—are respected and valued.

- Learners are actively involved and receive feedback.
- Learners apply knowledge to enduring and emerging issues and problems.
- Learners integrate discipline-based knowledge and general skills.
- Learners understand the characteristics of excellent work.
- Learners become increasingly sophisticated learners and knowers.
- Professors coach and facilitate, intertwining teaching and assessing.
- Professors reveal that they are learners, too.
- Learning is interpersonal, and all learners—students and professors—are respected and valued.

FIGURE 2–1   Hallmarks of Learner-Centered Teaching

LEARNERS ARE ACTIVELY INVOLVED
AND RECEIVE FEEDBACK

Learning is an *active search for meaning* by the learner—constructing knowledge rather than passively receiving it, shaping as well as being shaped by experiences (Joint Task Force on Student Learning, 1998a, p. 2).

Over the past 20 years, psychological researchers have documented that the human mind actively creates what it knows. Cognitive psychologists tell us that from the very first moments of life humans begin to interact with and explore the world, actively searching for meaning, constructing and reconstructing mental representations of what it's all about (Copple, Sigel, & Saunders, 1984; Gardner, 1991). Humans seem insatiable for new information and driven to make sense of it. This theory of learning is called constructivism (Bransford, Brown, & Cocking, 1999; Brooks & Brooks, 1993; Duffy & Cunningham, 1996; Fosnot, 1996).

Children, of course, who have less experience than adults and different ways of processing information, develop different perspectives as they grow. But their urge to make their own kind of sense out of what they experience is never ending. As shown in the following examples, cartoonists have made careers out of this characteristic, making us laugh at the unexpected statements of the children in their cartoons, statements that from an adult's perspective are "misconceptions."

- Dennis the Menace, dressed up and sitting in his booster seat at a fancy restaurant, looks at the large menu and says to his parents, "Is this one of those *slow-food* places with carrots on the menu?" (Ketcham, 1997a)
- Dennis the Menace looks up at the lifeguard on the beach and says, "I say, what flavor are the jellyfish today?" (Ketcham, 1997b)
- The little girl in The Family Circus stands by the flowers in the garden and patiently explains to her younger brother, "Butterflies are quiet, but bumblebees have motors" (Keane, 1997).
- The little girl in The Family Circus looks up as she eats her hamburger and says, "If I planted sesame seeds, would I grow hamburger buns?" (Keane, 1998)

All of these are unmistakable examples of children's attempts to construct an understanding of the world that incorporates what they see, hear, and experience. For example, in the first cartoon, Dennis the Menace is using his existing knowledge of fast-food restaurants—their typical environment, menu, and dress—to reason that the current restaurant, which seems different in every way, must be a "slow-food" place. In the words of the Joint Task Force on Learning quoted at the beginning of this section, his existing knowledge about restaurants "is shaping" his current experience. On the other hand, his existing knowledge about restaurants is in turn being shaped by his experience of a formal dining environment. His understanding of the concept "restaurant" is being forever altered.

Experts know now that this process of creating understanding continues throughout a lifetime. This may come as no surprise to modern day followers of Socrates, but to those who approach teaching as though students' minds are blank slates waiting for inscription, it has far-reaching consequences.

For example, it has profound implications for those of us who teach in colleges and universities. Rather than focusing on learners, our traditional approach to teaching has focused on the professor. How organized is the lecture? How accurate and up-to-date is the information in it? Is it well-paced and timed to maintain the needed level of student interest? Teachers "pour in" knowledge, and students are expected to give it back as received. This is the traditional paradigm of teaching: teachers with all the answers performing to passive students.

Those among us who espouse traditional approaches to teaching feel responsible for imparting to students the most current information in our fields. We typically use the lecture method of instruction that requires the professor to seek out new information, integrate it with existing knowledge, organize it for presentation to students, and explain it orally to the class. Students are expected to listen carefully, perhaps asking an occasional question, but basically receiving the information of the lecture in a passive fashion for later regurgitation in a subsequent assessment, probably a test.

From a constructivist perspective, the individuals learning the most in this classroom are the professors. They have reserved for themselves the very conditions that promote learning: actively seeking new information, integrating it with what is known, organizing it in a meaningful way, and having the chance to explain it to others. In fact, all of us who have taught a class more than once know that each time we teach it, our understanding of the material deepens.

Interestingly, the traditional approach to teaching intellectual skills and concepts is not used in performance-oriented areas like the arts or sports. No one would ever think of teaching violin or basketball by having students watch and memorize, whether they watched the teacher or memorized rules. Watching and memorizing simply aren't enough to support learning. Students must be actively involved to learn the concepts and practice the skills.

One more key ingredient of effective learning is present in performance-oriented areas. Students receive constant feedback on their performance.

Sending students out on the basketball court to try to shoot baskets or to explore the game doesn't ensure mastery. Students will undoubtedly have fun, and they will surely learn something. But they'll never master the many interrelated skills of the game unless they get feedback about how they are doing. Providing that feedback is what coaching—teaching and assessing— is all about.

Therefore, students in learner-centered environments learn course material in a way that promotes deep understanding. They are told the intended learning outcomes of their course or program (see Chapter 4), and they are encouraged to formulate their own learning goals (see Chapter 8). As will be discussed in Chapter 7, they complete assignments (assessments) that require them to seek out, organize, describe, and use new information as these activities are carried out in their disciplines. They explore, research, make choices, and explain, and this helps them develop an understanding of the discipline that matches that of experts in the field. In addition, they receive continuous feedback that keeps them on track to make continuous improvements in performance (see Chapter 6).

The learner-centered examples in Figures 2–2 through 2–6 illustrate this hallmark. In each example, the active involvement of the learners helps them make sense of the course material and develop a deeper understanding than they would if they passively listened to a lecture. Feedback to learners is provided through discussion with peers and the professor, through the use of criteria describing excellent work, or through summaries of student responses to in-class surveys.

Reflections

As you create your own meaning from the ideas in this section, begin to think about . . .

- How do I typically think about the students I teach? How would I describe them?
- At what times do I think of them as an audience to whom I play?
- At what times do I think of them as a collection of inquiring minds, each actively engaged in constructing understanding?

- In what ways do I expect my students to defer to me as an expert and an authority?
- In what ways do I work with students as partners in learning?
- When preparing for class, how much emphasis do I give to accurate and well-delivered lectures?
- How much emphasis do I place on activities in which students must *use* course material?

LEARNERS APPLY KNOWLEDGE TO ENDURING AND EMERGING ISSUES AND PROBLEMS

> Learning is enhanced by *taking place* in the context of *a compelling situation* that balances challenge and opportunity, stimulating and utilizing the brain's ability to conceptualize quickly and its capacity and need for contemplation and reflection upon experiences (Joint Task Force on Student Learning, 1998a, p. 1).

In learner-centered teaching, students are asked to do important things worth doing. They don't just acquire knowledge for knowledge's sake. They complete assessments designed around real-world problems (see Chapter 7), and in this way, they experience the compelling challenges typically faced by professionals in their disciplines. The problems they address are ill-defined, that is, they have no right answer and their structure is not always apparent. Some ill-defined problems are enduring (e.g., how to ameliorate world hunger) while others are emerging (how to use the capabilities of technology in an ethical manner). These enduring and emerging issues and problems are fraught with the complicating factors of real life (e.g., politics, value clashes, ambiguity, etc.).

Assessments in which students address ill-defined problems—authentic assessments—are engaging to college students who are making the transition from adolescence to adulthood. Most students enroll in college voluntarily, and they seek to develop an adult identity through the majors they have chosen. Real-world assessments reinforce students' desire to learn and achieve, and they help students develop the direction and identity they seek.

Completing ill-defined problems leads to the understanding that adults are judged on their ability to grapple with the unknown, using the known. As a professor of agriculture pointed out after returning from several years working in industry, "In my undergraduate and graduate education, I was taught using a black and white approach. When I went to work in industry, everything was gray. I know now that my task is to teach 'gray' when working with my own students" (T. Polito, personal communication, 1996).

In traditional educational environments, students typically encounter "black and white" problems that we refer to as "well defined." Well-defined problems are found at the end of most textbook chapters, and they have right answers that are keyed in the back of the book. These problems have been carefully constructed so that some problem elements are present and other problem elements are missing. In other words, the "messiness" of real life is removed so that students will be guided to apply a particular structured algorithm leading to a correct answer.

Well-defined problems are helpful for developing skills that involve many steps. When students complete them, they repeat the steps over and over so that they eventually become habits that can be used when needed. However, just solving well-defined problems doesn't help students know *when and how* the habits and skills should be *used*—and knowing *when and how to use* knowledge is critical to success in adult life. In other words, solving only well-defined problems in college does not prepare students to address the ill-defined problems that adults face daily in their personal and professional lives. Thus, the more we use authentic assessments in our teaching, the more we prepare students to use their knowledge effectively in the future.

Using authentic assessments has other advantages as well. For example, when students complete ill-defined problems, they have an opportunity to reveal their uniqueness as learners. Students bring different talents and learning styles to college, and learner-centered teaching and assessing honors them. Well-defined problems or traditional tests like multiple-choice tests require all students to respond in a uniform way. However, assessments that involve ill-defined problems allow each student to approach, solve, and communicate about the problem in his or her own way.

In addition, involving students in addressing real-world problems frequently leads to opportunities for students to work in teams. Learning is enhanced when it takes place in an environment in which cooperation instead of competition is cultivated. The process of working with others allows students to develop their own ideas through sharing them with others and listening to their feedback. It develops collaborative skills that will benefit them throughout life.

In the first three learner-centered examples (Figures 2–2 through 2–4) students are actively involved with complex issues and problems that are of current concern to practitioners in their discipline: processes for developing effective long-range strategic plans (Business Management), preparing successful bids for contracts (Construction Engineering), and understanding the implications of land management decisions (Forestry). Their ill-defined nature allows students to make errors and learn from them, developing a deeper understanding of their discipline as it is practiced in the real world.

Professor Sanchez teaches a capstone course for Business Management students. She assigns a long-term project for students to work on during the second half of the semester. The project describes a company whose profits have been steadily declining over recent years and requires students to design a process that management can use to develop a long-range, strategic plan. Students are expected to complete the project in teams.

Professor Sanchez outlines her expectations for the type of work students are to produce, and her expectations are based on criteria used in the business world. The purpose of the project is to design a process for developing a long-range, strategic plan that is feasible, defensible, and responsive to the particular company described. In order to do so, students must gather information about relevant legislation, common practice, company needs, and basic management protocol. In teams of three, students assign tasks to each other, discuss findings, brainstorm recommendations, and react to each other's ideas. Through the processes of inquiry, idea generation, and discussion, each student develops a deeper understanding of various aspects of the field of Management.

Feedback is provided when students react to each other's ideas in structured feedback sessions set up by the professor and in the final evaluation of the project. In the feedback sessions, two teams of students present their proposed process and its rationale to each other with one team defending and the other questioning their recommendations. The professor plays devil's advocate or prompts thoughtful reflection by questioning the team's proposals. When students find out, for example, that a certain proposal violates business standards, their understanding of good business practice increases. When each group completes their final project, it is presented to the professor and teaching assistants at which time further questioning takes place, and additional feedback is provided.

(Adapted from Ulrichson, 1998)

FIGURE 2–2   A Learner-Centered Example from Business Management

Reflections

As you create your own meaning from the ideas in this section, begin to think about . . .

- What *enduring* issues and problems do students address in my course? How do they address them?
- What *emerging* issues and problems do students address in my course? How do they address them?

- Where and how do students have opportunities to solve *well*-defined problems in my courses?
- Where and how do students have opportunities to solve *ill*-defined problems in my courses?
- How do my students see the connection between what they learn in my courses and how that information is used in real-world applications?

For several years, Professor Jahren has been teaching his Construction Engineering students how to prepare bids for construction projects like building a bridge or grading a highway. For most of his career, he lectured about the cost estimating process and assigned homework problems and labs that were meant to help students develop necessary skills. His exams included problems and essay questions to test students' understanding of the basic knowledge and skills involved in preparing bids that meet specifications and are feasible, cost-effective, and technically sound. In recent years, however, he followed the lead of his senior colleagues and developed a simulated bid opening for his final lab in which students incorporated a myriad of subcontractor and supplier quotes into their bids and tendered their completed bids to him.

Professor Jahren was pleased by his students' enthusiasm for the simulated bid opening. He received many compliments on student evaluations as well as requests to make the simulation more realistic. Therefore, when local construction industry leaders suggested that his students submit mock bids at an actual state transportation bid-letting, he quickly agreed. The industry people had seen students participating in a similar activity in a neighboring state. They pointed out that the activity helps students learn to work in groups under stress and correctly make last minute modifications to a complicated analysis. In addition, it allows engineers in industry to share an important part of their job that is little understood by the general public.

Professor Jahren developed the activity into a special project course. In the course, students get credit for preparing bids for actual construction projects (e.g., replacing bridges, grading, paving) designed by state, county, and municipal transportation agencies around the state. Students present their bids to transportation officials as mock bids at the same time that local contractors submit their actual bids. The students' mock bids are examined and evaluated along with the real ones, and students receive feedback on their work.

In executing this project, sophomore through senior students work in teams of three or four with seniors serving as team leaders. They design the construction process on paper, using the same information that is available to other professionals in the community. Next, students estimate the cost of implementing their design. In this phase of the project, they have access to a local company whose staff have been assigned to act as mentors. Interacting with the mentors provides an opportunity to develop skills in professional interaction. Finally, students submit their project to the transportation officials according to the same deadline and standards followed by local contractors.

Professor Jahren and his practitioner colleagues have developed criteria for judging the students' work (e.g., timeliness of the proposal, quality of materials used, adequacy of structural design, ability to respond to changing conditions, effectiveness of written and oral communication). They share these criteria with students when the project is assigned, and each semester the students themselves help improve the criteria.

Over time, students have begun to use the criteria as guidelines for developing their project. Professor Jahren meets with students periodically for progress reports about their project. He and the students use the criteria to assess what they are doing well and where they need to improve. In the future, Professor Jahren plans to have students rate the final version of their project using the criteria and hand in their ratings with the project. Both students and professors in the program have come to a clearer understanding of how to prepare effectively for bid-letting competitions in the real world of engineering.

(Jahren & Kipp, 1999)

FIGURE 2–3   A Learner-Centered Example from Construction Engineering

The faculty in a Forestry program organize their sophomore students into cohorts, and each cohort takes a five-course sequence of courses together. The courses in the sequence are taught by Forestry professors and are designed to integrate general education skills and disciplinary knowledge in Forestry. In each course professors teach and evaluate knowledge and skills related to inquiry, teamwork, application of mathematics, and oral and written communication, as well as standard course content.

Students complete a team project that gets them actively involved in addressing the political, environmental, economic, and social implications of land management decisions. Students gather data in the field, analyze it, and communicate their findings through oral and written reports. They confer regularly with the professor and participate in feedback discussions about their progress. At the conclusion of the project, students reflect about how well the team functioned as a whole and about how well they contributed individually to the team's success. They discuss together how they might do a better job working together in the future.

(Department of Forestry Faculty, 1998)

FIGURE 2–4   A Learner-Centered Example from Forestry

LEARNERS INTEGRATE DISCIPLINE-BASED KNOWLEDGE AND GENERAL SKILLS

Learning is fundamentally about *making and maintaining connections*: biologically through neural networks; mentally among concepts, ideas, and meanings; experientially through interaction between the mind and the environment, self and other, generality and context, deliberation and action (Joint Task Force on Student Learning, 1998a, p. 1).

Assessments designed around ill-defined problems typically take the form of projects, papers, performances, portfolios, or exhibitions. Students completing them have to call upon and develop their disciplinary knowledge, as well as their skills in the areas of inquiry, reasoning, problem solving, communication, and perhaps teamwork. In other words, authentic assessments require that students make connections between the abilities and skills they have developed in the general education curriculum and the discipline-based knowledge and skills they have acquired in the major. When authentic assessments are used, the evaluation issue changes from, "Are students getting the right answers?" to:

- Can students demonstrate the qualities we value in educated persons, the qualities we expect of college graduates?
- Can they gather and evaluate new information, think critically, reason effectively, and solve problems?

- Can they communicate clearly, drawing upon evidence to provide a basis for argumentation?
- Do their decisions and judgments reflect understanding of universal truths revealed in the humanities and the arts?
- Can they work respectfully and productively with others?
- Do they have self-regulating qualities like persistence and time management that will help them reach long-term goals?

In sum, can students use the skills and abilities that the general education curriculum has been designed to develop?

Even more important, authentic assessments allow us to ask, "Can students demonstrate the characteristics we expect from professionals in our disciplines? Can students think and behave like biologists, statisticians, landscape architects, teachers, and so on?"

At this point, assessment questions become more refined. Rather than the general question, "Can students communicate clearly?" we ask the more specific question, "Can students communicate like professionals in their fields?" Clearly, communication and problem-solving skills, as well as others like the application of ethical principles, change from discipline to discipline. To some extent, the communication skills required of engineers are different from those required of journalists. To some extent, the ethical questions facing geneticists are different from those facing teachers. Authentic assessments provide excellent opportunities to tailor students' learning to the fields in which they will work.

Obviously, learner-centered teaching gives greater prominence to "process" abilities and skills like communication and reasoning than traditional teaching practices may have done. However, learner-centered teaching does not de-emphasize basic knowledge in the discipline. As Resnick and Resnick (1992) point out, students who have greater command of the knowledge of their discipline can reason and communicate more effectively than those with less knowledge. Professors who take a learner-centered approach do not shortchange students in basic knowledge—they help them *use* it.

The projects in the first three examples (Figures 2–2 through 2–4) require the integration of disciplinary knowledge and numerous skills and abilities from the general education curriculum in the areas of inquiry, communication, problem solving, and teamwork. They provide the means through which students can actually *use* the knowledge of their discipline.

Reflections

As you create your own meaning from the ideas in this section, begin to think about . . .

- How do I emphasize critical thinking and problem solving in my courses?
- How do I help students integrate the skills and perspectives they learn in general education with the content of my discipline?
- How do I help students make connections between my course and other courses they have had or will have in the curriculum?

- How do I help students think and behave like members of the discipline?
- How comfortable or uncomfortable am I with this idea?
- What do I think about focusing on communication, critical thinking, teamwork, and so forth, with students as they learn the content of my discipline? How will these skills help them learn content more effectively?

PAUSE FOR AN EXAMPLE: DIFFERENCES BETWEEN TYPICAL TEACHING PRACTICE AND THE FIRST THREE HALLMARKS

Thus far, we have emphasized the active involvement of learners in activities and assessments that integrate discrete skills and abilities. We have also focused on the importance of helping students make connections between existing knowledge and new information and between what they learn in college and what takes place in the world of practice in their disciplines. How do these suggestions differ from the typical student experience? The following is an example.

Professors in most statistics departments probably expect their graduates to be able to explain statistical findings clearly to an educated audience that is not trained in statistics. This requires knowledge of statistical theory and practice, ability to use modern computing techniques, writing ability, and oral presentation skills (Department of Statistics, 1996).

Recognizing this, statistics faculty at most institutions have designed the curriculum so that students acquire the needed skills and understandings. Students take several courses in both parametric and nonparametric statistical theory. Some courses include computer applications that make use of modern computing technology. Built into the program is the general education requirement of a freshman writing course, and some students take a speech communication course as an elective. Does this ensure that the faculty's goal for graduates will be achieved? Probably not.

As it turns out, three difficulties occur with this approach. First, the important intended outcome of having graduates "explain statistical findings clearly to an educated audience that is not trained in statistics" is approached in the curriculum by having students take separate courses in statistics, computing, writing, and speaking. The writing and speech communications courses are probably outside their department. When important activities are divided up in this way, students learn the parts in isolation, but they receive no practice integrating the parts into a new, more complex "whole" (Resnick & Resnick, 1992). In this example, students are never asked to write and speak about statistics in their undergraduate program.

Second, the components tend to be taught outside the real-world context in which the performance typically takes place (Resnick & Resnick, 1992). Students lose the opportunity to see the real-world application for what they are studying; that is, they miss the forest for the trees. Motivation and a sense of direction are lost. In the example given, it probably never occurs to students in statistics classes that someday they will be asked to use their expertise to explain real-life data to "lay" audiences. They probably focus more on getting the right answers on tests than on integrating their statistical knowledge and communication abilities into a valued professional skill.

Third, the basic assumption that students will automatically apply knowledge when needed has turned out to be false. Research has shown that students can learn facts, theories, or individual tasks, but without the opportunity to use the knowledge or skill to achieve a goal, it is recalled only in the context in which it was learned (Bransford & Vye, 1989). In other words, the knowledge is "inert" (Whitehead, 1929).

This phenomenon helps explain why students who acquire knowledge and/or skills in one course seem unable to effectively use them in the next course. It may account for the extensive amount of on-the-job learning that college graduates typically need. They probably acquired the theory or some skills relevant to their job, but they need experienced co-workers to help them make the theory-to-practice connection. The public is becoming increasingly impatient with the training employers are required to provide for college graduates. Taxpayers today have higher expectations for higher education institutions, and they are demanding accountability.

A learner-centered solution to the statistics problem would retain the intended learning outcome of the statistics faculty ("Students should be able to explain statistical findings clearly to an educated audience that is not trained in statistics") because it focuses on student learning and reflects an important achievement valued by practicing statisticians. An additional step would be to reveal this intended learning outcome to students themselves in the college catalog and in course syllabi. (See Chapter 4 for a discussion of intended learning outcomes.)

The next step would be to provide opportunities for students to integrate the components of the outcome (statistical knowledge, computing, writing, and speaking) as students are learning about them. For example, as students learn about new statistical techniques in their statistics courses, they should not only solve numerical statistical problems, but they should also complete writing or speaking assignments interpreting the results. When this is done in beginning statistics courses, students will be relatively unsophisticated in integrating statistical knowledge, computing, writing, and speaking. The components will seem somewhat separate (Loacker, Cromwell, & O'Brien, 1986). However, by the time students have completed several courses, they will have developed rather sophisticated and well-coordinated abilities to "explain statistical findings clearly to an audience that is educated but not trained in statistics."

A related step for statistics faculty would be to teach students how to identify opportunities to apply their newfound skill in real-life applications and how to carry it out appropriately in different settings. In other words, statistics professors who want graduates to communicate effectively about statistics should ask students to do so while they are enrolled in their statistics courses.

We will now return to a consideration of additional hallmarks of learner-centered teaching and assessing.

Reflections

As you create your own meaning from the ideas in this section, begin to think about . . .

- What practices in my program reflect a learner-centered approach to teaching?

- What practices in my program interfere with a learner-centered approach to teaching?
- How could these practices be changed to reflect the hallmarks of learner-centered teaching and assessment?

LEARNERS UNDERSTAND THE CHARACTERISTICS OF EXCELLENT WORK

Learning requires *frequent feedback* if it is to be sustained, *practice* if it is to be nourished, and *opportunities to use* what has been learned (Joint Task Force on Student Learning, 1998a, p. 3).

In a learner-centered culture in which students seek to address enduring and emerging issues and problems, we must develop a focus on the quality of work expected and allow students to make errors as they seek to achieve it.

Solving ill-defined problems rather than problems with one right answer means that students *will* make errors. In learner-centered teaching, however, mistakes are opportunities on which to capitalize, rather than events to avoid.

> *Errors are part of the process of problem solving, which implies that both teachers and learners need to be more tolerant of them. If no mistakes are made, then almost certainly no problem solving is taking place. Unfortunately, one tradition of schooling is that perfect performance is often exalted as the ideal. Errors are seen as failures, as signs that the highest marks are not quite merited. . . . Perfect performance may be a reasonable criterion for evaluating algorithmic performance (though I doubt it), but it is incompatible with problem solving (Martinez, 1998, p. 609).*

Thus, a key ingredient in learner-centered teaching is allowing students to make mistakes and learn from them. In order for students to learn from their errors, we must create an environment of honesty without fear (Deming, 1986). We must provide students with a clear vision of what excellent work is like and help them use feedback to continually improve their own work and performance. We must develop clearly stated, public criteria in the form of scoring rubrics that describe excellent work and that can be used as the basis for feedback. Having clear standards of performance—that is, being able to describe the defining features of excellent work—is essential for improvement (Loacker, Cromwell, & O'Brien, 1986; Wiggins, 1993).

As will be discussed in Chapter 6, criteria in the form of rubrics can be developed by the professor or by the professor and students together. When public criteria are available and discussions about the quality of work are common, students don't have to wait for the first test to figure out what aspects of learning the professor considers important. They know right from the beginning. Using available criteria, students can assess and judge their own work, even in the early stages of formulation, and they are thus more motivated to take ownership of their own learning. Furthermore, students can work with each other to critique their work, judging it not simply by their own idiosyncratic standards, but also by the standards the professor has shared or developed with the class.

Most importantly, students can use the criteria to self-correct, because improvement in learning is what assessment is all about.

> *We've heard a lot during the past ten or fifteen years in both the higher education and K-12 settings about the importance of student self-assessment. Despite the importance of the idea, it is a misleading phrase. Self-assessment is not the goal. Self-adjustment is the goal (Wiggins, 1997, p. 35).*

The opportunity to self-correct and try again is essential to self-improvement and the development of lifelong learning skills; this is the underlying premise of continuous improvement. With rapid changes in the workplace due to the technology explosion, employers expect graduates to be able to learn independently. They must be flexible, skilled at making adjustments, and willing to take responsibility for making improvements.

In our role as professors, we can also use scoring criteria to give feedback about student work as it evolves. Furthermore, we can use the criteria to evaluate the final product. Assessing with clearly described criteria that have been publicly revealed is very different from assessing using an answer key that specifies "right" answers. We are able to evaluate qualities such as organization, communication, creativity, and ability to apply a known body of knowledge. We can allow students to approach assignments in unique ways, but we judge all work by the same criteria. By revealing standards of excellence, we remove barriers to learning. Of course, for many reasons, not all students will perform at the level of excellence, but revealing the standards held by educated people and by practicing professionals enhances students' chances of success.

Does this make assessments more subjective than tests that can be objectively scored by machines? Of course. But students will be judged subjectively throughout their adult lives. The important task is to let them know the standards shared by educated people and by individuals in their profession. In other words, assessment that is *subjective but public* may be more important than assessment that is *objective but private*.

In a learner-centered course, all students know the standards for excellence and therefore have a chance to produce excellent work. The instructor is not the only, or even perhaps the most important, evaluator. All engaged in the learning process have a stake in serving as assessors. Having public standards creates an environment that is fundamentally fair, downplaying the current need to figure out the system. This benefits all students, but it may be particularly helpful to nontraditional students who are faced with the need to "learn the ropes" on many fronts at college, creating barriers to learning. Learner-centered teaching helps circumvent those barriers. As the student population becomes increasingly more diverse, public standards of excellence ensure fairness for all.

The clearest example of this hallmark is found in Figure 2–3. In this Construction Engineering example, students and professors initially develop criteria for judging students' completed work. However, they soon find that the criteria are useful tools for students to use as they develop their work. The criteria are also a good basis for discussion when students talk about their progress with the professor. The professor in this example eventually decides to structure students' own assessment of their achievement into the project requirements.

Reflections

As you create your own meaning from the ideas in this section, begin to think about . . .

- How do my students and I view student errors? Are they something to avoid or are they learning opportunities?
- Do I expect excellent performance from all my students? How do I help them reach this level?

- How do I reveal to students the qualities that make an assignment excellent?
- Do I ever ask students what they think excellent work is like? Do we work together to develop the grading criteria on which their work will be judged?
- How can I encourage students to evaluate their own work, developing ideas about what they do well and where they could improve?

LEARNERS BECOME INCREASINGLY SOPHISTICATED LEARNERS AND KNOWERS

Learning involves the *ability of individuals to monitor their own learning*, to understand how knowledge is acquired, to develop strategies for learning based on discerning their capacities and limitations, and to be aware of their own ways of knowing in approaching new bodies of knowledge and disciplinary frameworks (Joint Task Force on Student Learning, 1998a, p. 3).

Learning is *developmental*, a cumulative process *involving the whole person*, relating past and present, integrating the new with the old, starting from and transcending personal concerns and interests (Joint Task Force on Student Learning, 1998a, p. 2).

Much learning takes place *informally and incidentally*, beyond explicit teaching or the classroom, in casual contacts with faculty and staff, peers, campus life, active social and community involvements, and unplanned but fertile and complex situations (Joint Task Force on Student Learning, 1998a, p. 3).

Learning is *grounded in particular contexts and individual experiences*, requiring effort to transfer specific knowledge and skills to other circumstances or to more general understandings and to unlearn personal views and approaches when confronted with new information (Joint Task Force on Student Learning, 1998a, p. 3).

In learner-centered teaching, students reflect upon what they learn and how they learn. Reflection is a powerful activity for helping professors and students understand the present learning environment and think of ways to improve it. Research has shown that students who reflect on their learning are better learners than those who do not (Cornesky & Lazarus, 1995; Cross, 1996). In a learner-centered environment, reflections may take the form of journals or learning logs. They may also be included when portfolios are used in assessment (see Chapter 8).

As students reflect upon their knowledge, they—and we—begin to realize that learning about the topic of a course doesn't begin on the first day of a course. Students have either encountered course topics before or have developed related or prerequisite skills and abilities through their life experiences or in earlier stages of their education. We also come to realize that student learning isn't confined to course settings. Students may be learning about and applying course content in a variety of settings on and off campus (Kuh, 1997).

When we take a learner-centered approach, we are sensitive to the fact that, through these previous and current experiences, students may have developed understandings of concepts that will serve as an effective springboard for new learning, or they may have developed understandings that are superficial or inaccurate (Wandersee, Mintzes, & Novak, 1994). They may have acquired skills that can support increasingly sophisticated performance, or their skills may be poorly developed or incompatible with highly-skilled performance. These prior learnings must be addressed in teaching, because students will construct new understanding and skills by integrating new information with existing structures.

Therefore, in learner-centered teaching, it is important when we introduce new material or applications that we have students discuss what they already know about a topic, as well as the experiences that led to their knowledge. It may also be helpful in some situations to have students discuss how they feel about a topic.

> *When certain topics or educational strategies are emotionally challenging for particular students, this situation should be acknowledged. For example, learning about atrocities conducted in a war in which a student's own relatives fought may make her wonder if her grandfather had been involved in such reprehensible conduct; studying about campus violence has made some men wonder if they have committed a rape. . . . To expect students to write detached, objective analyses of situations for which they have unresolved or emerging personal issues is to deny that students are multifaceted individuals, not just "talking heads," and that emotionally powerful questions may serve as barriers to reflective thinking on particular issues (King & Kitchener, 1994, p. 246).*

Such discussion helps students become aware of their knowledge and feelings. When current concepts, skills, and attitudes are compatible with or supportive of new learning, discussion assists students as they attempt to make sense of new information.

When current concepts and habits are incompatible with progress in the discipline, we can engage students in inquiry (Kurfiss, 1988), providing opportunities for them to confront new information that challenges their existing view. We can guide students to new understandings that are in harmony with the best knowledge in the field. As Resnick and Klopfer (1989) point out, "Before knowledge becomes truly generative—knowledge that can be used to interpret new situations, to solve problems, to think and reason, and to learn—students must elaborate and question what they are told, examine new information in relation to other information, and build new knowledge structures" (p. 5).

Both before and after instruction, we may wish to anticipate common misunderstandings that students develop. For example, Wiggins and McTighe (1998) include "Misconception Alert" boxes throughout the chapters of their book. In these boxes, they expand upon what they meant in certain sections and point out what they didn't mean. We can use similar strategies to detect common misunderstandings when we interact directly with students. "Teaching for understanding requires time, a deep understanding of the subject on the part of the instructor, and a perceptiveness in diagnosing students' problems in understanding" (Kurfiss, 1988, p. 36).

In addition to issues associated with students' prior learning, there is another critical aspect of learning that we should attend to in learner-centered teaching. It derives from the fact that, over time, students change not only in terms of *what* they know, but also in terms of *how* they know (Baxter Magolda, 1992, 1996; King & Kitchener, 1994). An important role for professors is to provoke more sophisticated ways of knowing on the part of students.

To elaborate, Baxter Magolda (1992, 1996) identified several types of knowers in her research with college students. For example, she found that most college freshmen believe that knowledge is certain and that there are absolute or right answers in all areas of knowledge. For them, learning is a process of obtaining knowledge from a teacher, and evaluation is an opportunity to show the teacher what they know. This way of knowing reflects and undoubtedly develops from the role students experience in the traditional paradigm.

In contrast, the most sophisticated knowers in Baxter Magolda's (1996) study "believe that knowledge is uncertain and that one decides what to believe by evaluating the evidence in the context in question" (p. 284). They believe that both learning and evaluation should consist of interactions between students and professors in which students can think "through problems, integrating knowledge, and applying knowledge in context" (p. 284). In Baxter Magolda's study, only two percent of undergraduates had reached this viewpoint as they neared graduation.

Individuals tend to reach this level of knowing in graduate schools and professional schools or in the workplace (Baxter Magolda, 1996). Faculty in graduate and professional schools foster this development by helping students relate course material to their own experiences, providing challenging situations in which students can extend their knowledge, and encouraging students to analyze and justify their beliefs. In the workplace, individuals are "expected to function independently, make subjective decisions, take on the role of authority, and work collaboratively with coworkers" (p. 286). If we bring many of these positive features into the undergraduate environment through adopting a more learner-centered approach, we may help students learn how to learn in a more sophisticated manner.

Another implication of Baxter Magolda's research is that the success of student learning in a course may depend on students' paradigms about learning as much as it depends on professors' paradigms (Warren, 1997). This suggestion was raised in Chapter 1. Students who believe that knowing is accumulating certain and true information (Baxter Magolda, 1996) will be more comfortable in the traditional situation in which the professor imparts such information to them. This type of environment confirms their beliefs about the nature of knowledge and how it is acquired, and they will undoubtedly feel that they learn best in this environment.

Such students will initially feel confused and threatened in a learner-centered situation in which we coach and guide them to construct their own knowledge. This type of learning environment is based on an epistemology that is different from the one they currently endorse, and they will probably resist our attempts to engage them in new roles. Thus, when we shift from the traditional teacher-centered paradigm to a learner-centered paradigm, it is important that we discuss the process and the reasons for it with students. For learning to be maximized, we and our students must shift paradigms together.

In learner-centered environments then, we seek to understand not only what students know, but also how they know it. We help students develop insight into the nature of their current understanding of a field. We also help them understand their beliefs about knowledge and how it is acquired. Learner-centered professors use teaching techniques that help students develop into more sophisticated knowers. As students develop epistemologically, they become increasingly able to think and reason in ways that correspond to society's expectations for college graduates.

The professors in the Business Management and Construction Engineering examples in Figures 2–2 and 2–3 provide ample opportunities for students to address ill-defined problems, to reason, and to share their reasoning with others. Students develop ideas and discuss them with their peers and with the professors themselves. Constant questioning and dialogue expose students to the ideas and ways of thinking of others, helping them develop insights about the uncertain nature of knowledge. Questioning and dialogue also challenge students to defend their own ideas more rigorously.

The Mathematics and Sociology examples in Figures 2–5 and 2–6 illustrate respect for students' knowledge and ways of knowing. When Professor Jackson (Figure 2–5) senses that calculus courses are ineffective, he takes a risk and adopts a new strategy for helping students take ownership of their own learning. When Professor Okere (Figure 2–6) tries out a new teaching

Faculty in the Mathematics Department are concerned about the low retention of students in introductory calculus classes, and they have been discussing ways to address the problem. Professor Jackson has heard about the base group technique of improving student involvement, and he decides to give it a try.

Professor Jackson divides his calculus students into teams of four—each is a base group—and tells them that the members of their base group *are expected* to work together on assigned out-of-class problems. Professor Jackson gives them some training on group effectiveness, covering topics like how to call a meeting, how to facilitate a meeting, and how to keep on task. The group is expected to turn in one completed assignment for the group, and all members are required to "sign off" that they participated and that they endorse the solutions submitted. When the group cannot come to consensus on a solution, they are expected to contact and work with another base group. They may also come to class and indicate that they are unable to move on to new material without more help. Some class time is occasionally devoted to having students work in base groups.

Over time, Professor Jackson observes a change in the course climate. Rather than feeling that he shoulders the burden for the achievement of the entire class, he begins to feel that the course is becoming the students' course. Students are spending more time on calculus, and they are partnering with him to determine the direction and pacing of the course. In-class participation has increased because students now know their peers personally and feel comfortable asking questions in front of them. Retention of knowledge improves, and grades on the final are dramatically better than those on the midterm.

(Adapted from the work of Keller, Russell, & Thompson, 1999)

FIGURE 2–5   A Learner-Centered Example from Mathematics

technique, she relies on students to help her understand if the technique really improves student learning. These approaches honor students' insights into their learning and convey trust and respect for students as learners.

Reflections

As you create your own meaning from the ideas in this section, begin to think about . . .

- What do I do to find out what students already know about the topics of my courses? How do I use this information?
- How can I learn more about students' beliefs about knowledge and the way it is acquired?

- How do I help my students reflect on what they know and how they know?
- How can I help students with traditional teacher-centered views of learning shift to a more learner-centered paradigm?
- How can I identify students' misconceptions about my discipline and help modify them?

Professor Okere received her Ph.D. in Sociology twenty years ago and has been teaching undergraduate students since then, even though during her graduate program she received no formal training in teaching. Last year, Professor Okere joined a faculty development program on campus in order to learn some new techniques to make her teaching more effective.

Of all the techniques she learned about, Cooperative Learning was the most appealing, and Professor Okere decided to use it in her course entitled Sex and Gender in Society. Following the principles she learned in the faculty development program, she organized the class into cooperative groups that met for part of each class session. At the end of every other week, she used an anonymous questionnaire to survey her students about the effectiveness of the groups and their satisfaction with learning using this new approach. Professor Okere summarized the students' responses and shared them with the students themselves, asking for their help in interpreting some of the reactions she observed. Based on student feedback, she made continual modifications throughout the semester in the organization and implementation of the groups, and she observed that student satisfaction with the cooperative approach increased steadily.

Professor Okere also observed that students became increasingly comfortable with their role as classroom assessors. Students began to contact her on their own with occasional suggestions for course improvement. Often, they felt comfortable enough to identify themselves when they left or sent their messages. Through comments that students included on course evaluation forms, Professor Okere learned that students appreciated her flexibility in incorporating their suggestions into the course format.

(Okere, 1997)

FIGURE 2–6   A Learner-Centered Example from Sociology

PROFESSORS COACH AND FACILITATE, INTERTWINING TEACHING AND ASSESSING

> Learning is strongly *affected by the educational climate* in which it takes place, the settings and surroundings, the influences of others, and the values accorded to the life of the mind and to learning achievements (Joint Task Force on Student Learning, 1998a, p. 2).

Previous sections of this chapter described new roles for students in learner-centered environments. When students are given new roles, professors have new roles as well. When teaching within the traditional model, we may be comfortable being the primary information givers and primary evaluators. However, shifting to a learner-centered approach challenges us to take risks and share these roles with students. Modifying traditional roles can be temporarily unsettling for us, but it does not mean that we "lose control" or lower our standards. Rather, by involving students in activities that enhance their learning, we more effectively control the direction and pace of learning in our courses. From a continuous improvement perspective, professors who are learner-centered:

> *view themselves as supporters rather than judges, as mentors and coaches rather than lecturers, as partners with students, administrators, teachers, businesses, and communities rather than isolated workers within the walls of the classrooms. We now understand that the only way to ensure our own growth is by helping others to grow; the only way to maximize our own potential is by helping others to improve little by little, day by day (Bonstingl, 1996, p. 5).*

When we take a learner-centered approach, we may also be considered leaders who facilitate and guide our students into new areas of understanding (Cornesky & Lazarus, 1995). Rather than simply imparting information, we make sure students understand and can *use* it. We provide a variety of opportunities for students to discuss and use new information.

For example, rather than lecturing for 30 minutes, a learner-centered professor may stop after several minutes to pose a question related to the material under consideration. The professor may then ask students to think for a minute about their own answers and to turn to another student to discuss their ideas and prepare an answer together. The professor can then call upon different students to share their answers with the class. The processes of sharing and of listening to and discussing the answers of others may reinforce students' own ideas, or they may provide an opportunity to modify them. In addition when students share their answers, professors can informally assess the depth of students' understanding.

When we participate in learner-centered teaching, we also guide students as they seek out information on their own. We teach students research skills and help them evaluate information and sources critically. As students share their findings, either orally or in writing, we can give feedback that students can use to improve their work. Other students can participate in giving feedback as well. Feedback is based on known standards for high quality work that we may have developed with students at the beginning of the course or project.

In this way, assessment in college courses changes from a process of occasionally monitoring student knowledge to one of providing continuous, meaningful feedback on important, valued characteristics. In the traditional paradigm, teaching and assessing are considered separate activities, with one following the other. Tests, the primary form of assessment, are scheduled at predictable times like midterm and finals week following several weeks of instruction. Their results give students a report about where they stand at any given point in time. However, "if assessment is viewed as a final judgment instead of a means to improvement, it can be a barrier to learning" (Griffith, McLure, & Weitzel, 1995, p. 1). Students not only fail to receive direction for improvement, but they also come to expect that learning can take place without it.

In a learner-centered environment, however, teaching and assessing are not separate, episodic events, but rather, they are ongoing, interrelated activities focused on providing guidance for improvement. If students are to develop important abilities and skills, they need to practice what they are learning and receive continuous feedback they can use to evaluate and regulate their performance. Students attempting to emulate practicing agronomists in the profession they aspire to join need feedback before midterm to know if they're on the right track. Both teaching and assessment must become ongoing activities that provide direction for learners.

When this happens, learning will be enhanced, but the learning environment will look and feel different than it has before. To individuals operating in the traditional teaching paradigm, it may seem unfamiliar.

A biology instructor was experimenting with collaborative methods of instruction in his beginning biology classes. One day his dean came for a site visit, slipping into the back of the room. The room was a hubbub of activity. Students were discussing material enthusiastically in small groups spread out across the room; the instructor would observe each group for a few minutes, sometimes making a comment, sometimes just nodding approval. After 15 minutes or so the dean approached the instructor and said, "I came today to do your evaluation. I'll come back another time when you're teaching" (Barr & Tagg, 1995, p. 17).

As the example illustrates, a learner-centered approach requires faculty, students, and administrators to shift their paradigms to an understanding that teaching is engaging students in the creation of meaning.

The Management and Construction Engineering examples in Figures 2–2 and 2–3 illustrate this hallmark. In each case, the professor departs from the traditional role of lecturer to meet with small groups of students, react to their ideas, play devil's advocate, and prompt student reflection through questioning. Feedback is given continually, and in one case, clear and publicly stated criteria of good work form the basis of feedback. In these unconventional roles, the professors continually teach and continually assess learning.

Reflections

As you create your own meaning from the ideas in this section, begin to think about . . .

- For how long do I lecture without interruption?
- When I give students an opportunity to talk to each other about what I have presented, how do I structure their discussions?
- What aspects of my teaching could be considered "coaching and faci-

litating" rather than "selling and telling?"

- What are students doing when I am coaching and facilitating?
- To what extent do I consider assessment to be a periodic event that is *separate from* teaching?
- To what extent do I consider assessment to be a continual activity that is *part of* teaching?

PROFESSORS REVEAL THAT THEY ARE LEARNERS, TOO

College instructors who have assumed that their students were learning what they were trying to teach them are regularly faced with disappointing evidence to the contrary when they grade tests and term papers. Too often, students have not learned as much or as well as was expected. There are gaps, sometimes considerable ones, between what was taught and what has been learned. By the time faculty notice these gaps in knowledge or understanding, it is frequently too late to remedy the problems (Angelo & Cross, 1993, p. 3).

Just as students need feedback to improve, so do the professors who provide the direction and guidance. We need to know what students understand and don't understand so that we can modify our own performance as teachers, if necessary. We also need to identify barriers to learning that students may be experiencing—even barriers that we may have inadvertently created. In other words, we need to adapt the definition of assessment presented in Chapter 1 to ourselves as teachers. We must use information from multiple and diverse sources to analyze, discuss, and judge our own performance in order to improve student learning.

Thus, when we take a learner-centered approach, we design assessments to gather opinions from students on a regular basis about how well they are learning and about how the course format helps or hinders their efforts (see

Chapter 5). The information helps us "analyze, discuss, and judge" our own performance in order to remove obstacles in students' paths and enhance their ability to learn. This information is typically collected from students anonymously and the results are shared with the whole class. By revealing to students that we are willing to use their input to improve the course, we create an atmosphere of partnership and trust. We use assessment to reveal that we are learners, too.

There are also other ways in which we are learners in learner-centered courses, and we can reveal them to students as well. We mentioned earlier that each time we teach our courses, our understanding of the course content deepens. In addition, we learn new information as we keep up with developments in our fields and share new information with students. We also learn from guest presenters whom we may invite to class, and we learn from students themselves. The questions students ask and the insights they share provoke our own learning. We can also learn from nontraditional students who may have had more practical experience in our discipline than we have had.

There are several benefits of revealing to students that we view ourselves as learners. It helps students develop an appreciation and understanding of the importance of lifelong learning. It can also deepen their sense that professors and students are partners in learning, thus helping them shift from the traditional paradigm of teaching to a learner-centered paradigm. Finally, students appreciate and respect professors who attempt to become better teachers.

In one sense, all the examples in Figures 2–2 through 2–6 illustrate the fact that professors are learners, too. In each, the professor uses an approach to teaching that actively involves learners in creating their own knowledge and sharing their ideas with others. Through dialogue with students, professors continually learn more about how their students learn and about the ways their discipline is understood by others. In addition, three of the examples (Construction Engineering, Mathematics, and Sociology) describe professors who are learning new approaches to teaching. Not only have they revealed that fact to students, they have also asked students to help them know what works and what does not work.

Reflections

As you create your own meaning from the ideas in this section, begin to think about . . .

- How do I reveal to my students that I need their help in order to improve my teaching or make the course more useful for them?

- How could I improve this process?
- How do I reveal to students that I am continually learning more about my discipline?
- How can I help my students view me as a partner in learning?

LEARNING IS INTERPERSONAL, AND ALL LEARNERS—STUDENTS AND PROFESSORS— ARE RESPECTED AND VALUED

> Learning is done by *individuals* who are intrinsically *tied to others as social beings*, interacting as competitors or collaborators, constraining or supporting the learning process, and able to enhance learning through cooperation and sharing (Joint Task Force on Student Learning, 1998a, p. 2).

We referred earlier to Baxter Magolda's (1996) research with students in graduate and professional schools in which they discussed factors that helped them learn. Two important themes emerged, reflecting the contention of Seymour and Chaffee (1992) that "both the process and love of learning are fundamentally social phenomena" (p. 28).

One factor that helped students learn was mutual respect between students and teachers. Students reported that effective professors treated them like adults and involved them in making decisions regarding the class direction and activities. Students felt central to the class environment. In this atmosphere, they "were freer to explore their thinking, connect knowledge to self, and use their experience in settings characterized by mutual teacher–student respect" (Baxter Magolda, 1996, p. 298).

Another factor that facilitated learning was collaboration among peers in exchanging perspectives. Students came to learn that experience is part of knowing, and this realization increased their interest in hearing about the diverse experiences of others. Sharing their own experiences with others helped students clarify their own perspectives—"what to believe, why they believed something, and how to act on their beliefs" (Baxter Magolda, 1996, p. 300). As trust among students grew, students "were able to take greater risks in exploring their beliefs and take advantage of diverse perspectives in knowledge construction" (Baxter Magolda, 1996, p. 300).

The importance of mutual respect between us and our students and among students themselves is reflected in W. Edwards Deming's (1986) Fourteen Points of Quality. As discussed in Chapter 1, these points were originally developed for business settings. However, they apply to educational settings as well (Greenwood & Gaunt, 1994), and Deming's eighth point, "Drive out fear," is especially relevant to a discussion of the interpersonal nature of learning. Deming believed that people cannot perform up to their potential unless they feel free to act without fear, free to express ideas, and free to ask questions. For improved quality and productivity, individuals must feel secure. When fear is used artificially to improve performance, performance is not improved. Instead, much effort goes into dealing with the fear at the expense of performance.

Fear prevents people from thinking. "It robs them of pride and joy in their work and kills all forms of intrinsic motivation . . . Fear is a motivator—but it does not motivate toward constructive action" (Aguayo, 1990, pp. 184–5). Reporting on recent brain research, Marchese (1997) says that "when humans confront a situation they perceive as threatening, their brain 'downshifts' . . . higher-order cortical functioning is supplanted by the more elemental limbic . . . the emotions come to rule" (p. 85). What educators need to think about is the norm of relying on "sticks and carrots" (p. 85) in the learning process. An environment that promotes competition and few rewards is commonplace and yet is not a healthy environment for learning. "High challenge, yes, . . . high anxiety, no" (p. 85).

In an environment in which our approach to assessment is focused primarily on grades, fear increases rather than decreases (Milton, Pollio, & Eison, 1986). Furthermore, "grading does not provide the necessary information required for improvement" (Tribus, 1994, p. 7). Instead of emphasizing grades in assessment, the focus should be on descriptive feedback for improvement. Feedback that focuses on self-assessment and self-improvement is a form of intrinsic motivation. According to Tribus (1994), we should promote joy in learning and cooperation; we should discourage competition among students.

Our goal should be to develop student self-awareness and self-knowledge for improvement, and to achieve this goal we must cultivate an environment based on trust. Trust is built with each and every interaction. By modeling honesty in our actions over a period of time, we can lay the foundation for helping students to trust or mistrust each other

A teacher who takes students seriously and treats them as adults shows that she can be trusted. A teacher who emphasizes peer learning shows that it's important to trust other students. A teacher who encourages students to point out to her anything about her actions that is oppressive and who seeks to change what she does in response to their concerns is a model of critical reflection. Such a teacher is one who truly is trustworthy (Brookfield, 1995, p. 26).

Removing fear should not be interpreted to mean diluting learning and lowering standards. Our efforts should be directed to creating an environment in which students are free to learn the skills they need for success in higher education and beyond. At times, this will mean allowing students to make mistakes so that they may learn from their errors. Trust, rather than fear, helps create this environment. In fact, standards should increase in a learner-centered environment because criteria that define excellence are known to all.

With this approach, college courses become settings in which personal and professional relationships develop between us and our students and among the students themselves (see Chapter 8). Students are treated as active partners, and their advice and input are sought. They become adept at giving feedback to others, and they learn to show respect for their fellow students and for professors by reacting to their work honestly and tactfully. The sense of mutuality that characterizes these relationships leads to enhanced learning (Baxter Magolda, 1995). Courses become communities of learners, and the institution is freed from the popular criticism that college courses are impersonal "sink or swim" challenges. "Frequent student–faculty contact in and out of classes is the most important factor in student motivation and involvement" (Chickering & Gamson, 1987, p. 4). Learner-centered environments promote retention by transforming institutions into welcoming places in which intellectual and personal growth takes place.

All of the examples in Figures 2–2 through 2–6 are designed to illustrate courses in which learning is interpersonal and all learners—professors and students—are respected and valued. What are the elements in each example that reflect this hallmark?

Reflections

As you create your own meaning from the ideas in this section, begin to think about . . .

- How often do I schedule time to talk with my students individually about what they know and how they know?
- How do I get to know my students as people and as learners?
- How can I determine if students feel fearful with some aspects of my courses?
- How do I help my students get to know each other? When and how do I provide time for them to talk to each other about what and how they are learning?

- How do I provide opportunities for students to work together?
- What activities can I incorporate into my courses so that students feel a sense of pride in their work and accomplishments?
- What changes could I make in the learning environment to decrease or minimize student fears?
- How can I give feedback to students in a way that reduces their level of anxiety?
- What do I do that leads students to feel that I respect them as people and as learners?

LOOKING AHEAD

As we shift paradigms, it is critical that we examine our own practice as teachers and learn more about how students learn. Also important is the need to examine the role of the teaching professor in the entire educational system that flows from the teaching mission of the institution. A current aspect of that system that has important implications for learning is the assessment movement that began in higher education in the 1980s. Chapter 3 discusses principles of good practice in learner-centered assessment.

TRY SOMETHING NEW

Completing the activities below will help identify aspects of your teaching you would like to change and the chapters in this book that are most relevant to your needs. You do not have to read the chapters in the order in which they are written. However, we would suggest that any efforts to change should start with Chapter 4, " Setting Direction with Intended Learning Outcomes." As the saying goes, if you don't know where you are going, you may never get there.

1. Review the hallmarks presented in this chapter, your responses to the Reflections questions, as well as Figures 1–1 and 1–2 at the end of Chapter 1. Make a list of the aspects of your teaching you would most like to change.
2. Using the list you developed above, read through the following chapter descriptions and decide which chapter would be the most useful starting place for you.
   Chapter 3: Basing assessment at the institutional, academic program, and/or course level on sound assessment principles.
   Chapter 4: Developing intended learning outcomes for your courses, academic program, or institution.
   Chapter 5: Identifying techniques for actively involving students in your courses and for gathering their feedback about how to improve the learning environment; learning how to receive and interpret feedback so that faculty and students can be partners in learning.
   Chapter 6: Identifying and communicating the characteristics of excellent work to help students shape and evaluate their work and to help faculty provide useful feedback for improvement; learning how to give useful feedback to students to improve their learning.
   Chapter 7: Developing assessments that evaluate students' abilities to think critically, solve enduring and emerging problems in their discipline, communicate effectively, work in teams, and so forth.

Chapter 8: Using portfolios in assessment so that faculty and students together can assess what students know and how they know it; helping students to become more sophisticated learners and shift to a learner-centered paradigm.

Chapter 9: Examining the organizational and individual implications of making a paradigm shift. Participating in a faculty development program that provides support and guidance for becoming learner-centered.

REFERENCES

Aguayo, R. (1990). *Dr. Deming: The man who taught the Japanese about quality.* Secaucus, NJ: Carol Publishing Group.

Angelo, T. A. (1994). Classroom assessment: Involving faculty and students where it matters most. *Assessment Update, 6* (4), 1–10.

Angelo, T. A., & Cross, K. P. (1993). *Classroom assessment techniques* (2nd ed.). San Francisco: Jossey-Bass.

Barr, R. B., & Tagg, J. (1995, November/December). From teaching to learning: A new paradigm for undergraduate education. *Change,* 13–25.

Baxter Magolda, M. B. (1992). Students' epistemologies and academic experiences: Implications for pedagogy. *The Review of Higher Education, 15* (3), 265–287.

Baxter Magolda, M. B. (1995). The integration of relational and impersonal knowing in young adults' epistemological development. *Journal of College Student Development, 36* (3), 205–216.

Baxter Magolda, M. B. (1996). Epistemological development in graduate and professional education. *The Review of Higher Education, 19* (3), 283–304.

Bonstingl, J. J. (1996). *Schools of quality.* Alexandria, VA: Association for Supervision and Curriculum Development.

Bransford, J. D., Brown, A. L., & Cocking, R. R. (Eds.). (1999). *How people learn: Brain, mind, experience, and school.* Washington, DC: National Academy Press.

Bransford, J. D., & Vye, N. J. (1989). A perspective on cognitive research and its implications for instruction. In L. B. Resnick & L. E. Klopfer (Eds.), *Toward the thinking curriculum: Current cognitive research, 1989 ASCD Yearbook* (pp. 173–205). Alexandria, VA: Association for Supervision and Curriculum Development.

Brookfield, S. (1995). *Becoming a critically reflective teacher.* San Francisco: Jossey-Bass.

Brooks, J. G., & Brooks, M. G. (1993). *In search of understanding: The case for constructivist classrooms.* Alexandria, VA: Association for Supervision and Curriculum Development.

Chickering, A. W., & Gamson, Z. F. (1987, March). Seven principles for good practice. *AAHE Bulletin, 39,* 3–7.

Copple, C., Sigel, I. E., & Saunders, R. (1984). *Educating the young thinker: Classroom strategies for cognitive growth.* Hillsdale, NJ: Lawrence Erlbaum Associates.

Cornesky, R., & Lazarus, W. (1995). *Continuous quality improvement in the classroom: A collaborative approach.* Port Orange, FL: Cornesky & Associates.

Cross, K. P. (1996, March-April). New lenses on learning. *About Campus,* 4–9.

Deming, W. E. (1986). *Out of the crisis*. Cambridge, MA: Massachusetts Institute of Technology Center for Advanced Engineering Study.

Department of Forestry Faculty. (1998). Unpublished program and course materials. Ames, IA: Iowa State University.

Department of Statistics. (1996). *Annual student outcomes assessment report*. Unpublished document. Ames, IA: Iowa State University.

Duffy, T. M., & Cunningham, D. J. (1996). Constructivism: Implications for the design and delivery of instruction. In D. H. Jonassen (Ed.), *Handbook of research on educational communications and technology* (pp. 170–198). London: MacMillan.

Fosnot, C. T. (Ed.) (1996). *Constructivism: Theory, perspective, and practice*. New York: Teachers College Press.

Freed, J. E., & Klugman, M. R. (1997). *Quality principles and practices in higher education: Different questions for different times*. Phoenix, AZ: American Council on Education and The Oryx Press.

Gardner, H. (1991). *The unschooled mind: How children think and how schools should teach*. New York: Basic Books.

Greenwood, M. S., & Gaunt, H. J. (1994). *Total quality management for schools*. London: Cassell.

Griffith, J., McLure, J., & Weitzel, J. (1995). Total quality management, assessment, and large class size. *Assessment Update, 7* (3), 1–7.

Jahren, C. T., & Kipp, R. (1999). A mock bid-letting for learning assessment. *Journal of Professional Issues in Engineering Education and Practice, American Society of Civil Engineers, 125* (3), 103–107.

Joint Task Force on Student Learning. (1998a). *Learning principles and collaborative action*. Washington, DC: American Association for Higher Education.

Joint Task Force on Student Learning. (1998b). *Powerful partnerships: A shared responsibility for learning*. Washington, DC: American College Personnel Association. http://www.aahe.org, http://www.acpa.nche.edu, or http://www.naspa.org

Keane, B. (1997, July 8). The Family Circus, *The Des Moines Register*, p. 5T.

Keane, B. (1998, May 19). The Family Circus, *The Des Moines Register*, p. 5T.

Keller, B. A., Russell, C. A., & Thompson, H. A. (1999). Effects of student-centered teaching on student evaluations in calculus. *Educational Research Quarterly, 23* (1), 59–73.

Ketcham. (1997a, July 5). Dennis the Menace, *The Des Moines Register*, p. 5T.

Ketcham. (1997b, July 14). Dennis the Menace, *The Des Moines Register*, p. 5T.

King, P. M., & Kitchener, K. S. (1994). *Developing reflective judgment: Understanding and promoting intellectual growth and critical thinking in adolescents and adults*. San Francisco: Jossey-Bass.

Kuh, G. (1997). Working together to enhance student learning inside and outside the classroom. In *Assessing Impact: Evidence and Action* (pp. 67–78). Washington, DC: American Association of Higher Education.

Kurfiss, J. G. (1988). *Critical thinking: Theory, research, practice, and possibilities*. (ASHE-ERIC Higher Education Report No. 2). College Station, TX: Association for the Study of Higher Education.

Loacker, G., Cromwell, L., & O'Brien, K. (1986). Assessment in higher education: To serve the learner. In C. Adelman (Ed.), *Assessment in American higher education* (pp. 47–62). Washington, DC: U. S. Department of Education. Office of Educational Research and Improvement.

Marchese, T. J. (1997). The new conversation about learning. In *Assessing Impact: Evidence and Action* (pp. 79–95). Washington, DC: American Association for Higher Education.

Martinez, M. E. (1998). What is problem solving? *Phi Delta Kappan, 79*, 605–609.

Milton, O., Pollio, H. R., & Eison, J. A. (1986). *Making sense of college grades: Why the grading system does not work and what can be done about it.* San Francisco: Jossey-Bass.

Okere, M. (1997). Unpublished course materials. Ames, IA: Iowa State University, Department of Sociology.

Resnick, L. B., & Klopfer, L. E. (1989). Toward the thinking curriculum: An overview. In L. B. Resnick & L. E. Klopfer (Eds.), *Toward the thinking curriculum: Current cognitive research, 1989 ASCD Yearbook* (pp. 1–18). Alexandria, VA: Association for Supervision and Curriculum Development.

Resnick, L., & Resnick, D. (1992). Assessing the thinking curriculum: New tools for educational reform. In B. R. Gifford & M. C. O'Connor (Eds.), *Changing assessments: Alternative views of aptitude, achievement and instruction* (pp. 37–75). Boston: Kluwer Academic Publishers.

Seymour, D., & Chaffee, E. E. (1992). TQM for student outcomes assessment. *AGB Reports, 34* (1), 26–30.

Tribus, M. (1994, June). *When quality goes to school, what do leaders do to put it to work?* Paper presented at the Annual AAHE Conference on Assessment and Quality, Washington, DC.

Ulrichson, D. (1998). Unpublished materials from Chemical Engineering 430. Ames, IA: Iowa State University, Department of Chemical Engineering.

Wandersee, J. H., Mintzes, J. L., & Novak, J. D. (1994). Research on alternative conceptions in science. In D. L. Gabel (Ed.), *Handbook of research on science teaching and learning* (pp. 177–210). New York: MacMillan.

Warren, R. G. (1997, March-April). Engaging students in active learning. *About Campus,* 16–20.

Whitehead, A. N. (1929). *The aims of education.* New York: MacMillan.

Wiggins, G. (1993). *Assessing student performance: Exploring the limits and purpose of testing.* San Francisco: Jossey-Bass.

Wiggins, G. (1997). Feedback: How learning occurs. In *Assessing Impact: Evidence and Action* (pp. 31–39). Washington, DC: American Association of Higher Education.

Wiggins, G., & McTighe, J. (1998). *Understanding by design.* Alexandria, VA: Association for Supervision and Curriculum Development.

▶ 3

Applying Principles of Good Practice in Learner-Centered Assessment

Assessment is a process in which rich, usable, credible *feedback* from an act—of teaching or curriculum—comes to be *reflected* upon by an academic community, and then is *acted* on by that community—a department or college—within its commitment to get smarter and better at what it does.... Assessment ... is a community effort or nothing, driven by a faculty's own commitment to reflect, judge, and improve (Marchese, 1997, p. 93).

A college must satisfy five conditions, at least, to validly claim that it has been transformed into a Learning Paradigm-governed college. First it must have identified its intended learning outcomes in detail. Second, it must have developed a system for measuring the achievement of these outcomes at both the individual student level and the aggregate class, program, and institutional levels. Third, its curriculum must have been built backward from the intended outcomes and must be developmental. Fourth, it must provide a wide range of powerful options for achieving required learning outcomes. Fifth and finally, it must continually and systematically investigate alternative methods for empowering students to learn (Barr, 1998, pp. 19–20).

Making Connections

As you begin to read the chapter, think about the ideas and experiences you've already had that are related to principles of good practice in assessment . . .

- How would you characterize the attitudes of faculty at your institution regarding assessment?
- How have you been involved in assessment efforts at your institution? What have you learned?

- What do you know about effective assessment?
- How do administrators at your institution support effective assessment?

What else do you know about applying principles of good practice in assessment?

What other questions do you have about applying principles of good practice in assessment?

In Chapter 1, we discussed the concept of assessment and the powerful role it can play in helping us shift to a learner-centered perspective. In Chapter 2, we examined a learner-centered environment, noting the many ways it is supported and nourished by assessment. In this chapter, we will discuss assessment from the point of view of good practice, asking ourselves how we can carry out assessment so that it will make a difference in student learning.

PRINCIPLES OF GOOD ASSESSMENT PRACTICE

Professional associations and accreditation agencies have developed lists of assessment principles or characteristics of successful assessment programs. Two are included in Figures 3–1 and 3–2. Figure 3–1 lists Principles of Good Practice for Assessing Student Learning developed by the American Association of Higher Education (AAHE) Assessment Forum (1992). Figure 3–2 lists Hallmarks of Successful Programs to Assess Student Academic Achievement included in the 1994–1996 *Handbook of Accreditation* of the Commission on Institutions of Higher Education of the North Central Association (NCA).

The two lists have several characteristics in common. For example, both focus on the importance of assessing for improvement and on the need to involve constituents across the institution in assessment. However, each list also provides unique insights into the assessment process. The AAHE Principles of Good Practice highlight the fact that assessment is most effective when it is part of a larger set of conditions promoting change, whereas the

1. The assessment of student learning begins with educational values.
2. Assessment is most effective when it reflects an understanding of learning as multidimensional, integrated, and revealed in performance over time.
3. Assessment works best when the programs it seeks to improve have clear, explicitly stated purposes.
4. Assessment requires attention to outcomes but also and equally to the experiences that lead to those outcomes.
5. Assessment works best when it is ongoing, not episodic.
6. Assessment fosters wider improvement when representatives from across the educational community are involved.
7. Assessment makes a difference when it begins with issues of use and illuminates questions people really care about.
8. Assessment is most likely to lead to improvement when it is part of a larger set of conditions that promote change.
9. Through assessment, educators meet responsibilities to students and to the public.

(American Association of Higher Education (AAHE) Assessment Forum, 1992)

FIGURE 3–1   Principles of Good Practice for Assessing Student Learning

NCA's Hallmarks of Successful Programs remind us of the need to assess the assessment process itself.

The remainder of the chapter has been organized around questions that derive from the principles in Figures 3–1 and 3–2. In the questions, the principles have been combined and reordered to enhance the flow of ideas.

Successful assessment:

1. Flows from the institution's mission.
2. Has a conceptual framework.
3. Has faculty ownership/responsibility.
4. Has institution-wide support.
5. Uses multiple measures.
6. Provides feedback to students and the institution.
7. Is cost-effective.
8. Does not restrict or inhibit goals of access, equity, and diversity established by the institution.
9. Leads to improvement.
10. Includes a process for evaluating the assessment program.

(North Central Association—Commission on Institutions of Higher Education, 1994)

FIGURE 3–2   Hallmarks of Successful Programs to Assess Student Academic Achievement

---

Reflections

As you create your own meaning from the ideas in this section, begin to think about . . .

• With what elements in these lists am I familiar?

• What elements in these lists surprise me?
• What elements in these lists do I want to know more about?

KEY QUESTIONS TO CONSIDER WHEN ESTABLISHING OR EVALUATING AN ASSESSMENT PROGRAM

Does assessment lead to improvement so that the faculty can fulfill their responsibilities to students and to the public?

In Chapter 1, we pointed out that many legislatures and accrediting associations have required or urged institutions to engage in the assessment of student learning. There are two aspects to this call for assessment, the need to assess for accountability and the need to assess for improvement, and these aspects are in continual tension. Both reasons for assessment are important— we must improve what we do, and at the same time, we must be accountable to our students, to the public, and to those who fund us. The tension between these assessment purposes results from the fact that they lead to two fundamentally different approaches to assessment.

On the one hand, when we assess to be accountable to external audiences, our primary motivation is typically to "put our best foot forward." We wish to showcase our successes and highlight the satisfaction of various stakeholder groups—students, parents, employers, alumni. Our assessment is dominated by the need to convince constituencies that funds are well spent, and this leads us to gather the type of assessment data that supports the contention that no change is needed.

On the other hand, assessing for improvement implies a focus not only on strengths, but also on areas in need of change. One assumption underlying an emphasis on improvement is that there are areas of programs and courses in which improvements can be made. Another assumption is that change, when needed, is desirable and should be embraced. For an improvement environment to develop, administrators must create trust by assuring faculty that no internal or external reprisals will result when they engage in assessment and identify areas in need of improvement. An atmosphere of trust encourages faculty to feel comfortable rather than threatened by change, and it provides a context within which faculty can feel free to identify weaknesses and address them. Trust allows faculty to apply a fundamental principle of continuous improvement, that data should determine the improvements to be made and thus drive decision making (Freed & Klugman, 1997).

Assessment is most likely to be useful to faculty and students when we resist the temptation to placate external audiences with glowing accounts of success and develop instead a more balanced approach that reveals both our strengths and weaknesses in helping students learn. Change is inevitable, and assessment takes time and effort. Our investments in assessment will have greater payback for us if the data help us determine what changes we need to make and how we can make them effectively.

Ultimately, improved student learning should satisfy constituencies outside the institution, and therefore, the need to be accountable to external audiences can be folded into the improvement process. However, this means that, in addition to collecting assessment data, we must complete the entire assessment process and use the results of data collection to make changes leading to better learning. Demonstrating that we are able to use assessment results to continuously improve student learning should fulfill our accountability requirements. Assessing for improvement is a must.

Reflections

As you create your own meaning from the ideas in this section, begin to think about . . .

- How does assessment in my courses, in our academic program, and at the institution lead to improvement so that my faculty colleagues

and I can fulfill our responsibilities to students and to the public?

- In what situations have my colleagues and I succumbed to the temptation to assess learning for accountability purposes—simply showcasing our successes—rather than for improvement?

Is assessment part of a larger set of conditions that promote change at the institution? Does it provide feedback to students and the institution?

To be effective, assessment should become integrated into existing processes like planning and resource allocation, catalog revision, and program review.

This puts student learning at the heart of the processes through which the institution does business.

Planning and Resource Allocation

The results of assessment should be as important in institutional planning as student–faculty ratios, credit hours generated, and fluctuating revenue sources. Data about the success of a particular unit in bringing about student learning should be influential in any decisions about the program. When decisions are made to add personnel or restructure a program, data about student learning should play a central role in developing the rationale for such changes. It is essential that assessment results are used for better decision making, leading to program improvement.

Curricular Change and Catalog Revision

At most U.S. institutions, the curriculum is delivered primarily in a course format, but other experiences like independent studies, practica, and internships are included. The process of curricular revision is embedded in a continuing catalog change process, and we reveal the results of the process to the public every time we develop a new catalog.

Ideally, when we participate in assessment, we begin to view the curriculum as an interrelated system of experiences through which students achieve the intended learning outcomes of the program. As mentioned in Chapter 2, students are driven to make sense of their experiences. When they experience a particular pattern of courses, they either develop greater understanding of their discipline or they become confused because they are unable to understand the essential features of the discipline and the relationships among them.

It is not uncommon for students to complain that they don't understand why a particular course is required or how it will help them in their field. As faculty, we can design curricula so that students develop an increasingly clearer understanding of the concepts and skills needed in their field, or we can inadvertently obscure these features, making it difficult for students to make connections among them. In so doing, we prevent students from achieving essential knowledge and skills, and we may cause students to become discouraged from pursuing a course of study.

Assessment data about student learning can help us keep a learner-centered perspective during curriculum development and revision. A primary use of assessment data should be to inform the decisions we make about curriculum. When we discuss assessment results, we come to understand what our students learned well and in what areas they need to improve. This may lead us to question the order in which courses are sequenced or the appropriateness of prerequisites. Every time a course description is modified, or the number of course credits is changed, or prerequisites are added or deleted, two questions should be asked: (1) How will these changes help our students reach the intended learning outcomes of the program? (2) What assessment data support this change?

As we strive to develop a curriculum that is coherent to students, we may decide to share the intended learning outcomes of the program with them. This can be done by listing them in the introductory narrative for each program in the catalog. In fact, course descriptions may evolve into a listing of what students should know, understand, and be able to do at the end of the course, rather than simply a listing of content topics.

Learning outcomes can also be shared in other important institutional and program documents such as those used in recruiting and marketing to students. Publicly revealing the student learning goals of a program communicates to various groups—students, parents, citizens, members of boards of trustees, and so forth—the types of achievement that are expected of students in the program. A public statement reveals that we, as program faculty, are intentional about promoting learning and that the curriculum is designed to enable students to reach our learning outcomes. Knowing the goals of the program provides students with a sense of direction and helps them take ownership of their own learning.

Certainly both program and course outcomes should be shared in course syllabi. In this way, we inform students about what we expect them to know, understand, and be able to do at the end of their program. We also help them understand how each course assists them in reaching overall program outcomes. Furthermore, it is helpful if students know which intended outcomes are the focus of each class period. Occasionally within a course, we should ask students to review the intended course and program outcomes and reflect on how well they are achieving them.

Program Review

Another process that promotes change on college campuses is program review. Assessment of student learning in an academic program feeds into the larger process of academic program review by providing a mechanism to assess and evaluate one aspect of an academic program—the student learning component. We should encourage our faculty colleagues to view assessment as a component of academic program review, not as a separate initiative on campus. Through the program review process, students and other important constituencies within the institution can learn about the effectiveness of student learning in a program. When the results of program reviews are shared with audiences like alumni, taxpayers, or boards of trustees, we fulfill both the need to assess for improvement and the need to be accountable to external stakeholder groups.

Reflections

As you create your own meaning from the ideas in this section, begin to think about . . .

- How is assessment in my program part of a larger set of conditions that promote change at the institution?
- How is it or could it be part of planning and resource allocation?

- How is it or could it be part of curricular change and catalog revision?
- How is it or could it be part of program review?
- How does assessment in my program provide feedback to students and the institution?

Does assessment focus on using data to address questions that people in the program and at the institution really care about?

If assessment is ultimately about making changes leading to improvement, we need to identify the questions we have about student learning at the beginning of the process. What do we want to know about our students' learning? What do we think we already know? How can we verify what we think we know? How will we use the information we get to make changes? Focusing on questions that have compelling interest for us as a faculty will help keep the assessment process moving toward its ultimate goal—using data for improved learning in our programs.

Identification of the questions that we and our colleagues care about will result only through discussion. The final identification of questions to be pursued in assessment should probably result from a formal decision of the faculty, but the process of generating and prioritizing questions about learning can occur in informal settings, in committee meetings, or in faculty development groups.

Does assessment flow from the institution's mission and reflect the faculty's educational values?

The mission and educational values of the institution should drive the teaching function of the institution. They should shape the intended learning outcomes of all programs on campus, providing the framework that characterizes what is unique and special about graduates of the institution's programs. As discussed at greater length in Chapter 4, the faculty should then use the intended learning outcomes as a guide when they develop their approach to teaching and assessment.

For example, Babson College focuses on preparing students for the business world, and its mission is "to educate innovative leaders capable of anticipating, initiating, and managing change" (Babson College, 1998, p. 23). In order to fulfill their mission, the Babson faculty have identified five areas in which students develop the skills they will need for career success and lifelong learning: rhetoric, numeracy, ethics and social responsibility, international and multicultural perspectives, and leadership/teamwork/creativity. Students' skills in the competency areas are developed throughout their program through coursework, field-based experiences, and continual assessment. In this way, various aspects of Babson's educational program, including assessment, flow from the institution's mission to prepare effective leaders. (The relationship between the institution's mission and its intended learning outcomes will be discussed at greater length in Chapter 4.)

Does the educational program have clear, explicitly stated purposes that can guide assessment in the program?

Faculty members at many institutions begin their assessment programs by trying to determine what measures they will use to assess learning, rather than by asking what it is that they want students to learn. As discussed in Chapter 1, the foundation for any assessment program is the faculty's statement of student learning outcomes describing what graduates are expected to know, understand, and be able to do at the end of the academic program. *When we are clear about what we intend students to learn, we know what we must assess.* Collecting data without a clear idea of what should be measured is likely to be inefficient because we will find it difficult to know how to use the information. We may find that we have measured the wrong thing, that the assessment data do not address the questions about student learning that we really care about. (Chapter 4 focuses exclusively on the important topic of developing intended learning outcomes.)

In addition, at the institutional and academic program levels, we should develop learning outcomes that target only the most important goals of the program. Addressing a small number of well-focused outcomes enhances the cost effectiveness of the assessment program. Taking on a burdensome, overly detailed and ambitious assessment program requires too much time and effort on our part—we are already busy people. Assessments at the program level should be as focused as possible on important aspects of learning in order to yield useful information without wasted effort. The process should "start small" in order to maintain realistic faculty commitment (Wehlburg, 1999).

Reflections

As you create your own meaning from the ideas in the previous sections, begin to think about . . .

- What questions about student learning do people in my program and at the institution really care about?
- How does assessment focus on using data to address these questions?
- What educational values of the faculty are represented in my institution's mission and other documents?

- How does assessment in my program flow from these educational values?
- Does my academic program have clear, explicitly stated purposes that can guide assessment in the program?
- If not, how can my colleagues and I develop these purposes or intended learning outcomes?

Is assessment based on a conceptual framework that explains relationships among teaching, curriculum, learning, and assessment at the institution?

The assessment process works best when faculty have a shared sense of how learning takes place and when their view of learning reflects the learner-centered perspective outlined in Chapter 2. This allows them to maintain a focus on what is most important, a perspective Deming (1986) refers to as constancy of purpose.

For example, at the University of Illinois at Springfield, the faculty work from a common set of learning goals: "(1) a solid foundation for lifelong learning, (2) a keen appreciation of intellectual and aesthetic achievements, (3) an enhanced capacity for critical thinking and oral as well as written communication, (4) a practical preparation for pursuing fulfilling careers, (5) a sound basis for informed and concerned citizenship, and (6) a productive commitment to improving their world" (University of Illinois at Springfield, 1996, p. 7).

In order to achieve these goals, faculty at the University of Illinois at Springfield are committed to the idea that students learn best through experience, both in formal courses and in the community. Classes are small, the faculty use a variety of teaching techniques, and student participation is viewed as central to learning. A public affairs perspective pervades every program. The curriculum includes Liberal Studies Colloquia, Public Affairs Colloquia, and Applied Study Terms (University of Illinois at Springfield, 1999).

At Alverno College, the faculty have developed a conceptual framework based on an ability-based approach to learning. They believe that "students should be able to do something with what they know" (Alverno College Faculty, 1994, 1996). Their ultimate goal is that each student will develop into an educated adult with "a sense of responsibility for her own learning and the ability and desire to continue learning independently, self-knowledge and the ability to assess her own performance critically and accurately, and an understanding of how to apply her knowledge and abilities in many different contexts" (Alverno College Faculty, 1996, p. 1).

In order to reach these ends, the faculty have identified eight specific abilities that they require students to develop in the context of their disciplines throughout students' undergraduate program (Alverno College Faculty, 1992, 1996):

- communication
- analysis
- problem solving
- valuing in decision making
- social interaction
- global perspectives
- effective citizenship, and
- aesthetic responsiveness.

Within each of these ability areas, the Alverno faculty (1996) have formulated a series of subgoals or levels to be pursued developmentally as the student progresses through the general education curriculum and into the major discipline. For example, the levels in the area of analytical capabilities are as follows:

In general education
- Level 1: Show observational skills
- Level 2: Draw reasonable inferences from observations
- Level 3: Perceive and make relationships
- Level 4: Analyze structure and organization

In majors and areas of specialization
- Level 5: Establish ability to employ frameworks from area of concentration or support area discipline in order to analyze
- Level 6: Master ability to employ independently the frameworks from area of concentration or support area discipline in order to analyze (p. 2).

The curriculum is designed so that students have ongoing opportunities to develop their abilities. Each course in the curriculum targets certain abilities, and knowing this, professors teaching the courses intentionally offer opportunities for students to develop them.

Assessment of abilities—at the level of both the individual student and the program or institution—is central to the Alverno faculty's view of learning. Students assess themselves throughout the program, a process that begins as soon as they arrive at Alverno. Faculty working with students assess and coach students in the eight ability areas throughout their program (Loacker, Cromwell, & O'Brien, 1986).

At Alverno College, the faculty collectively embrace a conceptual framework about learning and all aspects of their program reflect it. Assessment will be more useful to those of us at other institutions when we and our colleagues develop our own conceptual framework for student learning. A conceptual framework ties together and gives shape to all the elements in the educational process—curriculum, teaching, learning, and assessment—allowing them to function as a continuous system of interrelated parts.

Reflections

As you create your own meaning from the ideas in this section, begin to think about . . .

- What conceptual framework, if any, do my colleagues and I espouse that explains the links between

teaching, curriculum, learning, and assessment at the institution?
- What is the role of assessment in our framework?
- How could our conceptual framework be improved?

Do the faculty feel a sense of ownership and responsibility for assessment?

The curriculum has typically been viewed as our prerogative as faculty in institutions of higher education. Because of this, assessing the success of the curriculum should be our prerogative as well. Assessment is carried out to improve student learning, as well as the curriculum and the teaching that takes place within it. As faculty members, we must decide on the intended learning outcomes of the curriculum and the measures that are used to assess them. We must use assessment data to make changes that are needed to strengthen and improve the curriculum. We also need to ask about the effectiveness of our teaching strategies—should we continue to lecture, use small group discussions, assign projects, give tests? What are the best methods to enhance student learning?

When we assess for improvement in this way, we begin conversations about student learning. This assertion has several intriguing elements. First, it suggests that assessment is a *beginning*. For many of us, this will come as a surprise. A traditional view of assessment is that it is a culminating or concluding activity rather than a beginning.

A perhaps even more intriguing element of the assertion is that assessment is the beginning of *conversations*. Assessment is usually perceived to be a private activity conducted by each of us in the "castle" of our classroom, and it rarely leads to communication with colleagues. Data are gathered and may take the form of grades to be submitted or statistics for reports. There is typically scant reference to the importance of conversation or dialogue about assessment results. However, talking about results should be built into the assessment process. Conversation and dialogue lead to enhanced understanding that is collectively derived by participants.

The final intriguing element of the assertion above is that assessment is the beginning of conversations about *learning*. This implies a close and intrinsic connection between learning and assessment, a connection that has been emphasized elsewhere in this book. However, this connection has not always been obvious. In the culture of higher education, assessment typically takes place within courses, following instruction. Grades are posted for students to see, and they are submitted to the administration to fulfill bureaucratic requirements. Students receive summative feedback rather than feedback that can guide their performance. Assessment rarely leads to enhanced understanding of learning, on the part of either students or faculty.

Assessment at all levels should generate conversations among faculty that will lead to deeper, collective understandings about the learning that students are experiencing in the program. These conversations should in turn lead to reasoned change and improvement.

Reflections

As you create your own meaning from the ideas in this section, begin to think about . . .

- Do faculty in my program (or at my institution) feel a sense of ownership and responsibility for assessment?

  - If not, how could we develop a sense of ownership?
  - How could conversations take place that would lead us to a better understanding of student learning?

Do the faculty focus on experiences leading to outcomes as well as on the outcomes themselves?

As indicated above, in the learner-centered paradigm, the curriculum is viewed as the vehicle for helping students reach our intended learning outcomes. Through the assessment results we obtain at the program level, we learn whether or not the curriculum has been effective.

The way students perform in program assessments reflects the experiences students have during their program. For example, students whose professors emphasize writing and who have had frequent opportunities to write and receive feedback, will undoubtedly learn to write better than those whose experiences have not included writing. Likewise, students' performance on program assessments will be influenced by the content and form of the assessments we use in our courses.

For example, assume that one of the goals of a graduate program is that students will be able to articulate central issues and concepts in the discipline, providing specific references to prominent theorists. If course assessments focus on details rather than central ideas, or if they do not evaluate students' ability to link names of theorists with the theories themselves, students may not be able to perform well on an assessment of program goals.

Even when course content matches the desired content specified in program goals, the form of assessment is also an issue. For example, if the program assessment is an oral exam, part of students' success will depend on the opportunities they have had during their program to talk aloud about central issues and prominent theorists. To the extent that their professors lecture in courses and require students to take written exams, students' ability to reveal their knowledge during the culminating oral exam will be compromised. Course assessment and program/institutional assessment are interrelated, mutually supportive activities that must be developed in harmony in order to enhance student learning on a college campus.

Is assessment ongoing rather than episodic?

Completing the assessment cycle in Figure 1–3 is a process that cannot be achieved in a short period of time. Assessment must become part of standard practices and procedures at the institution and in each program. It should not be an activity that "starts up and stops" at midterm and finals week or near the end of a five-year program review cycle or a ten-year accreditation cycle. Rather, it should respond to the ongoing need for information about our chief responsibility as teachers—learning. Cycles that are part of this responsibility such as catalog revision should be coordinated with assessment. For example, it would be helpful for the faculty to have recent assessment data collected and analyzed at the program level during the semester in which they are deciding on revisions in the next catalog.

In order to help us maintain ongoing attention to assessment, we may find it helpful to complete the matrix in Figure 3–3. The matrix has been completed to guide a faculty in Architecture as they develop and implement program-level assessment; however, the matrix can be completed at the course, program, or institutional level. In column 1, each of the intended learning outcomes of the program is listed. For each outcome, the relevant experiences (e.g., courses, practica, internships, labs) that the faculty provide to help students reach the learning goal are listed in column 2. Column 3 specifies the measure(s) faculty have identified or developed to assess each learning goal. In column 4, the results obtained from administering the measures are summarized, and in column 5 any changes that have been made based on results are listed. Column 6 identifies stakeholders who have been informed about the process.

In some institutions, programs are required to submit assessment reports in order to fulfill accountability requirements. In this situation, the matrix format in Figure 3–3 could be used to structure the report. The matrix not only summarizes the process that has been completed, but it also educates faculty about key elements in the assessment process.

Reflections

As you create your own meaning from the ideas in the previous sections, begin to think about . . .

- In my program, how do my colleagues and I focus on experiences leading to outcomes—teaching, the curriculum, out-of-class experiences of students—as well as on the outcomes themselves?
- What opportunities do we provide for students so that they can achieve our intended outcomes?
- What type of content do we emphasize in our course assessments and how does the content affect students' ability to achieve the intended learning outcomes of our program?
- What forms do our assessments take and how do they affect students' ability to achieve the intended learning outcomes of our program?
- Do our assessment efforts tend to be ongoing or do they lapse into periodic efforts?
- What aspects of the matrix in Figure 3–3 would be useful to me and my colleagues?

Is assessment cost-effective and based on data gathered from multiple measures?

The question, "Have our graduates learned what we intend them to learn?" is ideally answered by gathering data using multiple methods of assessment. No one assessment measure can provide a complete picture of what and how students are learning.

The multiple methods of assessment should contain both direct measures of student learning, as well as indirect measures of learning. Direct measures of learning take the form of projects, products, papers/theses, exhibitions, performances, case studies, clinical evaluations, oral exams, interviews, locally developed tests, and licensure exams. They directly measure the knowledge and skills that students have acquired in a course or program, and they are thus more valuable measures of learning than indirect measures.

Intended Outcome	Relevant Experiences	Measures	Results	Changes Based on Results	Stakeholders Informed
Architecture students should be aware of the values, behaviors, and traditions of diverse cultures and individuals.	Courses: 221, 222, 301, 302, 351, 421, 423, 467. Study Abroad Semester.	a. External examiners. b. Senior diploma project review.	a. " . . . exceptional strength . . . a model program in this regard." b. Favorable review.	None.	Students, alumni.
Architecture students should be able to gather and integrate information about history, context, site, users, project goals, codes, forms, structures, and materials to generate architectural form.	Courses: 102, 240, 301, 302, 401–404, 448, 458, 465.	Senior diploma project review.	Overall satisfactory work, but some weakness in theory was noted.	Revised course in architecture theory and methods.	Students and practitioners on department advisory committee.

Architecture students should be able to write, speak, listen, and use a variety of media effectively.	Courses: 102, English composition sequence, 230, 232, 240, 334, 335, 351, all 400 level courses.	a. Review of applicants' portfolios. b. External examiners. c. Senior diploma project review.	a. Continued concern about communication skills of entering students. b. External examiners noted high quality of graphics. c. Need for improvement in writing and oral communication.	Continued emphasis on communication at all levels. Integration of speaking and writing into courses in the discipline. Partnering with English faculty.	Students and alumni.

(Developed in part from Department of Architecture, 1996)

FIGURE 3–3   Sample Matrix for Assessment Planning, Monitoring, or Reporting

Indirect measures like student self-report surveys or interviews, alumni surveys, or employer surveys provide suggestions about student learning, but they don't measure learning itself. Nevertheless, they can be useful in understanding how important stakeholders in the learning process (e.g., participants or beneficiaries) perceive an academic program. In the early stages of assessment at the program level, indirect assessments may already be in place, and because of this, they may be considered easier to implement than direct assessments. A collection of assessments that measure learning only indirectly, however, does not constitute an effective assessment repertoire.

In program-level assessment, the most efficient manner of gathering data using direct measures of learning is to use assessments that are embedded in the courses we teach. Course-embedded assessments are much more cost-effective than program-wide assessments that are administered to students outside the course system. Out-of-course assessments are layered onto the program and are by definition inefficient. Using them raises problematic questions about how to ensure that the students who participate in them are motivated to do their best work.

When course-embedded assessments are used, they should address overall program outcomes and not just those for a specific course. The professor teaching the course will use the assessments to give feedback to individual students in the course and to determine course grades. However, samples of student work can be taken randomly from the course and reviewed separately by program faculty members. Program faculty can use the samples to determine whether students in the program are achieving at desired levels and to decide whether curricular adjustments or improvements need to be made.

At King's College, the faculty use course-embedded assessments to assess students' ability to think critically in the major. Through the use of the Sophomore–Junior Diagnostic Project and the Senior Integrated Assessment, individual students receive feedback about their progress and about areas in which they need further development (King's College Faculty, 1997). Program faculty use the results of the assessments to judge whether changes should be made in individual courses or in the curriculum as a whole.

For the Sophomore–Junior Diagnostic Project, each department designs a project for students to complete in a required course in the major (O'Brien, Bressler, Ennis, & Michael, 1996). In the project, students address problems typically faced by professionals in their chosen disciplines, and they are evaluated in terms of their expected knowledge of the major to date and their ability to use the liberal arts skills developed in the general education curriculum. The project usually takes place in the sophomore year, but sometimes it begins in response to an assignment in a sophomore course and is completed in the junior year, allowing students the opportunity to work on it during the summer (Farmer, 1993).

The Senior Integrated Assessment is similar to the Sophomore–Junior Diagnostic Project in its real-life focus. However, in the senior project students have the opportunity to exhibit a "sophisticated command of the subject matter and methodology of the major as well as competence at advanced levels in the transferable skills of liberal learning appropriate to a student about to graduate" (King's College Faculty, 1997, p. 2).

Whether assessments are direct measures of learning such as those used at King's College or indirect measures of learning, they should focus on the faculty's intended learning outcomes. This may mean that some existing indirect measures will have to be revised to focus on student learning. Rather than asking alumni how effective their academic program was in preparing them for the world of work, faculty may wish to list the knowledge and skills developed in the program and have respondents rate their achievement of each one separately. If alumni participated in a program that had quite different intended learning outcomes than those focused on in the current program, an important role for them may be to provide feedback on the appropriateness of current program outcomes. As participating members of society and the professions, they can provide an invaluable perspective about the future needs of current students.

Course evaluations are not typically considered tools for assessing learning because they focus on aspects of course delivery—inputs—rather than outcomes. However, a simple revision of items could turn them into outcomes assessment instruments. Items like, "How well did your writing improve in this course?" could be added to provide information about learning outcomes that are programmatic in scope but developed in particular courses. (Redesigned course evaluation forms are discussed in Chapter 5.)

We should interpret data from the multiple measures used in assessment in terms of the type of academic program we offer and the context of the institution. Students cannot achieve outcomes unless they are given opportunities to do so. When assessment results indicate that achievement is not at the expected level, we should review all aspects of the program.

- Do our students have the necessary skills and abilities when they enter the institution?
- If not, what remedial experiences do we offer?
- Are the remedial experiences effective?
- Is the curriculum structured appropriately?
- As professors, are we working together to deliver a coherent program?
- Are we using approaches to teaching and assessing at the course level that are appropriate for the types of programmatic outcomes we desire?
- Are our intended outcomes appropriate for our type of institution?

A thorough discussion and analysis of assessment results can help provide direction for needed changes that will make a difference in student learning.

Reflections

As you create your own meaning from the ideas in this section, begin to think about . . .

- How do my colleagues and I gather data using multiple measures, some of which measure learning directly?
- Which direct measures of learning do we use in our courses?

- Which direct measures of learning do we use in program assessment?
- Which indirect measures of learning do we use in our courses?
- Which indirect measures of learning do we use in program assessment?
- From which assessments have we gathered the most useful data?

Does assessment support diversity efforts rather than restrict them?

Taking responsibility for the learning of nontraditional as well as traditional populations of students presents a challenge for many of us. Students whose life experiences differ from those of traditional students may learn differently and at different rates. As learners, they may make new demands on us.

One approach to ensuring that students achieve our intended learning outcomes is simply to change admissions standards so that only those students who have succeeded in the past are admitted. This, however, would be inadvisable and would conflict with other goals of the institution. It would also be incompatible with the underlying philosophy of an outcomes approach.

An outcomes approach to teaching commits us to taking up the challenge that a diverse group of learners presents. An outcomes approach means that we strive to promote and enhance the learning of all students whom the institution has admitted. Assessment data help us understand what students are learning, where they are having difficulty, and how we can modify instruction and the curriculum to help them learn better. Admissions standards are not changed simply to make the process of reaching intended outcomes easier.

Is the assessment program itself regularly evaluated?

Because assessment is a long-term process directed at fundamental aspects of institutional functioning, it is critical that we evaluate the effectiveness of our institution's approach to assessment. Is the institution or academic program reaching its goals for assessment? Have we formulated intended learning outcomes in a timely fashion? Have the principles in Figures 3–1 and 3–2 been effectively implemented? How do course and program assessment complement each other? Have we completed the assessment cycle for at least some of our learning outcomes? If not, what changes are needed in assessment itself?

Ongoing attention to evaluating our assessment efforts helps maximize the cost-effectiveness of assessment in that faculty and student efforts are used productively. When we initiate new approaches to assessment at the course, program, or institutional levels, we should plan at the outset to evaluate them.

Reflections

As you create your own meaning from the ideas in the previous sections, begin to think about . . .

- In what ways do students today seem to learn differently than students in the past?
- How well are my colleagues and I using data to enhance the learning

of all students, nontraditional as well as traditional?

- How could I evaluate the approach to assessment that I use in my courses?
- How could my colleagues and I evaluate our assessment efforts at the program level?

Does assessment have institution-wide support? Are representatives from across the educational community involved?

Administrators who set the tone for the institution and implement its policies play a critical role in creating the type of culture of evidence that will allow assessment to flourish. Simply mentioning the importance and role of assessment when chief academic officers address the faculty sends a powerful message of support for a learner-centered approach to teaching. Nevertheless, an even more active stance is recommended, and Figure 3–4 outlines two roles that administrators can play at the institutional and program levels in supporting assessment—administrative leadership and educational leadership.

Administrative leadership

Through their administrative leadership, administrators can organize the faculty to take ownership of the assessment process and carry it out in an efficient and effective manner. Involving as many faculty as possible in assessment is fundamental to its success. Dzimadzi (1997) found that the more faculty were involved in assessment, the more they knew about it and the more likely they were to have positive attitudes about it. For the most

---

Provide administrative leadership: Organize the faculty

- Lead the faculty in developing an assessment plan.
- Develop faculty ownership by insisting that the faculty develop and implement the plan.
- Acknowledge and reward faculty involvement.
- Make resources available.
  - time
  - money
- Be persistent.

Provide educational leadership: Coach the faculty

- Understand assessment concepts and articulate them to faculty.
- Maintain a focus on improvement rather than accountability.
- Make resources available.
  - literature
  - consultation
- Foster connections with related department initiatives.
  - program review
  - catalog change
  - planning, budgeting, and personnel decisions
  - learning communities
- Generate conversations about student learning.
  - What kind of learning do the faculty value for students?
  - What are their shared goals for learning, the intended learning outcomes of the academic program or the institution?
  - Who are their key partners at the institution? (Student Affairs staff, English faculty, Library faculty?)
  - How can faculty involve these partners?
  - What are the best ways to assess the learning faculty value?
  - What is the relationship between assessment in courses and assessment at the program level?
  - What do assessment data reveal about learning in the program?
  - What improvements, if any, are indicated by assessment data?
  - Who should know about assessment results?

FIGURE 3–4   Suggested Roles for Administrators in Assessment

part, faculty knowledge and attitudes did not differ by rank or by the professors' preference for teaching over research. Only involvement in assessment activities was related to what professors knew about assessment and how they felt about it. This finding highlights the importance of acknowledging and rewarding faculty participation in assessment at every stage of the process.

In order to promote faculty involvement, administrators can guide the faculty in the development and implementation of an assessment plan. Some key elements of an effective assessment plan are shown in Figure 3–5. Although faculty members themselves should develop the plan, administrators can be extremely helpful to the process by keeping faculty focused on the first

- Emphasize improvement rather than accountability.
- Conceptualize assessment in terms of the mission of the institution.
- Identify leaders and responsible parties.
- Clarify role of institution, colleges, departments, programs.
- Specify a timetable to achieve the following objectives:
  - Develop statements of intended learning outcomes at both undergraduate and graduate levels.
  - Present a matrix linking intended learning outcomes and the courses/experiences in which outcomes are to be attained.
  - Identify measures to be used to assess each outcome.
  - Describe who will use results and for what purpose.
  - Collect, analyze, interpret, and use data for improvement.
  - Establish feedback loops to key stakeholder groups.
  - Evaluate the assessment program according to AAHE's Principles of Good Practice for Assessing Student Learning.

FIGURE 3–5   Key Elements in an Assessment Plan

element of a plan—assessing for improvement rather than accountability. The temptation to view assessment in accountability terms is strong, and succumbing to it undermines the usefulness of the entire process.

Administrators can also encourage the faculty to review the institution's mission and discuss the educational values it expresses. These values should be reflected in course, program, and institutional assessment, thus keeping them in alignment with each other.

From a practical point of view, administrators can identify leaders and responsible parties to move the assessment process along. Will a faculty committee develop the assessment plan and present it to the faculty as a whole? Which committee will have this responsibility? Who will have oversight for implementing the plan? Will it be an existing committee such as the curriculum committee or will a separate committee be established? Administrators can also help clarify the role of various units within the institution in order to develop an approach to assessment that is comprehensive but avoids duplication, e.g., in relation to assessment in general education.

Administrators provide leadership when they encourage the faculty to include in the plan a timeline for achieving important steps in the assessment process. By what date will the faculty develop and adopt a set of intended learning outcomes? When will they have developed or selected their assessment measures in order to provide for data collection? When and how will data be analyzed? Who will use results, when will they use them, and for what purposes? When and how will interested parties be informed about assessment results? When and how will the assessment process be evaluated? Answering questions like these helps establish a program in which assessment is an ongoing activity rather than a series of occasional events.

Most importantly, administrators can create forums for discussion (regular faculty meetings, special retreats, and so forth) to ensure that the results of assessment are used by the faculty to improve the curriculum, as well as the teaching that takes place at the institution or in the program. When areas of student weakness are identified, adminstrators can allocate resources (e.g., new hires, support personnel, additional sections to reduce class size, and so forth) to strengthen those areas. When planning for the future takes place, they can include information about student learning in the planning process, and they can make sure that assessment results are examined when programs are reviewed.

Finally, administrators can play an important leadership role by simply being persistent in guiding the faculty to take the next step in assessment. Establishing an effective assessment program is a long-term activity in which faculty members have much to learn and in which mistakes will be made. Being persistent in helping the faculty make incremental improvements in assessment—encouraging them to look forward rather than backward—is a key leadership contribution.

Educational leadership

In addition to attending to the administrative aspects of assessment, administrators can also exercise educational leadership for assessment. In this role, administrators help faculty understand key assessment concepts, and this means that administrators must understand them as well. Administrators may find it useful to allocate resources for consultants who can facilitate increased understanding of the assessment process among all members of the institution or program. Administrators may also wish to seek out and share with the faculty useful information sources in the assessment literature.

As previously mentioned, one key aspect of an administrator's role is to help the faculty focus on assessing for improvement rather than for accountability, resisting the tendency to impress external audiences with data reflecting only positive features of the program. Administrators can also help faculty understand the connections between assessment and other important initiatives on campus—catalog change; program review; planning, budgeting, and hiring; and other educational interventions like learning communities.

Adminstrators can lead faculty in discussing important issues that both undergird the assessment plan and are central to an effective assessment program, such as those listed at the bottom of Figure 3–4. Such discussions can foster faculty ownership of assessment and lead to assessment programs that reflect principles of best practice. Furthermore, they can encourage partnerships with other individuals on campus who contribute to student learning and who thus can play a helpful role in assessment, e.g., faculty and staff in student affairs, the library, and so on. Administrative support is essential for effective faculty ownership of an assessment program.

Reflections

As you create your own meaning from the ideas in this section, begin to think about . . .

- What institution-wide support do my colleagues and I have for our assessment efforts?

- How do we involve appropriate colleagues from other parts of the institution?
- How do administrators support us in our assessment efforts?

LOOKING AHEAD

In Chapters 4 through 9, we examine specific techniques to support and enhance learner-centered assessment at an institution. Chapter 4 describes intended learning outcomes, their benefits, and the characteristics of those that are effectively stated.

TRY SOMETHING NEW

1. Using the guidelines in this chapter, evaluate the way
   a. you assess learning in your courses,
   b. you and your colleagues assess learning in your program, or
   c. your institution's faculty and staff assess learning at the institution.
2. Discuss your findings with colleagues who are also interested in or responsible for assessment. Together decide what needs to be done to improve assessment at the course, program, and/or institutional levels.

REFERENCES

Alverno College Faculty. (1992). *Liberal learning at Alverno College.* Milwaukee, WI: Alverno College Institute.

Alverno College Faculty. (1994). *Student assessment-as-learning at Alverno College* (3rd ed.). Milwaukee, WI: Alverno College Institute.

Alverno College Faculty. (1996). *Alverno College ability based learning program.* Milwaukee, WI: Alverno College Institute.

American Association of Higher Education (AAHE). (1992). *Principles of good practice for assessing student learning.* Washington, DC: AAHE Assessment Forum.

Babson College. (1998). *Undergraduate program guide.* Wellesley, MA: Babson College.

Barr, R. B. (1998, September–October). Obstacles to implementing the learning para-digm—What it takes to overcome them. *About Campus*, 18–25.

Deming, W. E. (1986). *Out of the crisis*. Cambridge, MA: Massachusetts Institute of Technology Center for Advanced Engineering Study.

Department of Architecture. (1996). *Annual department report on student outcomes assessment*. Unpublished document. Ames, IA: Iowa State University.

Dzimadzi, C. B. (1997). *Faculty knowledge, attitudes, and evaluation of student outcomes assessment at a U.S. research university*. Unpublished master's thesis, Iowa State University, Ames.

Farmer, D. W. (1993, January–February). Assessment in an era of empowerment. *Assessment Update, 5* (1), 8, 10–11.

Freed, J. E., & Klugman, M. R. (1997). *Quality principles and practices in higher education: Different questions for different times*. Phoenix, AZ: American Council on Education and The Oryx Press.

King's College Faculty. (1997). *King's College: The core curriculum and assessment*. Wilkes-Barre, PA: King's College.

Loacker, G., Cromwell, L., & O'Brien, K. (1986). Assessment in higher education: To serve the learner. In C. Adelman (Ed.), *Assessment in American higher education* (pp. 47–62). Washington, DC: U.S. Department of Education, Office of Educational Research and Improvement.

Marchese, T. J. (1997). The new conversations about learning. In *Assessing impact: Evidence and action* (pp. 79–95). Washington, DC: American Association for Higher Education.

North Central Association–Commission on Institutions of Higher Education. (1994). *Handbook of accreditation (1994–1996)*. Chicago: North Central Association.

O'Brien, J. P., Bressler, S. L., Ennis, J. F., & Michael, M. (1996). The Sophomore–Junior Diagnostic Project. In T. W. Banta, J. P. Lund, K. E. Black, & F. W. Oblander (Eds.), *Assessment in practice: Putting principles to work on college campuses* (pp. 89–99). San Francisco: Jossey-Bass.

University of Illinois at Springfield Faculty. (1996). *University of Illinois at Springfield vision statement*. Springfield, IL: University of Illinois at Springfield.

University of Illinois at Springfield. (1999). *University of Illinois at Springfield under-graduate/graduate catalog*. Springfield, IL: University of Illinois at Springfield.

Wehlberg, C. (1999, May). How to get the ball rolling: Beginning an assessment pro-gram on your campus. *AAHE Bulletin*, 7–9.

4

Setting Direction with Intended Learning Outcomes

Badly needed . . . is a set of agreements on what self-regulation in higher education ought to be fundamentally *about* . . . One is the community's own assurance of academic quality. This means first and foremost a predominant focus on the assessment of outcomes and results . . . Focusing on outcomes as the centerpiece of recognition also forces us to address (and eventually develop a satisfactory answer to) legitimate questions about the common meaning of academic awards given in common. What the baccalaureate really is supposed to *mean* in terms of knowledge, skills, or other attributes is a question increasingly asked by both society and ourselves. It is a question that deserves an answer and it is one that in the long run we cannot duck (Ewell, 1994, p. 29).

Making Connections

As you begin to read the chapter, think about the ideas and experiences you've already had that are related to intended learning outcomes . . .

- What are the *essential features* of your *institution* and how do they help shape the ideas, values, and attitudes of your students?

- What are the *essential features* of your *academic program* and how do they help shape the ideas, values, and attitudes of your students?

Continued

Making Connections   *Continued*

- What is *unique* about your *institution* and how are your graduates different because of that uniqueness?
- What is *unique* about your *academic program* and, as a result, what unique qualities do your graduates possess?
- What should graduates of your academic program know, understand, and be able to do when they leave the institution?

- How do you as a faculty member contribute to the development of the skills and abilities of your program's graduates?

What else do you know about intended learning outcomes?

What questions do you have about intended learning outcomes?

Answering the questions in Making Connections is the first step in creating the type of learner-centered environment discussed in Chapters 1 through 3. It is also the first step in helping an institution fulfill its teaching mission effectively. Students change in many ways during their college years. Their ability to think and reason is affected by the college experience (Baxter Magolda, 1996; King & Kitchener, 1994), as are their attitudes, values, aspirations, and self-concepts (Astin, 1993). Considerable research indicates that a variety of environmental factors influence the type of change that occurs, including factors associated with the curriculum, pedagogy, peer group interactions, and faculty attitudes toward students (Astin, 1993). Being clear about the desired outcomes of college can help faculty structure experiences that will lead to those outcomes.

INTENDED LEARNING OUTCOMES

Focusing on student learning requires that we specify the goals or intended outcomes of the experiences students have at our institutions. Intended learning outcomes can be written at a variety of levels, for example, for

- a course,
- an academic program, or
- an entire institution.

Intended learning outcomes describe the kinds of things that students know or can do after instruction that they didn't know or couldn't do before. Formulating such outcomes may require a change of mindset.

For example, if asked, "How would you describe your current teaching goals?" most of us would offer responses similar to the following:

- to provide the best course I can
- to provide a stimulating environment for learning
- to provide opportunities for students to experience the central ideas of my field.

Notice the focus of these goals. Who is the implied key player? Who will provide the best course, the stimulating environment, and the opportunities to experience central ideas? The professor. That's logical in one sense because our goals are important and worth pursuing. However, in learner-centered instruction, we also need to focus on learners in goal-setting. In other words, we need to ask, "If I provide the best possible course for students, creating a stimulating environment for learning with opportunities to explore central ideas,

- What will my students know?
- What will they understand?
- What will they be able to do with their knowledge at the end of the course?"

Our answers to these questions constitute our intended learning outcomes.

Learning outcomes for a course are typically developed by the professor or professors teaching the course. Developing learning outcomes for an institution or an academic program is a task for faculty to complete collectively, and it is a task that takes time and deliberation.

We may use a variety of strategies to develop learning outcomes. For example, as we work together with our colleagues to develop outcomes for an academic program, we may find it helpful to examine existing course descriptions and syllabi in order to review what is currently being taught in our program. Searches of the literature and the World Wide Web can provide us with the learning outcomes of programs at other institutions [e.g., see the University of Colorado outcomes at http://www.colorado.edu/outcomes/ or a list of other internet resources at http://www2.acs.ncsu.edu/UPA/survey/resource.htm (Schechter, 1999)]. Rogers (1991) suggests that reports from national commissions and professional associations in various disciplines may include desirable learner outcomes. Or we can simply brainstorm about our own ideas and values about student learning.

Reflections

As you create your own meaning from the ideas in this section, begin to think about . . .

- How familiar am I with the concept of intended learning outcomes? How comfortable am I with this concept?
- What are my intended learning outcomes? Have I written them down or are they just in my head?

- What are some of the desired learning outcomes that I want students in my program or my courses to achieve?
- Under what circumstances have I discussed learning outcomes with my colleagues?
- What learning outcomes are considered important in my discipline?

BENEFITS OF FORMULATING INTENDED LEARNING OUTCOMES

Three benefits of formulating intended learning outcomes are shown in Figure 4–1. Each is discussed below.

Intended learning outcomes form the basis of assessment at the course, program, and institutional levels

As discussed in Chapter 1, assessment refers to our efforts to evaluate the learning component of all academic and nonacademic programs on campus. We defined assessment as the "process of gathering and discussing information from multiple and diverse sources in order to develop a deep understanding of what students know, understand, and can do with their knowledge as a result of their educational experiences; the process culminates when assessment results are used to improve subsequent learning."

Intended learning outcomes

- form the basis of assessment at the course, program, and institutional levels.
- provide direction for all instructional activity.
- inform students about the intentions of the faculty.

FIGURE 4–1   Benefits of Formulating Intended Learning Outcomes

The fundamental question that drives a clearly focused assessment program is a simple one: "Have our graduates learned what we intend them to learn?" This is a learner-centered question, which implies the following:

- As program faculty, we have intentions about what students in the program should learn.
- As program faculty, we develop collective expressions of our intentions in statements of intended learning outcomes.
- As program faculty, we develop curricula and instructional experiences in order to ensure that students have opportunities to learn what we intend.
- Students have experienced learner-centered instruction throughout their years at the institution.

To the extent that our instruction is learner-centered, we can assess students in our courses in ways that help students learn while they are being assessed. Well-designed course assessments provide feedback on our important intended outcomes at every step along the way. If the intended outcome of a program is that students critically analyze and interpret information, then during the program, students must participate in assessments that require the critical analysis and interpretation of information. If the intended outcome is that students understand and are able to apply fundamental principles of the discipline, then students must participate in assessments that require the application of those principles.

For example, Julian (1996) describes the way in which eight intended learning outcomes were used in the Speech Communications Department at the University of Tennessee, Knoxville, to design a comprehensive assessment approach in a newly designed capstone course for majors. Faculty developed a matrix in which they mapped eight learning outcomes (write clearly, effectively; speak effectively, intelligently; work constructively in groups; make reasoned decisions; use the library effectively; critically evaluate what is read; sketch rhetorical history and theories; understand theories and perspectives) onto six different assessments (a symposium speech, abstracts, an annotated bibliography, a final paper, an oral critique, and midterm/final exams). All but two of the outcomes were assessed by two or more assessments. This approach gave a clear focus to both the course and the assessment process.

The feedback students receive from assessments should deal directly with the learning to be acquired, whether it be knowledge or skills. In this way, assessments will result in feedback that learners can use, not only to know how well they are doing, but also to improve their performance. If students receive constant feedback that they can use throughout the program, they should perform well on both course and program assessments.

This may be a new view of assessment for many of us because our institutions make minimal demands on us in the area of assessment. Faculty members are required only to submit a final grade for each student. Grades are needed for bureaucratic reasons only—to certify a student's completion of a course and to indicate a student's general level of achievement in the course. In other words, the assessment represented in the grade is used to *monitor* students' levels of achievement. Although the administration undoubtedly assumes that grades are based on the collection of assessment data throughout a course, the collection of data itself is not really required by the institution.

In this book, we contend that the bureaucratic or monitoring aspects of assessment should be secondary to the instructional, diagnostic aspects. For learning to occur in a program, assessments must be employed primarily to give students feedback they can use to improve their performance. The individual professor's intended learning outcomes outline the knowledge, abilities, and skills on which assessments should be based. When assessments measure intended outcomes, students learn better, particularly when they know what the outcomes are.

The benefits of basing assessments on the individual professor's learning outcomes can extend well beyond the individual student. When the professor's goals reflect the intended outcomes developed collectively by faculty at the academic program and institutional levels, assessment that takes place within a course can enhance the effectiveness of the program and of the institution in fulfilling their teaching missions. The teaching function of the institution becomes an effective system of interrelated parts in which the nature and quality of each faculty member's assessment techniques affect the nature and quality of student learning, whether it is assessed at the course, program, or institutional levels.

Intended learning outcomes provide direction for all instructional activity

Because intended learning outcomes form the basis for ongoing assessment, they also form the basis for planning and implementing instruction each time a course meets. Knowing the characteristics that an institution's faculty desire in all graduates *of the institution* helps program faculty know, in part, what students in their program should be like when they complete it. Knowing what students are expected to achieve *at the end of their program* helps individual faculty members decide, in part, what students should achieve at the end of each course. In turn, knowing what students are expected to achieve at the end of a course helps us decide what students should achieve at the end of each section of the course, or indeed, at the end of each class period.

In other words, a learner-centered approach to teaching helps us develop a new mindset as we think about and plan our courses. No longer do we prepare courses or lessons by asking, "What material do I want to cover?" Rather, the organizing question becomes, "What do I want students to learn in the course?" or "What do I want students to learn today (or this week)?"

Answering these questions leads us to consider what content should be covered during a particular time period. It also prompts us to consider the ways in which students should be able to *use* the content. This in turn leads to a consideration of the kind of experiences students must have in the course or during the class period in order to be able to know and do what we expect.

Intended learning outcomes inform students about the intentions of the faculty

Perhaps the most important role of intended outcomes is to reveal to students the intentions of the faculty. When students know the goals of an institution, an academic program, or a course, they are able to make more informed decisions about whether the institution, program, or course will meet their needs. They are also in a better position to profit from the experiences they have in the settings they choose.

King (1999) points out that, for students, attending college is like putting together the pieces of a jigsaw puzzle without having the picture on the box to guide them. In her metaphor, the puzzle pieces are students' many collegiate experiences, both in and outside courses. The picture on the box is the kind of person we hope our students become as revealed in our intended learning outcomes.

> Clearly, for both educational and ethical reasons, we need to share this picture with our students and explicitly communicate the knowledge, skills, and attitudes we hope they will acquire as a result of the collegiate experiences. And as we go along, we need to ask them to look at this picture from different angles, in different lights, and from among different groups of people. We should also prepare them to revisit the question of the type of person they wish to become and the type of life they wish to lead (p. 3).

Thus, it is important for students to know our intended learning outcomes, and it is important for us to know theirs. In a learner-centered environment, we should seek to know students' goals so that we can help them achieve them within the context of the course or program.

The intended learning outcomes of the institution or program can be revealed to students in documents such as the catalog or other admissions material. The intended outcomes of a course should always be included in course syllabi that are distributed to students at the beginning of the course. Sharing outcomes helps students develop a sense of direction as they participate in class, study, and complete assignments. Learning outcomes can also serve as a basis for ongoing self-assessment as the course develops. Students can review the outcomes, asking themselves whether or not they have achieved them.

Reflections

As you create your own meaning from the ideas in this section, begin to think about . . .

- What would I have to do differently if intended learning outcomes formed the basis of assessment in my courses?
- What would I have to do differently if intended learning outcomes formed the basis of all instructional activity in my courses?
- How would my students react if I shared with them a list of my intended learning outcomes?
- How would my students react if I asked what they hoped to learn from the course?

CHARACTERISTICS OF EFFECTIVE INTENDED LEARNING OUTCOMES

Figure 4–2 summarizes the characteristics of effective learning outcomes. Each of them is discussed in a following section.

Effective statements of intended learning outcomes

- are student-focused rather than professor-focused.
- focus on the learning resulting from an activity rather than on the activity itself.
- reflect the institution's mission and the values it represents.
- are in alignment at the course, academic program, and institutional levels.
- focus on important, non-trivial aspects of learning that are credible to the public.
- focus on skills and abilities central to the discipline and based on professional standards of excellence.
- are general enough to capture important learning but clear and specific enough to be measurable.
- focus on aspects of learning that will develop and endure but that can be assessed in some form now.

FIGURE 4–2   Characteristics of Effective Intended Learning Outcomes

Intended learning outcomes are student-focused rather than professor-focused

"What will my students know? What will they understand? What will they be able to do with their knowledge at the end of the course?" When we answer these questions with sentences that begin, "Students should be able to . . . ," we have formulated intended learning outcomes. With those in hand, we can intentionally go about the business of helping students achieve them. Intended learning outcomes provide direction for both us and for our students. They establish the basis for assessment.

The following intended outcomes, taken from a variety of major disciplines, are examples of goals that have been formulated to focus on student learning. They describe what students should know, understand, or be able to do with their knowledge at the end of a course or program.

Students will

- organize ideas in a way that increases the effectiveness of a message.
- analyze and interpret qualitative and quantitative social science research data.
- work effectively on problem-solving teams.
- make decisions consistent with moral and ethical principles.
- develop interior design solutions using creative problem-solving techniques.
- develop an erosion control policy based on plant, soil, water, and climate principles.

Intended learning outcomes focus on the learning resulting from an activity rather than on the activity itself

A learning outcome that reads, "Students will study at least one non-literary genre of art," describes a curricular experience that students will have, rather than the learning outcome that will result. We should ask, "If students study at least one non-literary genre of art, what will they know, what will they understand, and what will they be able to do with their knowledge?" Possible responses that would be appropriate can be found in two of the intended outcomes for the general education program at The College of St. Scholastica (The College of St. Scholastica, 1999).

- The student will arrive at an analytical and reasoned appreciation of a specific art form.
- The student will be able to communicate the appreciation to others either in written or verbal form or in the artistic medium itself.

Reflections

As you create your own meaning from the ideas in these sections, begin to think about . . .

- How can my colleagues and I make the intended learning outcomes of our *program* more focused on student learning?

- How can I make the intended learning outcomes of my *courses* more focused on student learning?
- What are the most effective activities that I use in my courses?
- What do I expect students to learn from each of them?

Intended learning outcomes reflect the institution's mission and the values it represents

Intended outcomes that we develop at the course, program, or institutional level should reflect our institutional mission. This assertion may seem surprising. Mission statements used to be tired documents, stored in file cabinets, pulled out and dusted off periodically for special occasions such as accreditation reviews. They were largely irrelevant to daily life at the institution, and as faculty, none of us would ever view our activities as being in any way circumscribed by the institutional mission.

Today, however, as the population of available students declines, institutions are struggling to attract students to their programs and to operate with declining resources. At virtually all institutions, this situation has forced a discussion about the institution's "competitive edge," what makes it unique, what makes it special. An increased emphasis on developing a clear and focused mission has resulted. Those things that the institution professes to achieve within its unique environment and with the particular resources it has available have important implications for educational programs and for the intended outcomes that faculty develop.

For example, the missions of The College of St. Scholastica, Babson College, Rutgers University, and Southern West Virginia Community and Technical College are shown in Figures 4–3, 4–4, 4–5, and 4–6, respectively. A review of the missions reveals that the institutions differ somewhat in focus. The College of St. Scholastica is a Catholic liberal arts institution, Babson College is an institution that prepares leaders for the business world, Rutgers is a state-sponsored land-grant research institution, and Southern West Virginia Community and Technical College is a two-year institution that provides vocational/technical programs. Although all these institutions focus on common aspects of students' intellectual development (e.g., communication skills, critical thinking), their missions reveal differences in educational values, and these differences are reflected in their learning outcomes.

Mission

The College of St. Scholastica is an independent, coeducational, comprehensive college with programs in the liberal arts and sciences and professional career fields. Founded in the Catholic intellectual tradition and shaped by the Benedictine heritage, the College stresses intellectual and moral preparation for responsible living and meaningful work. The curriculum serves the Mission of the College by providing undergraduate and graduate education that is grounded in the liberal arts and sciences. The entire College is committed to an educational process requiring students to meet rigorous academic standards, to broaden the scope of their knowledge, and to be accountable to both self and society. The College has a special commitment to bring its Mission to the people in the region through programs and services.

General Education

The General Education program at the College seeks to broaden students' grasp of the accumulated wisdom of the past so that the challenges of the present—racism, global conflict, injustice, dehumanization, spiritual emptiness—may be met with wisdom, faith and imagination. Integrated with their professional studies, General Education courses remind students that their professional lives will be touched, complicated, even shaped by these larger issues. The mission of General Education at The College of St. Scholastica is to help students envision the connection between the practice of their profession and the practice of their humanity.

General Education Outcomes

1. Outcome: Problem solving

   Problem solving is a process that incorporates the ability to analyze a situation; select, find, and evaluate appropriate information; and create one or more possible solutions to improve/correct the situation. It requires observation, information gathering, critical thinking, and communication skills. Problem solving is required in all academic disciplines and employment situations a student will face. A general education will provide students the opportunity to analyze and improve their problem solving skills.

   The student will:

   A. analyze a situation (either real or hypothetical) to identify a problem;
   B. use multiple resources to gain additional information regarding the problem;
   C. develop a procedure to solve the problem using a sufficient knowledge base;
   D. propose and critique a viable solution to the problem;
   E. communicate the problem statement, the solution steps and the eventual outcomes.

2. Outcome: Value-based decision making

   Broadly conceived, values have to do with ideas, motives, and standards that a society considers good and essential for sustaining life. Making decisions based on values involves developing analytical skills and moral reasoning, understanding the

   Continued

FIGURE 4–3   The College of St. Scholastica Mission and General Education Outcomes

sources of our personal and community value assumptions, and fostering the disposition and capacity to learn from the insights and experiences of others who perceive the world differently. Ultimately it involves making decisions to act based on values which are well suited to achieving well-being for the individual and the community and the environments on which they depend.

The student will:

A. understand his/her own value system and how these values have been influenced by his/her personal experiences and decisions;
B. differentiate between his/her own personal values and the value systems of others;
C. appraise personal and communal values in the light of new knowledge, recent experience, and insight;
D. defend value-based decisions as ultimately serving the common good.

3. Outcome: Social responsibility

As a Catholic and Benedictine institution, the college has a particular obligation to share with students why it believes in the worth and dignity of all persons, why it places importance on exhibiting hospitality toward those in need, and why it works for peace and justice. Equally important is helping students to be better informed citizens who take the responsibility of citizenship seriously, for a democratic society is dependent upon the active participation of all of its people.

The student will:

A. identify specific issues that call for social responsibility;
B. evaluate the complexity of social justice issues;
C. evaluate differing points of view on social responsibility;
D. evaluate the moral and social obligations to respond to injustice and to work for social change;
E. understand the responsibilities of citizenship;
F. demonstrate a beginning commitment to active citizenship.

4. Outcome: Effective Communication . . .

5. Outcome: Disciplinary Understanding . . .

6. Outcome: The Aesthetic Response . . .

7. Outcome: Living with Diversity . . .

(The College of St. Scholastica, 1999)

FIGURE 4–3   (*Continued*)

For example, The College of St. Scholastica purports to stress "intellectual and moral preparation for responsible living and meaningful work. . . . The entire College is committed to . . . requiring students to meet rigorous academic standards, to broaden the scope of their knowledge, and to be accountable to both self and society." The general education outcomes of The College of St. Scholastica address learning in seven areas: problem solving, value-based decision making, social responsibility, effective communication,

---

Mission

Babson's mission is to educate innovative leaders capable of anticipating, initiating, and managing change. The undergraduate program carries out this mission by developing responsible and effective professionals who are broadly educated, think creatively and analytically, and take entrepreneurial initiative.

(Babson College, 1998, p. 23)

Competencies

- **Rhetoric**—The ability to communicate effectively in speech and writing is essential in the business world.
- **Numeracy**—Effectiveness in quantitative work is vital in nearly all areas of business, and helps improve the ability to think creatively and analytically.
- **Ethics and social responsibility**—Awareness and development of ethics is a foundation for a successful business career. Volunteer work and giving back to the community are key to personal development.
- **International and multicultural perspectives**—Exposure to different cultures is important in an increasingly global world of business and personal relationships.
- **Leadership/teamwork/creativity**—Learning to lead within the structure of a team is a crucial element of success in business today, as is creative entrepreneurial thinking.

(Babson College, 1998, p. 4)

FIGURE 4–4   Babson College Mission and Competencies

disciplinary understanding, the aesthetic response, and living with diversity. Some of these areas are those that all baccalaureate degree-granting institutions have in common (e.g., problem solving and communication). However, other areas in the general education outcomes (e.g., value-based decision making and social responsibility) focus on aspects of personal development related to morality and responsibility. Figure 4–3 presents the college's learning outcomes in the areas of problem solving, value-based decision making, and social responsibility.

Alternatively, Babson College (Figure 4–4) focuses on leadership development in a changing world with a particular emphasis on "entrepreneurial initiative." As a result, Babson College's competency areas include leadership, teamwork, and creativity.

Rutgers (Figure 4–5) seeks to prepare students to be responsible citizens and productive contributors to society. Because it is a comprehensive, multi-campus, state university with a wide variety of majors, the institution has adopted learning outcomes that are broadly stated goals defining "common curricular ground" uniting the university. They are grouped in three areas: intellectual and communication skills; understanding human behavior, society, and the natural environment; and responsibilities of the individual in society.

Mission

As the sole comprehensive public research university in the New Jersey system of higher education and the state's land-grant institution, Rutgers University has the mission of instruction, research, and service. Among the principles the university recognizes in carrying out this three-fold mission are the following:

- Rutgers has the prime responsibility in the state to conduct fundamental and applied research; to train scholars, researchers, and professionals; and to make knowledge available to students, scholars, and the general public.
- Rutgers should maintain its traditional strength in the arts and sciences, while at the same time developing such new professional and career-oriented programs as are warranted by public interest, social need, and employment opportunities.
- Rutgers will continually seek to make its educational programs accessible to an appropriately broad student body.
- Rutgers is committed to extending its resources and knowledge to a variety of publics, and bringing special expertise and competence to bear on the solution of public problems.

(Rutgers University, 1998, p. 1.10)

University-Wide Learning Goals

The goals define the common curricular ground that unites the university. They are purposefully broad so that the various campuses, colleges, and schools can continue to develop their unique identities through varying ways in which the goals are met, given the mission of the academic unit. They allow for the multiple creative implementation methods that can be tailored to different types of student and faculty strengths and interests.

The goals define the skills and knowledge that all Rutgers students will acquire to support their development as responsible citizens and as productive contributors to society in their workplaces and in their intellectual, cultural, and social endeavors. The goals are grouped in three areas. Intellectual and communication skills are the basic skills necessary for acquisition, analysis, and communication of information. These skills include critical thinking, communication skills, mathematical reasoning analysis, scientific inquiry, and information and computer literacy. Goals in the area of understanding human behavior, society, and the natural environment focus on the major areas of knowledge necessary to function effectively in our society. These include historical understanding, multicultural and international understanding, understanding of literary and artistic expression, understanding the bases of individual and social behavior, and understanding of the physical and biological world. Goals in the area of responsibilities of the individual in society address the skills and knowledge essential to effective citizenship in a democratic society and to ethical social functioning. These include citizenship education and social and ethical awareness.

(Rutgers University, 1998, p. 3.9)

FIGURE 4–5   Rutgers University Mission and University-Wide Learning Goals

Finally, Southern West Virginia Community and Technical College prepares students for further education or for work and career experiences. Its general education goals are similar to those of the baccalaureate degree-granting institutions above. However, in each of its divisions, the general education goals are interpreted as intended student learning outcomes that reflect the emphasis of the division. As Figure 4–6 shows, students enrolled

---

Mission

Southern West Virginia Community and Technical College is a comprehensive community college located in a rural environment. The College strives to fulfill current and future higher educational and vocational/technical needs of southern West Virginia, its service area, and beyond. Our College emphasizes student-oriented, transferable learning, enabling students to achieve work, career, and personal success.

Our College provides high quality, affordable, student-friendly, and easily accessible educational services. We are highly effective and flexible in responding to state and community demands, and in adapting to a global socio-economic system.

(Southern West Virginia Community and Technical College, 1998a)

General Education Goals

Southern West Virginia Community and Technical College is committed to providing a general education program that helps students develop the qualities and skills associated with college-educated adults. Southern's general education program promotes the development of independent, critical and conceptual thinking skills and those skills necessary for the effective communication of one's thoughts. Southern's general education program provides students with an integrated view of knowledge and prepares them for their role as productive and responsible members of society.

Students who have completed the general education requirements of an associate degree will gain the competencies to understand, be effective, aware and have sufficient knowledge in the following:

Critical Thinking Skills

Oral and Written Communication Skills

Mathematical Skills/Competencies

Informational Access/Literacy Skills

Scientific Inquiry and Research Skills

A Cultural, Artistic and Global Perspective

(Southern West Virginia Community and Technical College, 1998b, p. 4)

Continued

FIGURE 4–6 Southern West Virginia Community and Technical College Mission and Learning Outcomes

Intended Student Learning Outcomes in the Division of Allied Health

The Division of Allied Health is committed to delivering the highest quality education using state of the art technology to all students enrolled in allied health programs. Students pursuing an associate degree or certificate will maintain the high standards set forth by their chosen profession. Primary to the success of the student is the ability to think critically and apply decision making skills appropriately. Analysis, synthesis, and evaluation of knowledge obtained in specific allied health programs is a vital link in the future success of the student.

All students enrolled in allied health courses will be required to possess excellent communication skills, both written and oral. Students will be able to effectively communicate with peers, faculty, members of the health care community, patients and their families. Additionally, communication and research through the use of modern technology is essential to success in a global society. Scientific inquiry and research skills are integral components of all allied health professions.

Students will be cognizant of diverse cultures and populations both locally and abroad. . .

A strong belief in life-long education will be instilled in the student from the first class throughout the program. Qualities of the allied health professional include staying abreast of current trends and changes through continued education.

(Southern West Virginia Community and Technical College, 1998b, pp. 10–11)

FIGURE 4–6   (*Continued*)

in the Allied Health Division in programs like Nursing, Medical Laboratory Technology, or Radiologic Technology are expected to be able to communicate effectively with fellow health professionals and with patients and their families. They are expected to apply their inquiry and critical-thinking skills as they use technology in their field. They are also expected to develop a commitment to the continuing education that will be a fundamental component of their professional lives.

Reflections

As you create your own meaning from the ideas in this section, begin to think about . . .

- When was the last time my colleagues and I reviewed our institution's mission?

- What values does the mission represent?
- What implications do those values have for our program and courses?

Intended learning outcomes are in alignment at the course, academic program, and institutional levels

The intended learning outcomes of a program or course should be compatible with the institution's intended outcomes—if they exist. The faculty and administration at all institutions expect that students will know more and be more skilled when they leave the institution than when they entered. However, not all institutions have formulated institution-wide learner-centered outcomes that describe what graduates should know and be able to do. As reflected in the previous section, the process of formulating institution-wide outcomes has taken place intentionally and with broad faculty input at some institutions. Typically, these intended outcomes address the outcomes of the general education portion of the institutional program because this is the component of the curriculum that all students experience in common.

Not all institutions have formulated learner-centered outcomes or have even considered doing so. But as discussed in Chapter 1, external forces such as legislatures and accrediting associations have prompted this approach by requiring institutions to conduct assessments of student learning. All institutions have missions, a developing sense of uniqueness, and some form of a general education program. These factors should be taken into account when formulating program and course outcomes.

Just as institutional faculty should consider the appropriateness of developing common learner-centered outcomes for all students, so academic program faculty should consider developing discipline-related goals or intended learning outcomes for the students in their program. Intended learning outcomes at the program level should reflect the type of knowledge and skills expected in members of the program's discipline, but they should be compatible with and support institutional outcomes. The intended outcomes of courses should be compatible with academic program and institutional outcomes.

This relationship is displayed in Figure 4–7 which is an offshoot of the early work of Spady (W. Spady, personal communication, October 28, 1998). In designing course outcomes, we start first with the broad outcomes expected of all students in the institution. We then work backward to design academic program outcomes that are in harmony with them. Finally, we design course outcomes that will lead to the achievement of both program and institutional outcomes.

On the other hand, when the program is delivered, students experience the system in reverse. They first participate in experiences that address lesson outcomes. The learning that results from these experiences accumulates as students proceed through the courses and other experiences in the program. When the curriculum is designed so that it provides a coherent set of experiences leading to the development of desired knowledge and skills,

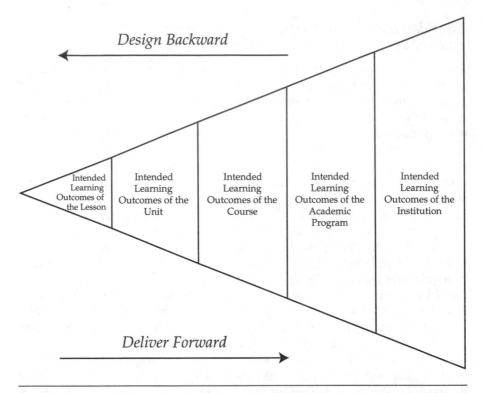

Design Backward

| Intended Learning Outcomes of the Lesson | Intended Learning Outcomes of the Unit | Intended Learning Outcomes of the Course | Intended Learning Outcomes of the Academic Program | Intended Learning Outcomes of the Institution |

Deliver Forward

FIGURE 4–7   Plan for Designing and Delivering Learning Outcomes

students show increasing levels of sophistication and integration of skills as they progress through the program. By the end of their college years, they should have achieved both academic program learning outcomes and institutional outcomes.

Figure 4–8 shows examples of institution-wide, program area, and course outcomes that address the topic of environmental awareness. The institutional outcome is a broadly stated learning outcome addressing students' understanding of physical and biological properties of the environment. This outcome could be achieved in general education science courses by students in many different major disciplines.

In some cases, achievement in a major discipline will reinforce and deepen students' understanding in an area addressed in an institutional outcome. For example, the academic program outcome shown in Figure 4–8 represents the type of achievement expected of graduates who major in Horticulture. It is compatible with the institution-wide outcome that addresses understanding of the physical and biological properties of the environment, but it is much more specific in its focus on the discipline of

Horticulture. It addresses student learning in the area of biotic and abiotic stresses and their relationship to plant development, and it also focuses on sensitivity to environmental concerns when reducing stresses. This is a culminating learning outcome of a major program, and more than one course in the curriculum would contribute to the achievement of this learning outcome.

The final outcome in Figure 4–8 addresses one aspect of the learning that might take place in a Horticulture course on Environmental Issues, that of the responsibility of the individual in the sustainable management of energy, soil, water, and plants. The learning outcome is narrowly focused, but it is compatible with both the academic program outcome and the institution-wide outcome. For Horticulture students, achieving this course outcome contributes to the achievement of program and institution-wide outcomes as well.

A program's outcomes should also address the general abilities and skills which are used in all academic disciplines, and they should reflect the unique ways in which they are applied in the program. For example, communication skills are desired in all students, but the way in which physicists communicate in their discipline is somewhat different from the way in which teacher education students communicate in theirs. Students in the arts will learn to communicate somewhat differently from students in engineering. This is illustrated in Figure 4–9.

Figure 4–9 presents an institution-wide outcome in the area of oral and written communication skills, followed by program outcomes in the area of

---

Institutional Outcome

Students will understand the physical and biological properties of the environment and how these properties are interlinked within ecological systems.

Academic Program Outcome (Horticulture)

Students will recognize common biotic and abiotic stresses, their potential effects on plants at various stages of plant development, and options for reduction of stresses with minimal disturbance to the environment and human beings (Department of Horticulture, 1996).

Course Outcome (Environmental Issues)

Students will be able to articulate the responsibility of the individual in the sustainable management of energy, soil, water, and plants.

FIGURE 4–8 Relationship Among Institutional, Program, and Course Outcomes: Example 1

Institutional Outcome

Students will be able to speak and write effectively.

Academic Program Outcome	**Academic Program Outcome**
(Political Science)	*(Psychology)*
Students can articulate principles and concepts of the discipline of political science (Department of Political Science, 1996).	Students can speak and write effectively in the discourse of psychology (Department of Psychology, 1996).
Course Outcome	**Course Outcome**
(Current Issues in U.S. Foreign Policy)	*(Psychological Measurement)*
Students can make an accurate and engaging oral presentation analyzing one current issue in American foreign policy.	Students can prepare a written summary and interpretation of standardized test results.

FIGURE 4–9   Relationship Among Institutional, Program, and Course Outcomes: Example 2

communication for the majors of Political Science and Psychology. Notice that one focuses on using communication skills to express the ideas of the discipline, whereas the other focuses on communicating in the manner of the discipline.

The course outcomes in Figure 4–9 list the type of communication that might be typical for professionals in each field. The course outcome for Political Science addresses the ability to make an accurate and engaging oral presentation on a current issue, whereas the course outcome for Psychology addresses the development of an understandable and useful written report of standardized test results. It is clear that members of both disciplines need excellent communication skills, but the content and sometimes the format of their communication will differ.

When the intended course outcomes in an academic program are compatible with institutional and program outcomes, those of us who teach the courses—individually and collectively—are at the heart of a system that intentionally and effectively helps students develop desired characteristics. This system becomes more effective when, at the program level, we examine program and course outcomes to decide how to best deliver the curriculum, including who will teach which courses and how.

For example, we may wish to structure experiences in the curriculum in order to intentionally help students integrate general skills with discipline-related knowledge in the program. We should sequence courses and establish appropriate prerequisites in such a way that student learning develops in a planned fashion.

In accomplishing this, it would be helpful for all of us to reflect on our individual strengths and weaknesses and determine the ways in which we are best able to contribute to the development of student learning. Those of us who are good communicators may take (or be given) the responsibility for emphasizing communication skills in the courses we teach in the discipline. Others may emphasize critical thinking and problem solving. This may be done informally, or it could be formalized by designating certain courses as "communication intensive" or "problem-solving intensive" (Green & Mullen, 1993).

Attending to the development of general skills and abilities may also cause us to design new organizational structures. At Alverno College, a faculty member is not only a member of an academic department, but he/she is also a member of an interdisciplinary group focused on one of the eight abilities the institution seeks to have students develop (Alverno College Faculty, 1992; Hakel, 1997). In a system with clearly formulated learning outcomes, each course and each faculty member can be envisioned in terms of their role in a curricular system of experiences that are interrelated and outcome-oriented.

It is possible for us to pursue learner-centered instruction without consideration of program and institutional outcomes, and we might be quite effective in helping students develop certain skills and abilities. However, as Chapters 1 and 3 point out, the ability of higher education institutions to serve society implies that faculty work in concert, developing a common vision of the desired qualities that our graduates should possess and a coherent curriculum to help students achieve them.

Reflections

As you create your own meaning from the ideas in this section, begin to think about . . .

- Have faculty at my institution formulated intended learning outcomes for all students?
- If so, what implications do they have for the outcomes in my program or courses?

- How would the intended learning outcomes of our program and courses differ if my faculty colleagues and I designed them backward, starting with institutional outcomes?
- As we deliver the curriculum forward, how are our courses helping students reach important institutional or program learning goals?

Intended learning outcomes focus on important, non-trivial aspects of learning that are credible to the public

One pitfall to avoid in formulating intended outcomes is focusing on easy-to-measure, but relatively unimportant outcomes like, "Students will recall the stages of mitosis." This can happen when we develop learning outcomes by carving up the content of the discipline into ever smaller pieces. Recalling the stages of mitosis may be important for some students, but it is probably more appropriate as an intended outcome of a class period than it is as a course or program outcome.

Statements of intended outcomes that "decompose" the content of the discipline into smaller parts are referred to by Erwin (1991) as "subject matter objectives" (p. 37). They tend to result from traditional, behavioral approaches to formulating learning goals and objectives that were advocated in the 1950s and 1960s. At that time, Bloom (1956) and others (Krathwohl, Bloom, & Masia, 1964; Mager, 1962) developed taxonomies of educational objectives and guidelines for developing them that encouraged teachers to think about student learning in terms of its cognitive, affective, and psychomotor components. The cognitive component focuses on the development of the intellect and related intellectual skills. The affective component focuses on the development of values and attitudes. The psychomotor area refers to the development of muscular skills and neuromuscular coordination.

Although it is helpful to think about these aspects of learning separately, it is important to remember that when students are engaged in learning, the cognitive, affective, and psychomotor aspects of their learning are inseparable (King & Baxter Magolda, 1996). All learning—even the acquisition of a new fact—requires the integration of new material with existing knowledge and is achieved through complex mental processes (Resnick & Resnick, 1992). Learning is influenced by feelings and attitudes, and in some cases, it involves feedback from muscular coordination. Thus, statements of intended outcomes at the course, program, and institutional levels should focus on desired outcomes with all of their complexities. They should address the integrated skills and abilities that are valued by educated people (Sizer, 1992; Wiggins, 1989).

This means that statements of desired outcomes should focus on the way the outcomes of the general education component of a student's program intersect with those in the major discipline. In general education, faculty help students to develop their skills and abilities in areas like communication and critical thinking. However, such abilities cannot develop in isolation from disciplinary content. One can learn effective communication and critical thinking skills only if one has something to communicate and think critically about. Furthermore, faculty should be helping students to communicate and think critically as members of their discipline. Process outcomes and content outcomes must be developed together, and the focus should be on *using* content effectively, not memorizing it. [See Chapter 7 for a discussion of Kurfiss's (1988) distinction between declarative knowledge and procedural knowledge.]

Marzano, Pickering, and McTighe (1993) have identified five types of learning outcomes that comprise the processes they believe will promote lifelong learning. The first category is that of complex thinking standards and includes students' ability to use various reasoning strategies and to translate "issues and situations into manageable tasks that have a clear purpose" (p. 19). The second is the area of information processing. Outcomes to be addressed in this area include using information-gathering techniques and resources, interpreting and synthesizing information, assessing the value of information, and knowing how and where additional information is needed. The third category is that of effective communication and includes communicating with diverse audiences in a variety of ways for different purposes. The fourth category addresses collaboration/cooperation outcomes, including effective performance in group situations, using interpersonal skills.

The final category, habits of mind, is concerned with students' ability to control their own thought processes and behavior. Marzano et al. (1993) include three types of outcomes in this category.

Self-Regulation

a. Is aware of own thinking.
b. Makes effective plans.
c. Is aware of and uses necessary resources.
d. Is sensitive to feedback.
e. Evaluates the effectiveness of own actions.

Critical Thinking

f. Is accurate and seeks accuracy.
g. Is clear and seeks clarity.
h. Is open-minded.
i. Restrains impulsivity.
j. Takes a position when the situation warrants it.
k. Is sensitive to the feelings and level of knowledge of others.

Creative Thinking

l. Engages intensely in tasks even when answers or solutions are not immediately apparent.
m. Pushes the limits of own knowledge and abilities.

n. Generates, trusts, and maintains own standards of evaluation.
o. Generates new ways of viewing a situation outside the boundaries of standard conventions (pp. 23–24).

King and Baxter Magolda (1996) support the importance of developing habits of mind in the college curriculum.

Developing thinking skills is only one aspect of achieving educational success in college . . . . For example, effective problem solving requires such attributes as awareness of the problem, the ability to gather and interpret relevant information, a willingness to try overcoming obstacles by making the best decision, and the personal "wherewithall" to implement the desired solution (p. 167).

Do students have the self-discipline to exert the appropriate amount of "time on task," the perseverance to see a problem or project through to completion, and the personal maturity to take responsibility for completing projects in a timely fashion. . . . The affective or personal development dimensions that affect student learning are painfully clear when the answer to questions like these is "no" (p. 168).

Some people react negatively to the suggestion that learning outcomes should focus on general abilities, "habits of mind," or attitudinal aspects of learning. They fear that a "process" focus will minimize the amount of content that students learn. However, these individuals may be confusing the amount of content that students *are exposed to* with the amount that they *actually internalize*. In traditional teaching, students are exposed to a great deal of content by professors, but the typical lament of professors is that students don't seem to understand or retain it. In courses in which students are expected to *use* content in meaningful ways, the amount of content internalized and recalled should actually increase.

Furthermore, students with little knowledge of the discipline will not be effective when they attempt to employ general abilities like communication, reasoning, and so forth. As Resnick and Resnick (1992) point out, the ability of individuals to think, reason, and make judgments like experts in the discipline depends on the amount of content they possess. Students who have mastered more content will be better able to think like members of their discipline. Thus, the focus is not on less content but rather is on what students can do with the content they have learned. Recall from Chapter 2 the problem of "inert knowledge" (Whitehead, 1929), stemming from the difficulty individuals have in knowing when, how, and where to use the information they acquire. When formulating intended learning outcomes, we should integrate the knowledge of essential facts and concepts with the development of habits of mind that will require their use.

This approach is compatible with a holistic model of college student development, one that blurs distinctions between cognitive and noncognitive achievements (Ewell, 1994). Outcomes that integrate content and thinking processes, as well as cognitive and affective components of learning, are referred to by Erwin (1991) as "developmental objectives" (p. 39). As Ewell points out, the conceptual foundations for an integrated developmental approach have been well established in the student development theories of Perry (1970), Chickering (1969), and Kohlberg (1981). The integrated developmental approach is becoming increasingly characteristic of curricular objectives on college campuses (Erwin, 1991).

The following intended outcomes are examples of learning outcomes that integrate intellectual skills and the use of disciplinary content.

- Students will reason using simplified economic models such as supply and demand, marginal analysis, benefit–cost analysis, and comparative advantage (Department of Economics, 1996).
- The student will be able to design and conduct original and independent biological research (Department of Biology, 1998).
- The student will be able to identify and present the implications of the various ethical and legal decisions facing Human Resources professionals and substantiate points of view with credible reasoning (Department of Human Resources Management, 1998).

These outcomes integrate intellectual and affective elements.

- Students will have greater respect for different races and cultures as their knowledge about them increases.
- As team members, students will reveal their commitment to the team through the effective use of group problem-solving techniques.

Reflections

As you create your own meaning from the ideas in this section, begin to think about . . .

- If a panel of educated people were to review the intended learning outcomes that my faculty colleagues and I have developed for our program and courses, which

ones would they agree are important?

- How do my colleagues and I focus on using knowledge rather than simply acquiring it?
- Which of our intended learning outcomes reflect an understanding that students are whole persons and not just minds?

Intended learning outcomes focus on skills and abilities central to the discipline and based on professional standards of excellence

Intended learning outcomes should be credible to members of the profession in which they are formulated. Many professors in disciplines like the arts perceive that an outcomes approach to assessment is a reductionistic attempt to "quantify" the elusive and important qualities they seek to develop in students. They feel that the "special quality" that makes a painting, a sculpture, or a landscape artistic is difficult to describe in observable terms, let alone quantify.

It is true that there is no need to quantify the unquantifiable in assessment. On the other hand, if faculty in the arts are going to participate in assessment that promotes learning, they must attempt to describe and measure the quality or qualities that make a work artistic, and their description should be convincing to members of their disciplines. Even though it is difficult to articulate and assess what is really central in the arts, it is critically important to do so. It doesn't make sense to simply "count" superficial aspects of artistic endeavor just to fulfill a requirement to assess.

Intended learning outcomes should be compatible with the best thinking in the discipline in terms of what is important to know and how information in the discipline should be taught. Most disciplines have developed standards for student learning. The National Council of Teachers of Mathematics is a notable example. In recent years, this organization has developed standards that focus on conceptual understanding, problem solving, and the use of mathematics in the context of application rather than simply on the acquisition of procedural information leading to right answers. We should all consider turning to our professional associations for guidance in developing learner outcomes.

Intended learning outcomes are general enough to capture important learning but clear and specific enough to be measurable

Attaining an appropriate level of generality or specificity is often a difficult challenge when we begin formulating intended outcomes. As a basic principle, institution-wide outcomes will be more general than academic program outcomes. Academic program outcomes will be more general than individual course outcomes, and within a course, we may formulate day-to-day intended outcomes that are more specific than the course outcomes they support. If a professor's course outcome is that teacher education students will learn to use instructional media effectively, the specific outcome for today or this week may be that students will learn to make and use transparencies that enhance the effectiveness of instruction.

Even though program and institutional outcomes will be stated more generally than course or lesson outcomes, they should still be framed in measurable terms. For example, the outcome, "Students will be able to solve problems," gives little guidance for assessment. On the other hand, considerable direction for assessment is provided when the outcome is phrased in the following manner:

> *Students will work effectively with others on complex, issue-laden problems requiring holistic problem solving approaches (College of Agriculture Curriculum Committee, 1994).*

This outcome can be assessed by developing assessments that require teams of students to develop solutions to complex, issue-laden problems, as defined by the discipline. They can be judged on the effectiveness of their team skills, the quality of their solution, and their ability to use holistic problem-solving approaches. Chapter 6 discusses the development of rubrics, tools that can be used to describe and judge student work in important areas like team skills, areas that many have considered too subjective to be measured validly.

Intended learning outcomes focus on aspects of learning that will develop and endure but that can be assessed in some form now

Another issue that can arise has to do with the point at which learners are expected to achieve intended outcomes. Many faculty claim that the goals of an education are not really achieved until many years after graduation when individuals have the opportunity to use their knowledge and apply their skills in the context of their adult life and professional development

This is probably true; however, it does not justify postponing the assessment of student learning until after graduation. We have a responsibility to gauge the extent of learning that can reasonably be expected to occur before students leave the institution. We also have the responsibility to assess whether or not it has occurred and how programs can be changed to make learning more effective.

Reflections

As you create your own meaning from the ideas in the previous sections, begin to think about . . .

- How do our intended learning outcomes reflect current thinking in our discipline?
- How would leaders in our discipline react to our intended learning outcomes?
- Do my colleagues and I have a clear idea of how we would mea-

sure the learning represented in our intended learning outcomes?
- How could we rephrase our learning outcomes to represent the type of learning that we have in mind?
- What aspects of our intended learning outcomes could be measured while students are still at the institution?
- What aspects can only be assessed later in students' lives?

LOOKING AHEAD

Once we have written learning outcomes that form the basis for assessment at all levels in the institution, provide direction for all instructional activity, and inform students about our intentions, it is important that we collect data about whether or not we are helping students achieve them. Classroom assessment techniques and continuous improvement activities provide us with numerous ways to gather feedback for the purpose of improving learning and teaching.

Chapter 5 explains several techniques commonly used by professors who are committed to assessing learning and continually improving. These techniques help teachers collect feedback to understand how students are progressing and to help them make adjustments to remove barriers to learning. Equally important is the need to communicate back to students about progress in learning and changes that will be made in order to create a feedback loop. This loop or system of continuous feedback helps create a learner-centered environment in which teaching and learning are inseparable activities that reinforce one another.

TRY SOMETHING NEW

1. Write five intended learning outcomes, and evaluate them according to the criteria discussed in this chapter and listed in Figure 4–2.
2. Write a set of intended learning outcomes for one of your courses and discuss them with students.

3. With a group of colleagues, formulate intended learning outcomes for your program and discuss how your courses help students reach them.

REFERENCES

Alverno College Faculty. (1992). *Liberal learning at Alverno College*. Milwaukee, WI: Alverno College Productions.

Astin, A. W. (1993). *Assessment for excellence*. Phoenix, AZ: Oryx Press.

Babson College. (1998). *Undergraduate program guide*. Wellesley, MA: Babson College.

Baxter Magolda, M. B. (1996). Epistemological development in graduate and professional education. *The Review of Higher Education, 19* (3), 283–304.

Bloom, B. (Ed.) (1956). *Taxonomy of educational objectives. Handbook 1: Cognitive domain*. New York: Longman.

Chickering, A. W. (1969). *Education and identity*. San Francisco: Jossey-Bass.

College of Agriculture Curriculum Committee. (1994). *Unpublished general education outcomes for the College of Agriculture*. Ames, IA: Iowa State University.

Department of Biology. (1998). *Competency growth plan in critical thinking for students majoring in Biology*. Unpublished document. Wilkes-Barre, PA: King's College.

Department of Economics. (1996). *Annual student outcomes assessment report*. Unpublished document. Ames, IA: Iowa State University

Department of Horticulture. (1996). *Annual student outcomes assessment report*. Unpublished document. Ames, IA: Iowa State University.

Department of Human Resources Management. (1998). *Competency growth plan in critical thinking for students majoring in Human Resources Management*. Unpublished document. Wilkes-Barre, PA: King's College.

Department of Political Science. (1996). *Annual student outcomes assessment report*. Unpublished document. Ames, IA: Iowa State University.

Department of Psychology. (1996). *Annual student outcomes assessment report*. Unpublished document. Ames, IA: Iowa State University.

Erwin, T. D. (1991). *Assessing student learning and development*. San Francisco: Jossey-Bass.

Ewell, P. T. (1991). To capture the ineffable: New forms of assessment in higher education. In G. Grant (Ed.), *Review of Research in Education, 17*, 75–125. Washington, DC: American Educational Research Association.

Ewell, P. T. (1994, November/December). A matter of integrity: Accountability and the future of self-regulation. *Change, 26* (6), 25–29.

Green, D. E., & Mullen, R. E. (1993). Doing it our way—revising a College of Agriculture curriculum. *Agronomy Abstracts*, 2.

Hakel, M. D. (1997, July–August). What we must learn from Alverno. *About Campus*, 16–21.

Julian, F. (1996). The capstone course as an outcomes test for majors. In T. W. Banta, J. P. Lund, K. E. Black & F. W. Oblander (Eds.), *Assessment in practice: Putting principles to work on college campuses* (pp. 79–82). San Francisco: Jossey-Bass.

King, P. M. (1999, March–April). Putting together the puzzle of student learning. *About Campus*, 2–4.

King, P. M., & Baxter Magolda, M. B. (1996). A developmental perspective on learning. *Journal of College Student Development, 37* (2), 163–173.

King, P. M., & Kitchener, K. S. (1994). *Developing reflective judgment: Understanding and promoting intellectual growth and critical thinking in adolescents and adults.* San Francisco: Jossey-Bass.

Kohlberg, L. (1981). *The meaning and measure of moral development.* Worcester, MA: Clark University Press.

Krathwohl, D. R., Bloom, B. S., & Masia, B. B. (1964). *Taxonomy of educational objectives. Handbook 2: Affective domain.* New York: Longman.

Kurfiss, J. G. (1988). *Critical thinking: Theory, research, practice, and possibilities.* (ASHE-ERIC Higher Education Report No. 2). College Station, TX: Association for the Study of Higher Education.

Mager, R. F. (1962). *Preparing instructional objectives.* Palo Alto, CA: Fearon Publishers.

Marzano, R. J., Pickering, D., & McTighe, J. (1993). *Assessing student outcomes: Performance assessment using the dimensions of learning model.* Alexandria, VA: Association for Supervision and Curriculum Development.

Perry, W. G. (1970). *Forms of intellectual and ethical development in the college years.* New York: Holt, Rinehart and Winston.

Resnick, L., & Resnick, D. (1992). Assessing the thinking curriculum: New tools for educational reform. In B. R. Gifford & M. C. O'Connor (Eds.), *Changing assessments: Alternative views of aptitude, achievement and instruction* (pp. 37–75). Boston: Kluwer Academic Publishers.

Rogers, B. (1991). Setting and evaluating intended educational (instructional) outcomes. In J. O. Nichols (Ed.), *A practitioner's handbook for institutional effectiveness and student outcomes assessment implementation* (pp. 168–187). New York: Agathon Press.

Rutgers University. (1998). *Middle States Association self-study: Assessing our vision for excellence.* New Brunswick, NJ: Rutgers, The State University of New Jersey.

Schechter, E. (1999). *Internet resources for higher education outcomes assessment.* http://www2.acs.ncsu.edu/UPA/survey/resource.htm

Sizer, T. R. (1992). *Horace's school: Redesigning the American high school.* Boston: Houghton Mifflin Company.

Southern West Virginia Community and Technical College. (1998a). *Mission statement.* Mount Gay, WV: Southern West Virginia Community and Technical College.

Southern West Virginia Community and Technical College. (1998b). *Plan for assessment of student academic achievement.* Mount Gay, WV: Southern West Virginia Community and Technical College.

The College of St. Scholastica. (1999). *Undergraduate and graduate catalog 1999–2000.* Duluth, MN: The College of St. Scholastica, Office of the Registrar.

Whitehead, A. N. (1929). *The aims of education.* New York: MacMillan.

Wiggins, G. (1989). A true test: Toward more authentic and equitable assessment. *Phi Delta Kappan, 70,* 703–713.

▶ 5

Using Feedback from Students to Improve Learning

If you are serious about quality, everybody has to know how they're doing (Marchese, 1991, p. 5).

You don't get good at anything without feedback—not feedback in the sense that an expert translates things for you, but feedback in the sense of watching the ball, where it goes and where it doesn't go, and realizing what the result means for your next actions (Wiggins, 1997, pp. 31–32).

Feedback is not praise or blame. It's what you did and did not do, whether you realized it or intended it. Assessment should make its chief business the confronting of performers with the effect of their work, including performers called teachers. And then performers must do something about the effect, either to explain it, to justify it, or correct it (Wiggins, 1997, p. 39).

Making Connections

As you begin to read the chapter, think about the ideas and experiences you've already had that are related to gathering feedback from students to improve learning . . .

- How do you collect feedback from your students to help you improve your teaching and their learning?

Continued

Making Connections   *Continued*

- What tools and techniques are you aware of to help you collect feedback from students?
- How would your students react if you asked them for feedback?
- When and how do you reflect on your teaching?

What else do you know about using assessment information to improve learning?

What questions do you have about using assessment information to improve learning?

Continuous improvement in education means constantly looking for new learning systems and processes. As we shift from a teacher-centered paradigm to a learner-centered paradigm, we must make fundamental changes in the way we teach. We also need to gather information about the effectiveness of the changes we make. Christensen (1991) claims that people "live life forward but understand it backward" (p. 99). Gathering feedback from others and spending time reflecting on our teaching are critical in helping us understand our practice as teachers.

To illustrate, think about your most recent learning experience. Was it learning how to write a grant proposal, swing a golf club, invest your money wisely, or something else? In all cases, you undoubtedly received feedback on your performance.

If you wrote a grant proposal, what did you learn when your grant proposal did or did not get funded? What did you learn from reviewers' comments? If you were seeking expertise on the golf course, what did you learn from the feelings you experienced when you either missed the ball completely or when you made a clean connection with it? How did your instructor's comments affect you? Finally, what factors have affected your investment strategies? Market fluctuations and their consequences? Feelings resulting from violating your level of risk tolerance?

Most importantly, in each case, what did you do because of the internal and external feedback you received? Did you decide to tailor your grant proposal more closely to RFP guidelines? Did you practice keeping your head down while swinging? Have you decided that the time is right to pursue growth as an investment goal? Useful feedback lets you know not only how you are doing, but what you should do next to improve.

Just as we all need feedback to help us understand how well we are learning to write proposals, play golf, or invest our money, we also need feedback to help us improve our teaching so that students in our courses will learn more effectively. Students can play an important role in providing the kind of feedback we need. According to Chaffee (1997),

Compared with other kinds of enterprise, universities and colleges are sys-tematically deprived of input from the people we serve . . . . An enterprise that cared deeply about the people it serves would mount an extensive sys-tem to gather feedback . . . . Instead, we typically have a weak system, with end-of-term surveys, if that—too late to improve a course while the student is still enrolled in it (p. 46).

Brookfield (1995) calls gathering information about the effects of our teach-ing on students "seeing ourselves through our students' eyes" (p. 92) and be-lieves that this is one of the trickiest, yet most crucial, tasks for teachers.

TECHNIQUES FOR COLLECTING FEEDBACK FROM STUDENTS

This chapter discusses several techniques we can use to involve and engage our students in providing data that can help us improve teaching and learn-ing. These approaches are in harmony with two key elements of quality im-provement, sometimes known as total quality management (TQM) or continuous quality improvement (CQI): involving and engaging participants and making decisions based on data (Chaffee, 1997; Cross, 1993; Freed & Klugman 1997). They allow us to gather assessment information from our students as a group *during* a course—formative assessment. This approach is quick and efficient, and most importantly, it helps us make immediate changes to our courses to improve student learning. Waiting until the end of the course to distribute course evaluation forms—summative assessment—is just too late to get feedback in a continuously improving culture.

It could be said that the techniques discussed in this chapter provide us with "fast feedback." *Fast feedback* is a term derived from management prac-tice, but it can be applied to education as well. Faculty who use the activities described in this chapter report learning more ways to improve their courses than they ever learned from end-of-course student evaluation forms (Bate-man & Roberts, 1992). The techniques described require a small amount of ef-fort, are easy to practice, are flexible, and use little class time. Feedback is a critical component if we are to learn how to become more effective teachers.

Using the techniques of this chapter benefits students directly as well. As discussed in Chapters 1 and 2, active involvement in learning promotes ex-cellence in undergraduate education (Cross & Steadman, 1996; Study Group on the Conditions of Excellence in American Higher Education, 1984). Re-search suggests that "the more time and effort students invest in the learning process and the more intensely they engage in their own education, the greater will be their growth and achievement, their satisfaction with their ed-ucational experiences, and their persistence in college, and the more likely they are to continue their learning" (Study Group on the Conditions of Excellence in American Higher Education, 1984, p. 17). Assessment techniques like the ones discussed in this chapter help students learn to become more effective learners.

In a learner-centered environment, "teaching and learning are inseparable parts of a single continuum—more Mobius strip than circle—of reciprocal giving and receiving . . . . All teach, and all learn" (Christensen, 1991, p. 99). Feedback and assessment are used to help both students and teachers continuously improve.

Reflections

As you create your own meaning from the ideas in these sections, begin to think about . . .

- What do I look like "through students' eyes"? How do I know? Do

I need better sources of information?

- Would I benefit by reflecting more frequently on my teaching?

Classroom Assessment Techniques (CATs)

Angelo and Cross (1993) have developed a number of classroom assessment techniques (CATs) to help faculty become better able to understand and promote learning, and they have described ways in which they can be used in a variety of disciplines. These techniques increase our ability to help students become more effective, self-assessing, self-directed learners.

Classroom assessment is based on the assumption that the best way to improve learning is to improve teaching. The question that drives classroom assessment is: What are students learning? "The purpose of Classroom Assessment is to make both teachers and students more aware of the learning that is taking place—or perhaps not taking place—in the classroom; it is an assessment of learning in process, during the semester, in a given classroom" (Cross & Steadman, 1996, p. xvii). When we observe students while they are learning and collect frequent feedback from them, we can learn much about how they learn and, more specifically, about how they respond to particular teaching practices (Angelo & Cross, 1993).

Cross and Steadman (1996) define classroom assessment as "small-scale assessments conducted continually in college classrooms by discipline-based teachers to determine what students are learning in that class" (p. 8). Data are collected with the understanding that results are shared with students. By using classroom assessment, both professors and students continually use information to improve their performance.

Characteristics of classroom assessment conform to principles of good practice for continuously improving student learning. According to Angelo and Cross (1993), classroom assessment is learner-centered, teacher-directed, mutually beneficial, formative, context-specific, ongoing, and rooted in good teaching practice. The model of classroom assessment is based on seven assumptions.

1. The quality of student learning is directly, although not exclusively, related to the quality of teaching. Therefore, one of the most promising ways to improve learning is to improve teaching (p. 7).
2. To improve their effectiveness, teachers need first to make their goals and objectives explicit and then to get specific, comprehensible feedback on the extent to which they are achieving those goals and objectives (p. 8).
3. To improve their learning, students need to receive appropriate and focused feedback early and often; they also need to learn how to assess their own learning (p. 9).
4. The type of assessment most likely to improve teaching and learning is that conducted by faculty to answer questions they themselves have formulated in response to issues or problems in their own teaching (p. 9).
5. Systematic inquiry and intellectual challenge are powerful sources of motivation, growth, and renewal for college teachers and Classroom Assessment can provide such a challenge (p. 10).
6. Classroom Assessment does not require specialized training; it can be carried out by dedicated teachers from all disciplines (p. 10).
7. By collaborating with colleagues and actively involving students in Classroom Assessment efforts, faculty (and students) enhance learning and personal satisfaction (p. 11).

Using CATs Effectively

In order to use CATs most effectively, we should follow three steps. The first is to *decide* which CAT will provide the information we really need or desire because each CAT has been designed to give somewhat different information from the others. At this step, we should also think about the kinds of changes that might be implied in students' responses and be sure we are willing to consider them.

The second step is to *implement* the CAT. Angelo and Cross (1993) give clear directions for implementing each CAT, as will be seen below. Most CATs are administered in the last few minutes of each class and require note cards or half-sheets of paper.

The third step is to *respond* to the feedback collected. After collecting data from students, we should review the responses before the next class and decide what changes, if any, need to be made in the course (e.g., revisit a topic already discussed, assign a new reading, use more small group discussions, etc.). At the next session, we should share a summary of students' responses with the class and explain what changes will be made based on the students' input. Although it is not necessary to respond to every suggestion students make, it is important to follow through when an area for improvement is clearly indicated. In this way, students learn that their feedback matters.

If we do not feel changes are warranted, we should explain *why* changes will not take place as a result of the feedback. In other words, feedback received from students is matched with feedback given by the instructor and a complete feedback loop is created.

Among the most commonly used CATs are the Minute Paper and its variation, the E-mail Minute, the Muddiest Point, the One-Sentence Summary, the Word Journal, Directed Paraphrasing, and Applications Cards. The three steps for using CATs effectively should be employed with all of them.

The Minute Paper

This technique is sometimes referred to as the One-Minute Paper or the Half-Sheet Response because it is a quick and simple way to obtain feedback on student learning. Angelo and Cross (1993) claim that "no other Classroom Assessment Technique has been used more often or by more college teachers than the Minute Paper" (p. 148). The popularity of this CAT is attributed to its simplicity. Faculty members who use the Minute Paper regularly comment that "it is the best example of high payoff for a tiny investment . . . . The payoff of the reflection required of students is often as great as the payoff of information provided for the instructor" (Cross & Steadman, 1996, p. 133). For the small investment of time and energy, the feedback received from students can influence the effectiveness of the learning process.

When using this CAT, we should stop the class two or three minutes early and ask students to respond to questions like:

1. What was the most important thing you learned during this class?
2. What important question remains unanswered? (Angelo & Cross, 1993, p. 148).

Students usually write their responses on index cards or half-sheets of paper and turn them in anonymously. In large classes, it is not necessary for all students to respond each time the Minute Paper is used. Some method of sampling can be chosen. For example, the professor might say, "Today I'd like all students with birthdays in March to respond."

The purpose of the Minute Paper is to make it easy and quick for students to give feedback, as well as easy and quick for faculty members to gather it. The feedback helps instructors decide if efforts should be redirected or if changes should be made during the course. The Minute Paper is so popular that many faculty members modify the questions to fit their needs, but the goal remains the same: to have students respond to a few questions in a short period of time. Other questions that could be asked include:

- How was the pace of the class?
- Were the examples clear?
- Were the topics presented sufficiently?
- What specific questions do you have?

The Minute Paper helps us know how well our students are understanding. It makes students aware that teachers are concerned about their learning. The Minute Paper is a simple way for faculty and students to become aware of barriers to the learning process so that they can be removed or at least minimized.

E-mail Minute

One modification of the Minute Paper is to combine it with electronic mail (e-mail). Using e-mail to encourage communication is well documented in the education and communication literature (Strasser, 1995).

The benefits of e-mail include allowing faculty or students to send or read messages at their convenience, a factor which is advantageous for commuting students. Basically, e-mail extends office hours by allowing more time for communication among students and instructors. Another important feature of e-mail is the ability to send one message to numerous addresses simultaneously by using a distribution list. This makes the process of communicating between faculty and students efficient.

The E-mail Minute works in one of two ways. In the first, students are asked to respond anonymously to two questions in the last two or three minutes of each class, using index cards or half-sheets of paper. Immediately after class, the professor reads through the responses looking for common themes and questions or comments that require a response. The professor sends a summary of the themes to the entire class using e-mail. Faculty members using this method report that this system opens up communication with students, and students tend to ask questions or send comments beyond the E-mail Minutes.

The other way to use this CAT is to distribute the two questions to students in class and have all or a sample of them answer the questions using e-mail. Students who prefer not to ask questions in class often feel more comfortable using e-mail which is more private.

Whatever method is used, the most important part of the process is to complete the feedback loop by discussing with students the themes that emerged in their feedback. When changes are made as a result of student feedback, students understand that the process has credibility and their input is valued.

Muddiest Point

Muddiest Point is perhaps the easiest and quickest CAT since it involves asking only one question: What was the muddiest point in _____? The focus of the question may be a lecture, a discussion, an assignment, or an event. As the title suggests, the point of this CAT is to find out what was least clear or what was somewhat confusing about the class. The feedback can be used to identify the concepts that students find most difficult to understand. Responses help determine which topics need further discussion and provide guidance for allocating time among topics.

Similar to the Minute Paper, the Muddiest Point question addresses a particular aspect of one class. It is asked during the last few minutes of class, and responses are written on index cards or half-sheets of paper and collected as students leave class. Again, it is important to respond to students' feedback during the next class period or as soon as possible. Responses can be grouped into themes if themes emerge. The focus should be on clearing up any "muddy" areas before moving on and introducing new concepts, theories, and practices (Mosteller, 1989).

A business professor from Florida State uses a variation on this technique, asking three questions:

1. Did you get what you came for today?
   a. If yes, what did you get?
   b. If no, what was missing?
   c. If not sure, please explain.
2. What was the muddiest point remaining at the end of today's class?
3. What percent of mud was due to:
   a. Unclear presentation by instructor?
   b. Lack of opportunity to ask questions?
   c. Your lack of preparation?
   d. Your lack of participation in class discussion?
   e. Other? (Bateman & Roberts, 1992, p. 18).

One-Sentence Summary

The One-Sentence Summary enables instructors to determine how well or whether students can summarize a large amount of information on a particular assignment. This CAT assesses comprehension by asking students to respond to the questions: Who does what to whom, when, where, how, and why (WDWWWWHW)? A particular topic or passage is the focus, and students synthesize their answers into a long summary sentence. The purpose is to find out how well students can identify critical points by focusing on these specific questions. This technique is quick and easy to administer because students are limited to one sentence. Students should be encouraged to make their sentences grammatically correct, factual, and complete. When this CAT is used consistently, it encourages students to focus on key questions when they read an assignment.

Word Journal

A CAT similar to the One-Sentence Summary is the Word Journal. First, students summarize an assignment (article, reading, text) in one word. Then, students write a paragraph or two explaining why they selected that particular summary word. Like the One-Sentence Summary, this CAT assesses how well students can condense large amounts of information by focusing on the key concept or thought in the assignment. It also encourages students to seek out the main points when reading an article.

Both the Word Journal and the One-Sentence Summary can be used to assess how well students understand the material they read and how well they can focus on the main points. It is possible to use these CATs instead of quizzes to evaluate student performance.

Direct Paraphrasing

In Direct Paraphrasing, students are asked to paraphrase for a particular audience part of a topic, concept, lecture, or article. This technique assesses how well students understand what they have learned and how well they can use their own words to explain it to individuals with different perspectives. Students can be asked to role-play (Assume you are the director of marketing . . . Imagine you are the teacher . . .) in order to direct their paraphrasing to an audience other than faculty and students. Because their paraphrase is for a specific audience, this CAT is extremely practical and applicable to building skills needed for the future. Students should be told how much time will be allowed for this assessment and about how long their paraphrases should be.

Direct Paraphrasing results can be analyzed by separating the responses into categories: confused, minimal, adequate, and excellent. They should also be examined for accuracy, relevance for audience, and effectiveness in satisfying the assignment. The rubrics discussed in Chapter 6 may be useful in giving students feedback about how well they are able to accomplish this CAT.

Angelo and Cross (1993) emphasize that Direct Paraphrasing is "useful for assessing the students' understanding of important topics or concepts that they will later be expected to explain to others" (p. 232). In fields such as marketing, social work, education, law, and others, success often depends on how well people can understand specialized and complex information and then effectively communicate this information to others.

Application Cards

After students have heard or read about an important principle, theory, concept, or procedure, the instructor hands out index cards and asks students to write down at least one real-world application for what they have just

learned. This is an instantaneous way to determine how students have con-
nected their new learning to prior knowledge and how well they understand
how to apply the concepts. This CAT helps students to see more clearly the
relevance of what they are learning.

At the beginning of class, students are asked to think about possible applications for topics as they are discussed. At the end of class, the professor
selects one concept, principle, theory, or procedure and asks students to write
down no more than three applications on an index card in three to five minutes. The professor collects the responses and shares a few of the applications
in the next class period. Because of the simplicity and flexibility of this CAT,
it can be used in almost any course of any size. Like Direct Paraphrasing, the
focus is on encouraging students to think about applications of the course material. It helps students make connections between what they are learning in
their course and in their experiences outside the class. It reinforces the relevance of their learning.

Continuous Quality Improvement Techniques

Continuous quality improvement (CQI) techniques from the business management literature are being adapted to improve learning and teaching
processes in education. Even though more progress has been made implementing CQI on the administrative side of institutions, interest in implementing quality principles continues to evolve on the academic side as
evidenced by the growing literature (e.g., Bonstingl, 1996; Chizmar, 1994;
Cornesky, 1993, 1994; Cornesky & Lazarus, 1995; Freed & Klugman, 1997;
Wolverton, 1994).

The assessment and continuous quality improvement movements are
both based on collecting feedback for improvement. The principles of continuous improvement parallel the themes of Classroom Assessment, and CQI
techniques are very similar to CATs. Both strive to accomplish the same goal:
to improve the learning of both teachers and students by collecting and sharing data.

Two-Way Fast Feedback
Similar to CATs, Two-Way Fast Feedback is a process of collecting feedback
and reversing the feedback so that students and professors work together in
the improvement of the learning processes and environment (Luechauer &
Shulman, 1996; Roberts, 1995). The name of this process emphasizes the fact
that faculty members "give feedback to students on the student feedback just
received, a new channel of communication opens up, hence two-way fast
feedback" (Roberts, 1995, pp. 517–518). The approach is "systematic, frequent, and focused on learning about specific problems that students may be
experiencing" (Bateman & Roberts, 1995, p. 250).

Date _____

	Little or nothing		A fair amount		A great deal
Overall, how much did you get out of today's class?	1	2	3	4	5

What was the most important thing you learned?

What was the muddiest point?

What single change by the instructor would have most improved this class?

Please comment briefly on the helpfulness of the advance reading assignments for today's class.

Your Preparation for Today's Class

	Little or nothing		A fair amount		A great deal
Overall, how much did you get out of your preparation for today's class?	1	2	3	4	5

What one thing can the instructor do to help you to improve your future class preparation?

What one thing can you do to help improve your future class preparation?

Your Progress on Your Project

	Behind Schedule		On Schedule		Ahead of Schedule
On balance, how are you doing on your project?	1	2	3	4	5

What one thing can the instructor do to help you make better progress on the project?

Continued

FIGURE 5–1   Sample Fast Feedback Questionnaire

What one thing can you do to help you make better progress on the project?

General
Is there any other feedback about any aspect of this course that you would like to learn more about?

Are you having problems unrelated to this course that the instructor should be aware of?

(Bateman & Roberts, 1995, p. 253)

FIGURE 5–1   (*Continued*)

In two-way fast feedback, students complete a one-page questionnaire at the end of a class meeting. (See Figure 5–1 for an example.) The results are simple and easy to summarize because the students merely circle a number on five, seven, or nine point scales, and summaries require only simple calculation of average responses or the percentage that chose each response. Space is allowed for students' comments, but the questionnaire is usually a page in length. Questions refer to issues like clarity of lectures, presentation skills, and student preparation outside of class.

The essential step in this process is the reverse feedback. After collecting feedback from the students, the professor responds to the group—either orally, in writing, or both as soon as possible. This may sound time-consuming, but Bateman and Roberts (1995) claim from experience that the process prevents "rework" for students and instructors. Since the questionnaires are completed anonymously, students feel comfortable responding in ways that may improve the course for them while they are still enrolled.

The point of this approach is not to find out from students what content to cover—this would be inappropriate. Rather, the technique is based on the assumption that students are capable of commenting accurately on the learning process. Students know when they are confused, bored, or uncertain, all of which decrease the effectiveness of learning.

Instantaneous Feedback
This is a modification of Two-Way Fast Feedback. At a point late in a class session—usually when 10–15 minutes remain in the class—say to students, "Reflect upon the class. In two minutes, think of any questions you wanted to ask or comments you would have liked to make and write them down on paper." Collect the anonymous papers in the remaining minutes of class, and answer the questions orally for everyone. The exercise does not need to take more than 15 minutes, and the rewards for students are well worth the time spent.

Using this process in about 75% of class meetings is enough to collect sufficient feedback and to indicate to students that you are serious about continuously improving the course (Reilly, 1995).

Plus/Delta Feedback Tool

This tool, sometimes referred to as Plus/Change, is used as a feedback tool at
the end of a class session to determine what processes to change and how to
change them. Using an index card, ask students to divide the card into four
quadrants and complete these two steps: 1) Identify the things that are working and should stay the same (Plus). 2) List the things that are not working
and should be changed (Delta).

Ask students to complete these two steps both for the teacher and the
course and for themselves, resulting in feedback in the four quadrants. The
essential step for the Plus/Delta is that students have to reflect upon their
own behavior and take ownership for their learning. Students ask themselves
what they need to keep doing for the course to be successful (Plus) and what
they need to change for the course to improve for them (Delta) (Helminski &
Koberna, 1995). Figure 5-2 is an example of Plus/Delta.

The LEARN Model

"The purpose of LEARN is to help students and faculty members work together to improve teaching and learning" (Baugher, 1995, p. 266). The model
utilizes a team of students who design, administer, and evaluate feedback
and then implement suggestions for improvement. The goal is similar to most
classroom assessment goals: to identify areas of strength and weakness. "The
difference in focus is at the heart of the LEARN process—to help students and

The Teacher/Course— What's Working?	The Teacher/Course— What Needs Changing?
The teacher stayed focused on objectives.	One student dominated discussion.
Class is enjoyable and the time goes fast.	We did not go over assignments.
Small group discussions are helpful.	The video was not helpful.
The Student—What's Working?	**The Student—What Needs Changing?**
I was prepared for class.	I need to participate more in class.
My attendance is good.	I should study more for exams.

(Adapted from Helminski & Koberna, 1995, p. 323)

FIGURE 5–2   Sample Plus/Delta Feedback Form

instructors begin to focus on continuous improvement of processes rather than to seek out and solve problems" (p. 266).

LEARN is an acronym for the steps in the process:

- Locate an opportunity for improvement.
- Establish a team to work on the process.
- Assess the current process.
- Research root causes.
- Nominate an improvement and enter the Plan-Do-Study-Act (PDSA) cycle (Baugher, 1995, p. 270).

The LEARN team works through this process several times during a course, identifying improvements and implementing suggestions.

The PDSA cycle, sometimes referred to as the Plan-Do-Check-Act cycle, is a simple, effective, data-driven tool for continuous learning and improvement.

- *Planning* requires collecting the data needed to understand the process to be improved and developing a plan for improvement. In teaching, this means moving beyond the typical measures of progress such as examinations, quizzes, and summative evaluations to a much more active, ongoing data collection process. Gathering and interpreting the data drives the cycle. The importance of data as a driving force in improving the process of learning cannot be overemphasized. "Data are the foundation for understanding this process and for planning and developing changes —the doing" (Sherr & Schwoerer, 1995, p. 454).
- *Doing* represents making changes based on data collected. Alternatives are generated from the data and changes are implemented on a test basis.
- *Studying* refers to monitoring the changes by collecting more data and evaluating. This step may lead to revisions or adjustments.
- *Acting* means that an effective change is permanently implemented when it seems appropriate. The cycle continues. To continuously improve, the cycle is repeated when needed (Sherr & Schwoerer, 1995).

The LEARN team acts as a quality improvement team that focuses on process improvement rather than problem solving and implements its own improvements. But the team does *not* dictate course content to the instructor, handle student grievances, or translate improvement to mean responding to all student demands or lowering course expectations. (For additional information on implementation, refer to Baugher, 1995.)

Critical Incident Questionnaire (CIQ)
The CIQ is a one-page form that is handed out to students to complete during the last 10 minutes of class. Five open-ended questions on the form ask

students to write down details about events that happened during the week. Rather than asking them what they liked or did not like, the focus is on specific, concrete events that were important to them. (Refer to Figure 5–3 for an example of a CIQ.)

The benefits of using CIQs include alerting professors to potential problems before they develop, encouraging students to be reflective learners, and building trust between teachers and students. As with other feedback techniques, it is important to report back to the students about the themes that emerge in the CIQs. When students witness their opinions, reactions, and feelings shared publicly and taken seriously, they know they have had some input into the process of improving the course (Brookfield, 1995).

Feedback from Teambuilding Techniques

In many disciplines, increasing importance is being placed on preparing students to interact collaboratively and cooperatively in the workplace. As a result, professors are increasingly structuring activities in which students work in teams. Training is provided in the interpersonal and problem-solving skills needed to create a successful team experience (Scholtes, 1988). Students learn about expectations, roles, and conflict resolution techniques.

Directions

Please take about five minutes to respond to each of the questions below about this week's class(es). Don't put your name on the form—your responses are anonymous. When you have finished writing, put . . . the form on the table by the door. . . . At the start of next week's class, I will be sharing the responses with the group. Thanks for taking the time to do this. What you write will help me make the class more responsive to your concerns.

1. At what moment in the class this week did you feel most engaged with what was happening?
2. At what moment in the class this week did you feel most distanced from what was happening?
3. What action that anyone (teacher or student) took in class this week did you find most affirming and helpful?
4. What action that anyone (teacher or student) took in class this week did you find most puzzling or confusing?
5. What about the class this week surprised you the most? (This could be something about your own reactions to what went on, or something that someone did, or anything else that occurs to you.)

(Brookfield, 1995, p. 115)

FIGURE 5–3   Sample Critical Incident Questionnaire (CIQ)

Some of the techniques used to prepare students to be successful team members can also be used to generate feedback about learning. Idea-generating tools such as brainstorming and the nominal group technique are examples of techniques that can be used in this manner.

Brainstorming

The team's goal in brainstorming is to generate as many ideas as possible. Members initially share ideas without judging their worth because the focus is on quantity not quality. One person acts as recorder or scribe and summarizes ideas using a flip chart. As pages are filled, they are taped in sequence to the wall or blackboard. This creates a team memory so that all ideas can be viewed simultaneously.

Professors can use this approach to gather information for course improvement. Students can work in teams to generate as many ideas as possible about changing the course to improve learning. This technique encourages creativity and provides the professor with a wide variety of suggested modifications to consider (Scholtes, 1988).

Nominal Group Technique

The Nominal Group Technique (NGT) is used to make decisions in teams. It is similar to brainstorming, but it has some unique features that facilitate efficiency. In advance of the meeting at which the technique is to be used, the question to be addressed is distributed to participants. Members thus come to the meeting prepared to share their responses. In a round-robin fashion, members give one response at a time, and the ideas are recorded on a flip chart, the board, or a transparency until all ideas are given. In this way, everyone has an equal voice, and the focus is on generating a complete list of ideas rather than on advocating for certain ideas.

Once this step is finished, a second tool, N/3, is used to help teams or groups arrive at a consensus quickly. The number of ideas that has been generated is divided by three, and the resulting number determines the number of ideas each person selects from the list. For example, if 15 ideas are generated, every person selects five in a round-robin fashion. Typically two or three ideas emerge as the most popular.

This second step of coming to consensus can also be used with data collected by other methods. It allows a group to prioritize any list of data in a short period of time because ideas emerge about which there is some agreement without having to discuss every idea (Freed & Klugman, 1997). In the case of gathering data to improve learning, NGT provides a process for finding out which of many ideas for course improvement are the most important ones to students.

Other Feedback Activities

Turn to Your Partner (TTYP)

Turn to Your Partner (TTYP) is a technique professors can use to enhance student learning at the same time they collect feedback about learning (Licklider, 1996). Adapted from the paired discussion activity of Johnson, Johnson, and Smith (1991), the purpose is to provide students with maximal opportunity to develop deep understanding by discussing what they're learning while they're learning it. It is a technique that can be used in large lecture classes, as well as small seminars.

In this approach, every student has a partner, typically an individual sitting beside him/her, and the partner is identified at the beginning of class. During the class session, the professor periodically asks the class questions about the topic under discussion, and then tells them to TTYP. First the members of the pair must formulate their individual answers to the question privately. Then each shares his or her answer with the partner. It is important for each student to listen carefully to the partner's answer. Then, through discussion, the pair creates a new answer to the question. The professor calls upon pairs at random, using this as an opportunity to get immediate feedback about how students are understanding the topic of the day.

Other purposes for this technique include focusing student attention at the beginning of class, regaining student attention when it appears to be waning, highlighting a key point, engaging students in open-ended thinking when it's desired, and allowing the professor to refocus him- or herself (Licklider, 1996). The technique reinforces the social skills of active listening, summarizing, paraphrasing, justifying and asking for justification, and asking good questions.

Tools for Teaching

Davis (1993) outlines several useful feedback activities in *Tools for Teaching*. The emphasis in all of the activities is on involving the students in improving their learning. This requires them to give input and to be engaged in the learning processes. We describe two of these tools as follows.

One tool is to ask students to give definitions, associations, and applications for complex concepts or ideas. During the last few minutes of class, distribute a short questionnaire based on the concepts covered that day. On the questionnaire, students complete the following or similar sentences:

- The main point of today's session was . . .
- A good example of an application of this idea is . . .
- I believe that the main point of today's lecture is most closely related to the following concepts, people, places, events, or things . . .
- I am most unclear about . . .

A second tool is to ask students to write a closing summary. At the end of a class session, ask students, individually or in pairs, to write a brief summary of the main ideas covered in class. Inform them that this is *not* a quiz but rather an assessment of their understanding of the material. Another approach is to ask students at the beginning of class to summarize the main ideas from the previous class and to write one question they would like to have answered. This helps students reflect on their learning and make connections between class periods.

Redesigned Course Evaluation Forms

Most end-of-course evaluation forms that faculty distribute to students reflect the traditional model of teaching. They focus on the professor (was he/she well-prepared, organized, etc.) and other inputs to the course (the textbook, other instructional materials, etc.). These are important aspects of the course to evaluate, but the end-of-course evaluation process could be strengthened if there were also questions that focused on student learning.

For example, students could be asked, "Which of your skills improved the most during this course?" Or, areas in which learning is expected to occur could be listed (e.g., understanding the concepts of the course, writing, critical thinking, speaking, analyzing, synthesizing) and students could rate their improvement, thus providing data to be used in making future changes in the course. By gathering data using questions that reflect each of the intended learning outcomes in the course, faculty can learn more about what they did well and what needs to be improved in their courses.

For example, the Instructor and Course Evaluation System (ICES) at the University of Illinois at Urbana–Champaign (Office of Instructional Resources, 1977) is comprised of a collection of items from which professors can select in developing a course evaluation form. The items fall into several categories (e.g., Course Management, Instructor Characteristics and Style, etc.), and one category is Student Outcomes of Instruction. Students respond on a five-point scale, and the anchors at the end of each scale have a verbal description. In the area of cognitive outcomes (p. 8), professors can select either general concept items (e.g., "How much have you learned in this course? A great deal/very little") or specific items (e.g., "Did you improve your ability to solve real problems in this field? Yes, significantly/No, not really"). Similarly, in the affective area (p. 9), one can select a general concept item ("Did this course increase your interest in the subject matter? Yes, greatly/No, not much") or a specific item ("Were you stimulated to do extra reading about the course material? Yes, very much/No, not really").

Figure 5–4 is an example of a course evaluation form that includes questions focusing on student learning. The form begins with traditional questions about the professor's characteristics (Section A). The remainder of the questions (Sections B through F) are designed to focus on learning outcomes and to encourage students to reflect upon their experiences.

Course Title and Number _____

Instructor _____

Semester _____

A. *For each of the five areas below, answer the question by placing a check in the appropriate column.*

In this course, to what extent was the instructor:	Very	Somewhat	Not at all
1. Knowledgeable about the subject?	___	___	___
2. Able to communicate well?	___	___	___
3. Organized?	___	___	___
4. Courteous and respectful to students?	___	___	___
5. Successful in bringing a variety of voices and perspectives into the course?	___	___	___

   6. What would you most like to say about the instructor's effectiveness as a teacher?

B. *Please describe the way in which this course affected your learning in each of the following areas.*

   7. Knowledge of the content of the discipline
   8. Critical thinking
   9. Writing
  10. Speaking
  11. Teamwork
  12. Other

[Note: Instructor can list other intended learning outcomes in this section.]

C. *Please complete the following statements.*

  13. My learning in this class was helped most by . . .
  14. My learning in this class was hindered most by . . .
  15. The aspect of this class that most helped me take responsibility for my own learning was . . .
  16. The factor that was most important in preventing me from taking responsibility for my own learning was . . .
  17. As a result of this class, I now understand that the area of my development as a learner that I most need to work on is . . .

D. *Please complete the following statements by checking one of the alternatives and briefly answering each related question.*

  18. In this course, I found that
      _____ many different teaching approaches were used.
      _____ some different teaching approaches were used.
      _____ very few teaching approaches were used.

     What are your feelings about the teaching approaches used?

Continued

FIGURE 5–4   Sample Redesigned Course Evaluation Form

19. In this course, I found that the instructor was responsive to students' concerns
    _____ always.
    _____ sometimes.
    _____ rarely.

    What are your feelings about this level of responsiveness?

20. In this course, I found that the teacher was successful in bringing about student participation
    _____ consistently.
    _____ sometimes.
    _____ rarely.

    What are your feelings about the amount of participation by students in this course?

21. In this course, I found that I received information about my learning
    _____ regularly.
    _____ occasionally.
    _____ rarely.

    What are your feelings about the frequency with which you received information about your learning and the quality of that information?

22. In this course, I found that democratic habits of equity, inclusion, and negotiation were practiced
    _____ regularly.
    _____ occasionally.
    _____ infrequently.

    What are your feelings about the level—or lack—of democracy in this class?

E. *Please complete the following two statements.*

    23. Overall, the moments in this course when I was the most engaged, excited, and involved as a learner were when . . .

    24. Overall, the moments in this course when I was most distanced, disengaged, and uninvolved as a learner were when . . .

F. *Please answer the following questions.*

    25. What would you most like to say about your experiences as a student in this course?

    26. What piece of advice would you most like to give the instructor on how to teach the course in the future?

    27. If there is anything else you would like to say about the experience of being a student in this class that you have not already said in response to previous items, please write it below.

(Adapted from Brookfield, 1995, pp. 268–270)

FIGURE 5–4 *(Continued)*

Course evaluation forms should be based on helping teachers gain a better understanding of how they are assisting learning and how their actions as teachers are being perceived. Too often forms continue to be used year after year without reflecting changes taking place in the field of pedagogy. Institutions and/or individual professors should regularly revise their course evaluation forms so that they accurately assess important characteristics of effective teaching.

Reflections

As you create your own meaning from the ideas in this section, begin to think about . . .

- Which of the feedback tools interest me the most? Why?
- Which techniques seem most conducive to my style and my students? Why?

- How can I systematically incorporate these techniques into my courses?
- How can I develop an approach for discussing assessment results with students that is comfortable for me?
- How can I ensure students that I am open to listening to their suggestions?

ENHANCING THE PROCESS OF GATHERING AND INTERPRETING FEEDBACK FROM STUDENTS

Chapter 2 began with a discussion of how people learn. The theory of constructivism suggests that all individuals actively create their own knowledge through a process of continually "making sense" of information and experiences. People create meaning by integrating new ideas with existing knowledge, and through this process, existing knowledge is reorganized and changed. The process of seeking to understand is not a choice; people are driven to create what they know and understand. Teaching and learning are two aspects of performance about which professors and students create meaning in a course.

One difficulty with creating meaning about one's own performance as a teacher or a learner is that the information on which interpretations are based is not always accurate. For example, when professors assess their effectiveness as teachers, some information is readily available to them (e.g., students' test scores) and other information is not (e.g., how students feel about a particular class experience or teaching technique). Similarly, when students assess their effectiveness as learners, some information is readily available to them (e.g., their test scores) and other information is not (e.g., specific suggestions about what and how they could improve).

Sometimes needed or helpful information comes too late (at the end of the course), and sometimes it never comes. Sometimes information is available but is too threatening to consider. For example, when information about performance is conveyed in a negative, harsh, or punitive manner, people pay less attention to it or minimize its importance. At other times, information may not be threatening, but it may be difficult to understand. For example, nonverbal reactions are often noticeable, but they may be ambiguous and thus difficult to interpret.

When clear, accurate, timely information is not available in a supportive manner that allows it to be heard, people's interpretation of their own performance suffers. As Wiggins (1993) points out, most learning situations do not provide what teachers and students need most: information designed to enable them to accurately self-assess and self-correct—so that assessment becomes a component of learning. After years of examining school systems and organizations, Gilbert (1978) observed, "I have almost never seen an ideal confirmation (feedback) system. Managers, teachers, employees, and students seldom have adequate information about how well they are performing" (p. 178). Thus, the goal of assessment should be to provide information to support learning.

Self-knowledge is empowering (Bateson, 1990) and feedback is the foundation of learning about ourselves and about the effect of our behavior on others. Christensen (1991) states it this way, "Self-knowledge is the beginning of all knowledge. I had to find the teacher in myself before I could find the teacher in my students and gain understanding of how we all taught one another" (p. 103). Ken Blanchard, author of *The One Minute Manager*, refers to feedback as the "breakfast of champions" because it is something which people need for growth and improvement and is something on which we thrive (Blanchard, 1984).

Although we may feel comfortable when we give feedback to students about their learning, we may be less comfortable when students give us feedback about our teaching. In higher education this type of communication has not been the norm. Recall from Chapters 1 and 2 that in the teacher-centered paradigm the professor is the expert information giver and the only evaluator in the course. Usually the direction of feedback during the course is from professor to student. In this environment, feedback is typically evaluative and judgmental rather than descriptive, and it may not be expressed in a manner that is constructive and helpful. Receiving feedback from students takes place only at the end of the course, and it is usually mandated by the institution.

Because of the timing, faculty members using a teacher-centered approach rarely have to face students immediately after feedback has been received. This is not the case when using CATs and CQI techniques. Fast feedback refers to faculty members quickly communicating back to the students regarding the data collected. Initially, this may not be easy to do if it has not been a common practice.

Similarly, students may be uncomfortable giving feedback to teachers. One reason may be fear of retribution. Another reason may be that they are not accustomed to being asked for their input on a regular basis. The role of giving feedback to the professor may conflict with the way they perceive their appropriate role in the course.

As professors and students shift from a teacher-centered to a learner-centered paradigm, ideas and practices will be put in place that support a comfortable view of mutual feedback. Professors will begin to view themselves more as partners in helping students learn than as expert information givers. They will welcome students' active involvement in their own learning, and students will learn new roles and take more ownership of their learning. Dialogue between professors and students will increase, and respect for students as people and as learners will be a more visible component of the course. As the course climate changes, the environment will be more supportive of a mutual feedback loop in which clear and accurate information is shared in a timely and supportive manner. There will be mutual trust, a perception that feedback is a joint effort, and the type of conversation that encourages the learner to be open and talk.

During the process of making the transformation to a learner-centered approach, however, some guidelines—presented in Figure 5–5—can be followed for facilitating the process of gathering feedback from students.

First, help students make the distinction between giving feedback to the professor and criticizing the professor. Feedback describes what took place

---

1. Help students make the distinction between feedback and criticism.
2. Allow students to provide feedback anonymously.
3. Focus questions—and encourage students to focus responses—on specific behaviors and processes instead of on personalities.
4. Maintain a focus on using data for improvement.
5. Learn to practice active listening skills:
   - Listen to the message.
   - Summarize your understanding of the message.
   - In the next class session, share your summary with students to be sure that the message heard is the message sent.
6. Identify changes you will make in the course and share them with students.
7. Reinforce an atmosphere of mutual respect by thanking students for their feedback.

FIGURE 5–5   Guidelines for Gathering Feedback from Students

and what did not take place in terms of the intended goal (Wiggins, 1997). Feedback is descriptive and criticism is evaluative. Useful feedback is value-neutral, without praise or blame. Praise is useful in learning because it encourages a learner (in this case, the professor) to keep going, but only feedback helps a learner improve (Wiggins, 1998). Useful feedback helps to build and maintain communication channels between students and professors.

Second, allow students to provide feedback anonymously. This will create an environment in which students feel comfortable giving feedback to professors. When students realize their input is valued, even though their suggestions may not always be feasible or realistic, their fears will be transformed into enthusiasm. When that happens, it is not unusual to find them signing their names to their suggestions. This level of comfort leads to more open channels of communication and increased dialogue in class discussions.

Third, focus questions—and encourage students to focus responses—on behaviors and processes instead of personalities. This makes the activity less personally threatening, and typically makes the recipient of the feedback more receptive.

Fourth, maintain a focus on using data for improvement. When students see that the information they share leads to discussions about improving learning, rather than to arguments about whether their perceptions are "right" or "wrong," they become more comfortable participating and sharing. Furthermore, an emphasis on improvement puts the process in perspective for professors. They seek out common themes and patterns in student responses instead of reacting to every variation in the system. As the old adage says, "You can't please all of the people all of the time." Therefore, the goal should be to address issues of concern to most students and to stay in touch with their progress in order to determine if additional adjustments are necessary.

Fifth, learn to practice active listening skills. In the traditional paradigm professors are information givers, but as the paradigm shifts, teaching becomes not only the art of thinking and speaking, it is also the art of listening and understanding. But listening is not just keeping still; effective listening is an art that must be practiced (Gragg, 1940).

Not surprisingly, one aspect of effective listening is to listen to the message. According to Covey (1989), "Seek first to understand, then to be understood" (p. 237). By this, he means that listening is a more important skill than speaking. It is important to be receptive to the idea of listening for input for the purpose of improvement. Because we are accustomed to being the primary speakers when we teach, actively listening to students may present a challenge.

Figure 5–6 points out that active listening requires us to be open to suggestions, interpreting student feedback by viewing the course through students' eyes. When students point out aspects of the course that may be

---

1. Try to view the situation through students' eyes.
2. Avoid acting defensively.
3. Avoid rationalizing any undesirable behaviors/processes students identify.
4. Accept responsibility for your actions.
5. Explore the feedback; look for recurring themes.
6. Avoid brushing off the feedback with misplaced humor or sarcasm.
7. Avoid putting yourself down, assuming that students are correct in all respects.
8. Identify constructive ways to use the feedback.

(Adapted from Stewart, 1997)

FIGURE 5–6   Guidelines for Interpreting Feedback from Students

interfering with learning, we should accept responsibility for our actions and avoid being defensive or rationalizing what we have done. We should explore and reflect on the feedback, resisting the temptation to brush it off or minimize it. Continuous improvement principles advocate that it is important to explore the feedback, listening for recurring themes. It is not wise to react to every comment, complaint, or suggestion, or to put ourselves down, assuming the need for improvement is a sign of failure. Use student suggestions as a springboard for creative modifications in the course.

It is also important to develop a summary of the feedback, focusing on positive as well as negative feedback. Students' suggestions for improvement can be grouped into categories such as

- those you can change this semester (i.e., decreasing the turnaround time for assignments);
- those that must wait until the next time the course is offered (i.e., the textbook);
- those that you either cannot or will not change for pedagogical or philosophical reasons (i.e., number of tests or assignments) (Davis, 1993, p. 349).

Another aspect of active listening is to be sure that the message heard is the one that was sent. Share summaries with students to ensure that their opinions were properly understood. It is critical that students believe their input was taken seriously, and it is important to convey this as soon as possible after the assessment was used, typically at the next class meeting. Keep the tone and attitude neutral, and avoid being defensive or unnecessarily apologetic. Ask questions to clarify or to receive more information.

Sixth, respond to students with proposed changes in the course. As mentioned several times in this chapter, this step convinces students that their input is valued and helps build trust in the learning environment. When students witness faculty members responding to their input, they interpret these actions as a serious commitment to continuous improvement. Students understand their feedback is important and they tend to increase the amount of feedback given. When systems are in place so that students can anticipate being asked for feedback on a regular basis, they typically become more engaged in the learning process, and they are able to shift more easily to a learner-centered paradigm.

Seventh, reinforce the atmosphere of mutual respect by thanking students for their feedback. Because feedback is not always easy to give, be appreciative of the time and effort students are taking to improve their learning processes and environment. Invite their continued participation in improving the course.

Giving feedback fosters self-responsibility, encouraging students to take more ownership in their learning. As partners in the learning process, students can help professors make changes so that learning is enhanced for everyone involved. As students begin to perceive that the course has improved as a result of their input, their expectations may rise. This should not be interpreted as dissatisfaction with the course or instructor, but rather as a sincere effort to continue to make the course better for this particular set of learners.

Continuous improvement practices focus on striving to satisfy or exceed customer expectations. However, because it may be difficult to view students as stakeholders or customers, we have not typically asked for student feedback on a regular basis in higher education. Nevertheless,

> *in many ways, college students are customers. They are customers because they have engaged in an economic agreement, a contract for goods and services and an opportunity to learn in an organization that is in the business of selling opportunities to learn. As a result, students should be given an opportunity to voice their needs, desires, and satisfaction with their learning environment and their voices should be heard (Groccia, 1997, p. 31).*

However, "students are learners as well as customers" (Groccia, 1997, p. 31) and the growth process does not mean that professors should simply give them what they want. Rather, the purpose of collecting student feedback through CATs, CQI techniques, and other activities is to engage the students in their learning, to encourage them to take more ownership of their learning, and to remove any unnecessary barriers to the learning processes.

Based on extensive experience and research on teaching as a profession, Brookfield (1995) makes these observations and challenges us to practice what we teach.

> *The most important thing I have learned from reading years of learning journals, portfolios, and classroom critical incident responses is that what we do as teachers has enormous significance in the eyes of our students. The degree to which you are prepared to take the risks you ask students to take and the extent to which you are genuinely open to new ways of thinking about teaching and learning will determine how far students are prepared to do these things themselves . . . How you model in your own life a continuous engagement in learning determines very significantly the extent to which students take learning seriously. And the only way you'll know how well you're modeling these values and processes is by seeing your actions through students' eyes (pp. 112–113).*

Finally, even though the feedback methods discussed in this chapter take class time, faculty members who systematically practice them report that the time is well spent. They reap rewards such as more class cohesion, increased class discussion, and enhanced learning because barriers to learning have been removed along the way (Roberts, 1995). Feedback becomes "the breakfast of champions" (Blanchard, 1984), and it is difficult to get enough because there is a desire for more. As faculty and student expectations go up, so does the quantity and quality of learning.

Reflections

As you create your own meaning from the ideas in this section, begin to think about . . .

- How do I feel about accepting suggestions for change from students?

- How do I typically react when students propose changes?
- How can I apply the guidelines suggested in this section to make the feedback process more useful?

LOOKING AHEAD

This chapter described techniques we can use to *solicit* feedback from our students about how well a course is meeting their needs as learners. Chapter 6 is also about feedback, but the focus of that chapter switches to techniques and issues associated with the process of *giving* feedback to learners about their learning.

TRY SOMETHING NEW

1. Select from this chapter at least one feedback technique you have never used and implement it sometime in the next few weeks. Make sure that you share with students the themes that emerged from the data.
2. Review your approach to gathering and interpreting student feedback. How could you improve it to create a climate even more conducive to student learning?
3. Examine the guidelines for gathering and interpreting student feedback in Figures 5–5 and 5–6. Select one from each list that represents an area in which you would like to improve. Decide what you need to do to begin the improvement process.

REFERENCES

Angelo, T. A., & Cross, K. P. (1993). *Classroom assessment techniques: A handbook for college teachers.* San Francisco: Jossey-Bass.

Bateman, G. R., & Roberts, H. V. (1992). *Total quality management for professors and students.* Unpublished paper, the Graduate School of Business, University of Chicago.

Bateman, G. R., & Roberts, H. V. (1995). Total quality for professors and students. In H. V. Roberts (Ed.), *Academic initiatives in total quality for higher education* (pp. 241–264). Milwaukee, WI: ASQC Quality Press.

Bateson, M. C. (1990). *Composing a life.* New York: The Atlantic Monthly Press.

Baugher, K. H. (1995). Listening to our coworkers: Using the LEARN process to improve teaching and learning. In H. V. Roberts (Ed.), *Academic initiatives in total quality for higher education* (pp. 265–278). Milwaukee, WI: ASQC Quality Press.

Blanchard, K. (1984). *The one minute manager.* London: Fontana.

Bonstingl, J. J. (1996). *Schools of quality.* Alexandria, VA: Association for Supervision and Curriculum Development.

Brookfield, S. (1995). *Becoming a critically reflective teacher.* San Francisco: Jossey-Bass.

Chaffee, E. E. (1997). Listening to the people you serve. In *Assessing impact: Evidence and action* (pp. 41–50). Washington, DC: American Association for Higher Education.

Chizmar, J. (1994). Total quality management (TQM) of teaching and learning. *Journal of Economic Education, 25* (2),

Christensen, C. R. (1991). Every student teaches and every teacher learns: The reciprocal gift of discussion teaching. In C. R. Christensen, D. A. Garvin, & A. Sweet (Eds.), *Education for judgment: The artistry of discussion leadership* (pp. 99–119). Boston: Harvard Business School Press.

Cornesky, R. (1993). *The quality professor: Implementing TQM in the classroom.* Madison, WI: Magna Publications.

Cornesky, R. (1994). *Quality classroom practices for professors.* Port Orange, FL: Cornesky & Associates.

Cornesky, R., & Lazarus, W. (1995). *Continuous quality improvement in the classroom: A collaborative approach.* Port Orange, FL: Cornesky & Associates.

Covey, S. R. (1989). *The 7 habits of highly effective people.* New York: Simon and Schuster.

Cross, K. P. (1993, February–March). Involving faculty in TQM. *AACC Journal,* 15–20.

Cross, K. P., & Steadman, M. H. (1996). *Classroom research: Implementing the scholarship of teaching.* San Francisco: Jossey-Bass.

Davis, B. G. (1993). *Tools for teaching.* San Francisco: Jossey-Bass.

Freed, J. E., & Klugman, M. R. (1997). *Quality principles and practices in higher education: Different questions for different times.* Phoenix, AZ: American Council on Education and The Oryx Press.

Gilbert, T. F. (1978). *Human Competence.* New York: McGraw-Hill.

Gragg, C. (1940). Teachers also must learn. *Harvard Educational Review, 10,* 30–47.

Groccia, J. E. (1997, May–June). The student as customer versus the student as learner. *About Campus,* 31–32.

Helminski, L., & Koberna, S. (1995). Total quality in instruction: A systems approach. In H. V. Roberts (Ed.), *Academic initiatives in total quality for higher education* (pp. 309–326). Milwaukee, WI: ASQC Quality Press.

Johnson, D. W., Johnson, R. T., & Smith, K. A. (1991). *Active learning: Cooperation in the college classroom.* Edina, MN: Interaction Book Company.

Licklider, B. (1996). *Project LEA/RN training manual.* Unpublished document. Ames, IA: Iowa State University.

Luechauer, D. L., & Shulman, G. M. (1996). Fast feedback permits students to assess faculty performance. In T. W. Banta, J. P. Lund, K. E. Black, & F. W. Oblander (Eds.), *Assessment in practice: Putting principles to work on college campuses* (pp. 288–291). San Francisco: Jossey-Bass.

Marchese, T. J. (1991). TQM reaches the academy. *AAHE Bulletin, 44* (3), 3–9.

Mosteller, F. (1989). The 'Muddiest Point in the Lecture' as a feedback device. *On Teaching and Learning, 3,* 10–21.

Office of Instructional Resources. (1977). *Instructor and course evaluation system (ICES).* Urbana–Champaign: University of Illinois at Urbana–Champaign, Division of Measurement and Evaluation.

Reilly, T. (1995). Instantaneous feedback. In H. V. Roberts (Ed.), *Academic initiatives in total quality for higher education* (pp. 333–334). Milwaukee, WI: ASQC Quality Press.

Roberts, H. V. (1995). Introduction. In H. V. Roberts (Ed.), *Academic initiatives in total quality for higher education* (pp. 1–16). Milwaukee, WI: ASQC Quality Press.

Scholtes, P. R. (1988). *The team handbook: How to use teams to improve quality.* Madison, WI: Joiner Associates.

Sherr, L. A., & Schwoerer, C. E. (1995). Continuous improvement in education: The process of learning in an introductory statistics class. In H. V. Roberts (Ed.), *Academic initiatives in total quality for higher education* (pp. 453–470). Milwaukee, WI: ASQC Quality Press.

Stewart, W. (1997). *An A–Z of counselling theory and practice* (2nd ed.). Cheltenham, UK: Stanley Thornes (Publishers) Ltd.

Strasser, S. E. (1995). E-Mail Minutes: The marriage of e-mail and the One-Minute Paper. In H. V. Roberts (Ed.), *Academic initiatives in total quality for higher education* (pp. 359–366). Milwaukee, WI: ASQC Quality Press.

Study Group on the Conditions of Excellence in American Higher Education. (1984). *Involvement in learning: Realizing the potential of American higher education.* Washington, DC: National Institute of Education.

Wiggins, G. P. (1993). *Assessing student performance: Exploring the purpose and limits of testing.* San Francisco: Jossey-Bass.

Wiggins, G. (1997). Feedback: How learning occurs. In *Assessing Impact: Evidence and Action* (pp. 31–39). Washington, DC: American Association of Higher Education.

Wiggins, G. (1998). *Educative assessment: Designing assessments to inform and improve student performance.* San Francisco: Jossey-Bass.

Wolverton, M. (1994). *A new alliance: Continuous quality and classroom effectiveness.* (ASHE-ERIC Higher Education Report No. 6). Washington, DC: The George Washington University, School of Education and Human Development.

▶ 6

Using Rubrics to Provide Feedback to Students

Learning increases, even in its serendipitous aspects, when learners have
a sense of what they are setting out
to learn, a statement of explicit standards they must meet, and a way of
seeing what they have learned
(Loacker, Cromwell, & O'Brien, 1986,
p. 47).

Assessment requires [faculty] to articulate ... explicit and public statements of criteria of performance. By
doing so, faculty refine their own understanding of expected abilities, clarify for their colleagues the basis of
their judgment, and enable students
to understand what performance is re-

quired (Loacker, Cromwell, & O'Brien,
1986, p. 51).

A number of reasons are often cited
for retaining "objective" tests (the design of which is usually quite "subjective"), among them: the unreliability
of teacher created tests and the sub-
jectivity of human judgment. However, reliability is only a problem
when judges operate in private and
without shared criteria. In fact, multiple judges, when properly trained to
assess actual student performance
using agreed-upon criteria, display a
high degree of inter-rater reliability
(Wiggins, 1989, p. 710).

Making Connections

As you begin to read the chapter, think about the ideas and experiences you've already had that are related to rubrics . . .

- What constitutes excellent work in your courses?
- Have you ever actually tried to describe the characteristics of excellent work—if only to yourself?
- Do your students know what you

consider to be excellent?
- How would it affect student learning if you told students what qualities you look for in their work?
- How would it affect student learning if you asked students what they consider to be excellent work?

What else do you know about rubrics?

What questions do you have about rubrics?

In previous chapters, we discussed learner-centered teaching as an approach that provides students with the guidance and feedback they need to learn to do important things. As learner-centered professors, we actively involve students in addressing enduring and emerging issues and problems in our disciplines, and we work in partnership with them so that they learn to produce high quality work (Chapter 2). We work with our academic program colleagues to gather information about how teaching and the curriculum can be improved (Chapter 3). In this environment, we are clear about what we expect students to know, understand, and do with their knowledge (Chapter 4). We ourselves seek continual feedback from students in our courses so that we can monitor student learning and make changes in pedagogy when needed (Chapter 5).

The focus of this chapter is on providing individual students with information they need to improve their work. In this chapter, as in Chapter 1, the terms "an assessment" or "the assessment" refer to an activity, assigned by the professor, that yields comprehensive information for analyzing, discussing, and judging a learner's performance of valued abilities and skills. Typically, the activity takes place over a period of time and results in a performance, project, product, portfolio, paper, or exhibition that will be judged and graded (see Chapters 7 and 8). One assumption is that students both learn and reveal their learning in an assignment of this type. Another assumption is that all learning requires feedback.

THE ROLE OF FEEDBACK IN STUDENT LEARNING

Chapter 5 presented numerous techniques that we can use to gather information to improve our teaching. Just as we need feedback to direct our learn ing, so students in our courses need feedback if they are to get better at what they're trying to do. When learners try something new and get a sense of how they're doing—either through their own observations or the comments of others—they use that information to improve their performance.

A key ingredient in learner-centered teaching is "active learning" (e.g., Silberman, 1996). The rationale for active learning is that students learn more and learn better when they explore a topic rather than when they watch and listen to a teacher. As authors, we agree—but we believe that more than activity is required. To be effective, students need feedback about how and what they're doing. Most importantly, they must learn how to use that feedback to improve performance.

Can fledgling writers improve without knowing if readers understand? Can accounting students learn to keep accurate records without knowing if bottom line figures are correct? Can philosophy students develop logical reasoning ability without knowing if others can follow their train of thought? Can dancers learn to inspire without reaction from an audience? We think not.

As pointed out in Chapter 2, however, many of us have been locked into the traditional teaching paradigm in which we have not provided the kind of continuous feedback necessary for continuous improvement. Using traditional assessment methods has prevented us from reaching our goals because traditional assessments provide little information to enhance student learning.

For example, test scores tell a student where he or she stands in terms of the total number of possible points (Jane scored 80 out of 102 points) or in terms of other students in the class (Bill received a higher score than 65% of the class). But even with test scores, students can't fully interpret them without looking at a variety of other factors. One factor is the difficulty of the test. What would Jane's score of 80 out of 102 points mean to her if the test were very easy? Or if it were very difficult? Another factor to consider in interpreting a score is the competitiveness of the other students in the course. Bill might be quite satisfied scoring better than 65% of his peers if they were a very precocious group, but he would probably be quite disappointed in his score if his peers were low achievers.

Even when information about factors like test difficulty and competitiveness of peers is available to help students develop interpretations of their work, there is little information available in the scores themselves to tell students *how* to get better. This information is essential to improvement, and it is not usually available.

Similarly, through grades, we convey messages to our students about our judgment of their work; their work is excellent, very good, satisfactory, unsatisfactory, or failing. This is helpful information for students to have, but alone, it gives them little direction as to what to do next. In other words, test scores and grades help professors and students *monitor* learning, but they do little to *promote* learning.

Reflections

As you create your own meaning from the ideas in this section, begin to think about . . .

- How can my students tell if they are learning well in my class?
- What kind of feedback do I give students about their performance?

- What do they learn from the feedback I give?
- How do I help students know how to improve?
- What else would students learn if they knew ahead of time the criteria for each major project?

USING ASSESSMENT TO *PROMOTE* LEARNING

To promote learning, assessments must incorporate genuine feedback that learners can employ in redirecting their efforts. In other words, assessment information must *reveal* to learners an understanding of how their work compares to a standard, the consequences of remaining at their current level of skill or knowledge, as well as information about how to improve, if improvement is needed.

Viewing assessment as a tool for "revealing" hasn't been typical. Many synonyms for assessment as we know it come to mind rather easily—information-gathering, testing, monitoring, evaluation. "Revelation," however, is usually not among them. But in order to provide useful feedback to learners, we must reveal many things that heretofore have been unspoken, invisible, or assumed aspects of teaching activity. Key aspects of "revelation" must occur before, during, and after an assessment.

Learners first need a clear sense of what they are trying to accomplish and why it is important. What intended learning outcome does the assessment address? What does the assessment task consist of? Do they understand it well? What can they do already that will help them? What new learning is required? Is there special knowledge required? Have they mastered that knowledge? How will their ability to perform the task well help them after graduation? Who values the knowledge and skill that this task requires? As professors, we must answer these questions, preferably *before* they are asked.

For example, if an engineering professor assigns a project in which students must design an engine, the purpose of the project should be discussed at the outset. Is it primarily technical or are other skills involved? If the professor will evaluate skills in several areas like teamwork, oral and written communication skills, as well as engineering practice, it helps students to know this from the beginning. They should know if they're expected to draw upon knowledge beyond that covered in the course. They should also know what the final product of the project will be—a paper, a diagram, a report and presentation to a fictional committee, or something else. They should know whether there is one final deadline or whether portions of the project are due at several stages along the way. Most importantly, they should know that the skills involved are valued by and useful to engineers in the field and that they don't just represent the idiosyncratic preferences of one particular professor.

Learners also need to know what constitutes good performance, not just in their courses, but in the adult and professional world. Addressing this issue provides professors with an opportunity to reveal to students the qualities and skills possessed by educated people and by professionals in their field. What is special about an excellent chemist or an excellent librarian? What are the standards of the profession students have chosen? These must be revealed in college courses.

Finally, as learners attempt to complete a task, they must receive ongoing information about the quality of their work vis-à-vis professional standards. They must also understand the consequences of operating at that level of quality. What happens when work is excellent? What happens when work is poor? Finally, they must know what to do next in order to improve.

Reflections

As you create your own meaning from the ideas in this section, begin to think about . . .

- When have I used assessment as an opportunity to reveal something to students?
- What do I reveal to students through assessment?

- How well do my students know the standards against which their work will be compared?
- How could I explain to students the real-life consequences of doing excellent or poor work?
- How can I help my students know how to improve if they need to improve?

RUBRICS DEFINED

This is where rubrics come in. What is a rubric? According to Webster, it is "an authoritative rule . . . an explanation or introductory commentary." As applied to assessment of student work, a rubric reveals, if you will, the scoring "rules." It explains to students the criteria against which their work will be judged. More importantly for our purposes, it makes public key criteria that students can use in developing, revising, and judging their own work.

Three sample rubrics are shown in Figures 6–1, 6–2, and 6–3. Figure 6–1 is a rubric used in assessing oral communication skills in a formal setting such as making a presentation to a group. It is an adaptation of a rubric developed by a graduate faculty committee in a Department of Educational Leadership (1998).

FIGURE 6–1 Rubric for Formal Oral Communication in a Graduate Program

	Levels of Achievement		
Criteria	3 Sophisticated	2 Competent	1 Not Yet Competent
Organization	Presentation is clear, logical, and organized. Listener can follow line of reasoning.	Presentation is generally clear and well organized. A few minor points may be confusing	Listener can follow presentation only with effort. Some arguments are not clear. Organization seems haphazard.
Style	Level of presentation is appropriate for the audience. Presentation is a planned conversation, paced for audience understanding. It is not a reading of a paper. Speaker is clearly comfortable in front of the group and can be heard by all.	Level of presentation is generally appropriate. Pacing is sometimes too fast or slow. The presenter seems slightly uncomfortable at times, and the audience occasionally has trouble hearing him/her.	Aspects of presentation are too elementary or too sophisticated for audience. Presenter seems uncomfortable and can be heard only if listener is very attentive. Much of the information is read.
Use of Communication Aids (e.g., Transparencies, Slides, Posters, Handouts, Computer-Generated Materials)	Communication aids enhance the presentation. They are prepared in a professional manner • Font on visuals is large enough to be seen by all.	Communication aids contribute to the quality of the presentation. Font size is appropriate for reading. Appropriate information is included. Some material is not	Communication aids are poorly prepared or used inappropriately. Font is too small to be easily seen. Too much information is included. Unimportant material

	• Information is organized to maximize audience understanding. • Details are minimized so that main points stand out.	supported by visual aids.	is highlighted. Listeners may be confused.

Content

Depth of Content	Speaker provides an accurate and complete explanation of key concepts and theories, drawing upon relevant literature. Applications of theory are included to illuminate issues. Listeners gain insights.	For the most part, explanations of concepts and theories are accurate and complete. Some helpful applications are included.	Explanations of concepts and/or theories are inaccurate or incomplete. Little attempt is made to tie theory to practice. Listeners gain little from the presentation.
Accuracy of Content	Information (names, facts, etc.) included in the presentation is consistently accurate.	No significant errors are made. Listeners recognize any errors to be the result of nervousness or oversight.	Enough errors are made to distract a knowledgeable listener, but some information is accurate. The presentation is useful if the listener can determine what information is reliable.

Use of Language

Grammar and Word Choice	Sentences are complete and grammatical, and they flow together easily. Words are chosen for their precise meaning.	For the most part, sentences are complete and grammatical, and they flow together easily. With a few exceptions, words are chosen for their precise meaning.	Listeners can follow the presentation, but they are distracted by some grammatical errors and use of slang. Some sentences are incomplete/halting, and/or vocabulary is somewhat limited or inappropriate.

Continued

FIGURE 6-1 *Continued*

	Levels of Achievement		
Criteria	3 Sophisticated	2 Competent	1 Not Yet Competent
Freedom from Bias (e.g., Sexism, Racism, Agism, Heterosexism, etc.)	Both oral language and body language are free from bias.	Oral language and body language are free from bias with one or two minor exceptions.	Oral language and/or body language includes some identifiable bias. Some listeners will be offended.
Personal Appearance			
	Personal appearance is completely appropriate for the occasion and the audience.	Personal appearance is generally appropriate for the occasion and audience. However, some aspects of appearance reflect a lack of sensitivity to nuances of the occasion or expectations of the audience.	Personal appearance is inappropriate for the occasion and audience.
Responsiveness to Audience			
Verbal Interaction	Consistently clarifies, restates, and responds to questions. Summarizes when needed.	Generally responsive to audience comments, questions, and needs. Misses some opportunities for interaction.	Responds to questions inadequately.
Body Language	Body language reflects comfort interacting with audience.	Body language reflects some discomfort interacting with audience.	Body language reveals a reluctance to interact with audience.

(Adapted from Department of Educational Leadership and Policy Studies, 1998)

FIGURE 6–2 Rubric for Engine Design Project

	Levels of Achievement			
Criteria	Excellent (A) 4 points	Good (B) 3 points	Needs Improvement (C, D) 2 points	Unacceptable (F) 1 point
Formulation of Design Problem				
Formulation and scope of problem	Design problem formulation is clear and well thought out. The problem scope is well defined.	The problem formulation is clear, but the scope is not well defined.	The problem formulation is unclear in some respects and does not appear to be well thought out.	The design problem is not formulated clearly.
Significance	The problem chosen represents a current challenge facing the engine industry. The potential market is large and clearly identified.	The problem represents a current challenge in the engine industry, but the potential market is small or is not clearly identified.	The problem does not represent a current challenge in the engine industry, and the market is small or is not clearly identified.	The problem does not represent a current challenge in the engine industry. There is no explanation about who would be interested in the product or why they should buy it. There is no evidence of the background work (e.g., market analysis) that is needed to design an engine.

Continued

FIGURE 6-2 Continued

Criteria	Levels of Achievement			
	Excellent (A) 4 points	Good (B) 3 points	Needs Improvement (C, D) 2 points	Unacceptable (F) 1 point
Engineering Skill Utilization				
Analysis	Engineering analysis is detailed and challenging and is used at every stage of the design process.	The engineering analysis is detailed and challenging, but some steps do not appear to be supported by calculations.	Some analysis is included, but it is not very detailed or challenging. Many steps are not supported by calculations.	Engineering analysis is infrequently used. When used, it appears trivial and leads to obvious conclusions.
Documentation	Documentation is thorough and complete.	There is some missing information in the documentation.	There is a great deal of missing information in the documentation.	Documentation is poor or nonexistent.
Assumptions	All assumptions are stated and justified.	Assumptions are stated, but some are not justified.	Assumptions are stated, but none are justified.	No assumptions are stated.
Extension of Knowledge about Internal Combustion Engines				
	Concepts beyond those in the prerequisite course are frequently used. The professor may have learned something new.	Prerequisite course content is used easily, and some material beyond the course is included.	Prerequisite course content is used, but new and unfamiliar areas are not introduced.	Prerequisite course content is not applied correctly. New areas are not included.

Team Skills

Group functioning	The group functions well. Peer review indicates good distribution of effort. All members are challenged and feel their contributions are valued.	The group functions fairly well. Some people in the group believe they are working harder (or less hard) than others, but everyone is contributing.	The group is still functioning, but each individual is doing his/her own work and ignoring the efforts of others. There are frequent episodes where one person's design will not fit with another's due to lack of communication.	The group functions poorly. All work is the product of individual efforts.
Regularity and productivity of meetings	The group meets regularly and the meetings are productive.	The group meets regularly, but meetings are not as productive as they could be. Some members are not prepared.	The group meets irregularly. Meetings are not as productive as they could be because several members are not prepared.	The group does not meet regularly, and when it does, some members are absent and no one is prepared.
Use of group problem-solving techniques	The group makes frequent use of brainstorming and group problem-solving techniques and documents the effect of these sessions.	The group uses brainstorming and group problem-solving techniques but does not always document the effect of these sessions.	Some attempt to use group problem-solving techniques is observed, but decisions are not based on results of problem-solving sessions.	No attempt to use group problem-solving techniques is made. Meetings are worthless.

Written Communication

Organization	Written work is well organized and easy to understand.	The organization is generally good, but some parts seem out of place.	The organization is unclear.	The report is disorganized to the extent that it prevents understanding of content.
Definition of terms	All new terms are defined.	Some terms are used without definition.	Many terms are used but not defined.	Terms are used without definition to the extent that understanding is inhibited.

Continued

161

FIGURE 6–2 *Continued*

	Levels of Achievement			
Criteria	Excellent (A) 4 points	Good (B) 3 points	Needs Improvement (C, D) 2 points	Unacceptable (F) 1 point
Integration of writing styles	The team developed a writing style that is uniform throughout the report. There is no indication that the report involved multiple authors.	There is some indication of multiple authors (e.g., different fonts, different paper, etc.).	There is ample indication of multiple authors (e.g., different fonts, different paper, etc.).	Report is clearly the work of multiple authors with different writing styles, margins, printer fonts, and paper types.
Grammar	The work has been thoroughly spell-checked and proofread by everyone in the group.	There are a few spelling and grammatical errors.	There is more than one spelling or grammatical error per page.	There are frequent misspelled words and serious grammatical errors, indicating that time was not taken to spell-check and proofread.
Use of appendices	Information is appropriately placed in either the main text or an appendix. Appendices are documented and referenced in the text.	Information is appropriately placed in either the main text or an appendix. Documentation and referencing in text are somewhat incomplete.	There is some misplacement of information in the text vs. the appendix. Appendices are poorly documented and referenced in text.	Considerable amount of material is misplaced. Appendices are not documented or referenced in text.

Oral Communication

Interest/ organization	Design presentation is clear, interesting, and well organized. It starts and ends well.	The design presentation is interesting, but some points are unclear. The introduction and/or conclusion are weak.	The design presentation has some interesting points but is difficult to follow. Either the introduction or conclusion is missing.	The design presentation is hard to follow and poorly organized. It appears to be off-the-cuff. There is no introduction or conclusion.
Visual aids	Visual aids are used frequently. They are easy to read and understand, and they are of professional quality.	Visual aids are good, but a few are sloppy or difficult to read.	Most visual aids are sloppy and hard to read.	There are too few visual aids, and those used are carelessly prepared.
Length	The presentation is within the assigned time limits.	The presentation is too short or too long by two minutes or more.	The presentation is too short or too long by five minutes or more.	The presentation is too short or too long by ten minutes or more.
Engineering analysis	Engineering analysis is presented with sufficient detail to be understood, but not so that it insults the audience.	Engineering analysis is poorly explained or so detailed that the audience falls sleep.	Engineering analysis consists of trivial calculations and is poorly explained.	No engineering analysis is presented.

(Van Gerpen, 1999)

FIGURE 6–3 Rubric for Economic Bill Writing Project

Levels of Achievement

Criteria	Exemplary 5–6	Proficient 3–4	Acceptable 1–2	Unacceptable 0
Understanding of Economic Principles	Your bill contains information which conforms to the correct application of principles of economics. The reader can tell that you understand these principles and have made them the central part of your bill.	Your bill contains information which conforms to the correct application of principles of economics. The reader can tell that you understand these principles but wishes you would have made more use of them to enrich your bill.	Your bill contains some references to principles, but they seem to be added as an attempt to include them without any obvious relationship to the point you are trying to accomplish.	No references to principles are found. The reader does not understand how your bill would affect the economy or the political situation concerning the economy.
Significance of Economic Problem	Your bill addresses a recognized economic problem which has macro application and would benefit the majority of the American people with its passage.	Your bill addresses a recognized economic problem, but it may be somewhat limited in impact, affecting only a small portion of people with its passage.	Your bill addresses an apparent economic problem, but it is not of sufficient importance to cause much impact on the economy with its passage. It could go unnoticed.	Your bill may have economic content, but it does not address a recognized or apparent economic problem. It would not be worth the time of Congress to consider it.
Feasibility of Proposed Bill	Your bill is realistic and workable. It takes into consideration current economic and political conditions and recognizes the limits to which the current situation can and will accommodate your recommendations.	Your bill is realistic and workable for the most part. You do consider current conditions, but you need to pay more attention to the limitations presented by current conditions.	Your bill is not unrealistic, but more consideration of current conditions would require revision of your bill before it would seem realistic to the reader. The reader is left with a feeling that the bill would not accomplish what you would like it to do.	Your bill is not realistic, either because it does not conform to actual situations or because it is too vague to help the reader understand how it would affect the political or economic situation.

Knowledge of Past Economic Decisions	Your bill reflects economic decisions which have worked in the past, is based on research involving comparisons of previous eras, and makes reference to actual events.	Your bill reflects economic decisions which have worked in the past, but your examples are limited. More examples would make your bill easily understood by the reader.	Your bill makes little reference to precedents from the past. You need to add some to help the reader decide if the bill would work and should be passed into law.	Your bill makes no reference to precedents from the past. The reader is left wondering if you know what past economic and political practice has been.
Knowledge of Procedures for Introducing a Bill	Your bill conforms to correct procedures for writing and introducing a bill as reflected in actual practice.	Your bill conforms to correct procedures for writing and introducing a bill with only a few minor omissions or commissions of error.	Your bill is presented with several errors in procedure. You need to observe rules more closely. Be sure you understand correct procedure.	You have not made an effort to follow accepted procedure for writing or presenting your bill. It does not receive consideration.
Factual Accuracy	No errors are made in fact. Your work will be very useful in aiding the reader to make a decision about whether this bill would make a significant contribution as a law to improve the economic situation within the current political arena.	No significant errors are made. The reader recognizes any errors as the result of hasty conclusions or oversights. Your work is usable for making economic/political judgments but would be considered more reliable if you were more careful in proofing your work.	Enough errors are made to distract the reader, but the reader is able to use the information to make some important judgments. The bill is useful if the reader is able to decide what evidence is reliable.	Your bill is rendered impassable because there are so many errors in fact. The reader cannot depend on this bill as a source of accurate information, or you have included so little information that the reader is not sure what the bill is all about. It will not be reported out of committee.

(Calvin, 1995)

Figure 6–2 is a rubric that Professor Jon Van Gerpen uses with his senior mechanical engineering students (Van Gerpen, 1999). The project he assigns requires a group of students to work as a team to formulate a problem that can be solved using a new engine. They then design an engine or an engine component to solve the problem, presenting their findings both orally and in writing.

Figure 6–3 is a rubric designed by Professor Linda Calvin for her high school integrated economics and government course (Calvin, 1995). The project requires senior honors students to develop a national economic program presented as a Congressional bill.

Rubrics are unfamiliar to most of us. They represent a way of evaluating student achievement that is radically different from the methods we have used in the past. However, shifting from teacher-centered courses to learner-centered courses is a change of culture that, at times, requires drastic modifications in the way fundamental activities are carried out. Making standards public facilitates a more trusting relationship between teacher and learners. No longer are grading criteria a secret that only perceptive learners can discover.

In Figures 6–1 through 6–3, there are two kinds of rubrics. One is a rubric describing a general ability, oral communication. The others are rubrics for particular assessments that professors have assigned. These rubrics include criteria that reflect general abilities and skills (like oral and written communication, teamwork, etc.). They also include criteria related to knowledge of content and some specific aspects of the assessment itself (e.g., designing an engine, writing a bill for Congress).

Reflections

As you create your own meaning from the ideas in this section, begin to think about . . .

- What are my first reactions to the idea of a rubric?

- How would my teaching change if I used rubrics with my students?
- How could I use rubics to reveal to students the caliber of their work?
- How could I use rubics to give students feedback for improvement?

ELEMENTS OF A USEFUL RUBRIC

There are several elements of useful rubrics, and each is discussed in turn below.

Levels of Mastery

Notice that each of the rubrics has three or four columns. At the top of each column is a label describing the level of student work. Figure 6–1, the oral communication rubric adapted from the Educational Leadership graduate program, includes three columns labeled Sophisticated, Competent, and Not Yet Competent. Figure 6–2 has four columns describing achievement in Professor Van Gerpen's course: Excellent, Good, Needs Improvement, and Unacceptable. The four columns in Figure 6–3 are labeled Exemplary, Proficient, Acceptable, and Unacceptable to describe the quality of work in Professor Calvin's course.

Dimensions of Quality

The rows of each figure list the dimensions of quality that the professor believes are important in reaching the goal of the project or program. These have been targeted as important for giving feedback. Note that the oral communication rubric (Figure 6–1) includes several aspects of oral communication from organization to responsiveness to audience. Professor Van Gerpen's rubric (Figure 6–2) includes both discipline specific characteristics (e.g., formulation of design problem, engineering skill utilization, and extension of knowledge in internal combustion engines), as well as characteristics related to general education (e.g., development of team skills, oral and written communication skills). Professor Calvin assesses a wide range of intellectual skills, from understanding economic principles and formulating a significant economic problem to knowledge of appropriate procedures for introducing a bill and knowledge of facts (Figure 6–3).

Organizational Groupings

For five of the six areas to be assessed in his engine design project, Professor Van Gerpen has detailed several aspects to be evaluated (Figure 6–2). By grouping these aspects together, Van Gerpen reveals to students the underlying characteristics of good work. This helps students understand that they will be evaluated on complex abilities that are multidimensional. For example, in the area of team skills, they will be assessed on group functioning, regularity and productivity of meetings, and the use of group problem-solving techniques.

Commentaries

For each aspect of quality, the rubric provides a commentary describing the defining features of work at each level of mastery. For example, in the commentaries, each professor describes excellent work. If students read all of the paragraphs in the Sophisticated (Figure 6–1), Excellent (Figure 6–2), or Exemplary (Figure 6–3) columns, they have a rich description of the standard of work they should strive to emulate. The task they face is still formidable—to produce work with these qualities. But knowing clearly what the standard is provides them with direction and with information to help them continuously improve.

Similarly, by reading all of the paragraphs in the Not Yet Competent (Figure 6–1) or Unacceptable (Figures 6–2 and 6–3) columns, students know clearly the standard they must exceed in order to produce minimally acceptable work. Bluffing is less likely because the professors have provided a clear description of poor work, characteristic by characteristic, in each row of these columns.

The commentaries in the columns between the highest and lowest levels of achievement reveal some of the weaknesses that professors have observed in student work over the years. Attending carefully to these descriptions can help students avoid common pitfalls.

Descriptions of Consequences

In many of the commentaries, the professors describe for students the likely consequences of performing at that level of quality in a real-life setting. Describing consequences is a form of feedback, encouraging students to think about what will happen in an applied setting if they perform at a particular level. This approach reveals to students that what they are learning will "count" after graduation. It helps them to develop goals beyond simply "getting a good grade."

Professor Calvin (Figure 6–3) is especially good at revealing consequences to her students and teaching lessons about professionalism, as the following examples show.

Rubric: "Your bill . . . would benefit the majority of the American people with its passage" (Row 2, Column 1).

Lesson: Good work pays off many times over.

Rubric: "Your bill addresses an apparent economic problem, but it is not of sufficient importance to cause much impact on the economy with its passage. It could go unnoticed" (Row 2, Column 3).

Lesson: Apparently good work may benefit you in the short term (i.e., your bill will be passed), but others will benefit only if your work is genuinely good.

Rubric: "[Your bill] would not be worth the time of Congress to consider it" (Row 2, Column 4).

Lesson: Poor work wastes people's time.

Professor Calvin's descriptions about factual accuracy also reveal important consequences and lessons to students.

Rubric: "No errors are made in fact. Your work will be very useful in aiding the reader to make a decision about . . . this bill" and "Enough errors are made to distract the reader . . . The bill is useful if the reader is able to decide what evidence is reliable" (Row 6, Columns 1 and 3).

Lesson: In the world of work, people read written reports to acquire new knowledge to be used in making decisions. You can either help them or you can harm them.

Rubric: "Your work is usable . . . but would be considered more reliable if you were more careful in proofing your work" (Row 6, Column 2).

Lesson: Others will judge you by the quality of your work.

Rubric: "[Your bill] will not be reported out of committee" (Row 6, Column 4).

Lesson: Poor work doesn't fly.

Reflections

As you create your own meaning from the ideas in this section, begin to think about . . .

- What are my reactions to the elements of a rubric?

- How would I go about writing a rubric?
- What materials do I already have that could be used in a rubric?
- What else would I need to do or prepare?

USING RUBRICS TO *REVEAL* IMPORTANT INFORMATION

Carefully developed rubrics can be used to accomplish two broad aims: to educate students and to judge their work.

Educating with Rubrics

We can educate students with rubrics in several ways. First, we can use rubrics to reveal to students the standards of our disciplines. When we develop rubrics in such a way that they inform students about commonly accepted criteria for excellence in a profession or in society in general, we help students internalize standards they can aspire to reach throughout their lifetime. In this way, we help students make connections between their current course of study and life after graduation.

Second, through rubrics, we can also inform students about the many qualities that comprise good—and poor—work, thus providing them with benchmarks for developing, judging, and revising their work. This enhances students' ability to self-assess and self-correct. By using rubrics in this way, we add a valuable feedback component to active learning.

Third, using rubrics can also involve students in *setting* standards (Wiggins, 1989). For example, prior to finalizing a rubric for a particular assignment, we can get students' input about what it should include. One way to do this is to share examples of good and poor work collected from previous students who have completed the same assignment. Then ask current students to examine and compare these examples and to identify the characteristics that distinguish them. We can then discuss these characteristics together and consider including them as criteria in the rubric.

A fourth way to educate with rubrics is to involve students in describing the criteria in the rubrics. The worksheet in Figure 6–4 shows one way to gather students' ideas about the properties of various criteria. These ideas can form the basis for class discussion and consensus building about the meaning of the criteria that will be used in assessment. As students develop descriptions of good vs. poor work, their descriptions can be included in the class rubric that will be used to both shape and judge their work. This focuses students on "how good" work should be, rather than simply on "how to" complete the assignment. Including students' ideas in the final rubric conveys respect for students as people and builds student ownership for learning.

Embedded in this approach is the need for us to take on a new role—becoming a repository for student work. This, of course, requires permission from the students whose work is shared with others. One professor we know includes the following on the syllabus she distributes at the first class meeting:

When students have an opportunity to examine assignments that differ in quality, they usually find that their own work is enhanced. As a result, I have developed a file of previous students' work that is ungraded. Some examples represent excellent work, and others represent work that could be improved. In this course, you will have access to this file as you develop your own assignments.

Because it is important to keep the student file current, I seek your permission to include your work in the file. Accordingly, when you submit your work to me to be graded, please submit two copies if you are willing to contribute to the file. One will be graded and returned to you. The other will be placed ungraded in the student work file. (B. Licklider, personal communication, April 20, 1998)

Course: Mechanical Engineering Graduate Seminar

Directions:

You have developed a topic, an abstract, and a reference list for your research project. The intended audience for your paper is people whose knowledge base is the same as yours and that of your classmates in terms of technical subjects. This is similar to the general population of practicing engineers with B. S. degrees.

What criteria should be used in developing and judging your papers? I listed five below and left spaces for you to add more. For each criterion, list some attributes that would be evident in a paper that meets the criterion.

Criteria   *Attributes*:

Appropriateness for audience

Organization and logic

Objectivity

Technical accuracy

Grammar and syntax

_____

_____

(Shapiro, 1998)

FIGURE 6–4   Student Worksheet for Developing Assessment Criteria

A fifth way to educate with rubrics is to use them to open channels of communication between us and our students and among students themselves. When we use a rubric as the basis of conversation with a student, we have an opportunity to engage in a mutual dialogue about learning. The student grows in understanding of course goals and standards of quality, and at the same time, the student can share information about how he or she learns best. We and our students can talk together, reflecting on the student's work and mutually assessing it using the rubric.

Conversations during the course of development of a project are particularly helpful to both us and our students. When students talk with us about their work as it is developing, we can use the rubric to help students understand how the work at its current stage differs from the target stage of development described in the most proficient column in the rubric. Students thus gain insights and information in time for them to make changes in their work. Conversations during the development of a project also allow us to learn if the student uses feedback effectively to revise work, a quality needed for effectiveness after graduation.

Students can also use the class rubric to review each other's work. This increases their understanding of professional standards. The likelihood of the uninformed leading the uninformed is lessened when students judge their peers' work according to public standards as opposed to their own idiosyncratic standards.

A sixth way to educate with rubrics is to have a variety of individuals give feedback to students about their work using a rubric. Through the process of obtaining feedback from us, their peers, and perhaps others (e.g., advisors, mentors, employers, parents), students learn that different individuals have different perspectives and that, throughout life, their work will be judged in different ways.

The intent of the rubric, of course, is to minimize differences in ratings, to focus everyone reviewing the work on the same set of standards. As will be discussed in the next section, this is particularly important when rubrics are used to *make judgments* about student work, rather than to educate them about standards and about learning. An example is when multiple raters (e.g., a professor and two graduate assistants) are involved in final scoring leading to a course grade. In this case, consistency in judgment about the quality of a student's work is especially important because grades carry with them important consequences—whether or not the student can take the next course in a sequence, enter a particular major, and the like.

Nevertheless, the process of making human judgments cannot be completely standardized, and from *an educational point of view*, students can benefit from the different viewpoints that others bring to their work. As discussed in Chapter 8, Paulson and Paulson (1991) point out that when Siskel and Ebert reviewed movies for us on television, we benefited from their disagreements as well as from their agreements; that is, we knew more about the movie by virtue of their different viewpoints. Similarly, when developing their work, students can benefit from hearing various reactions to it. Each individual commenting on the work will have a unique perspective that causes him or her to focus on one or more aspects of the work. From a collection of reactions, then, students gain deeper insights into their work, much like a graduate student benefits from having a diverse graduate advisory committee. Consistency in judgment is not the ultimate goal in all life situations.

There are also several ways in which we ourselves can learn from using rubrics. For example, one educational benefit of using rubrics is that we gain information to use in rubric revision. Writing useful rubrics that clearly reveal the standards we may have kept private for so long is really difficult. One hallmark of using rubrics is that they are continuously being improved. When students question the wording in part of a rubric, when students don't understand our rating on one dimension of the rubric, when we experience difficulty scoring student work using the rubric—these are signals that sections of the rubric are not clearly stated and must be revised.

Second, we can also share rubrics with our colleagues and use them in discussions about teaching, curriculum development, and assessment. In fact, when colleagues begin sharing rubrics, they often discover that they are looking for the same qualities in their students' work and they gain insights from talking with each other. This leads to collaboration in developing rubrics, a process that both saves the faculty time and effort and undoubtedly results in stronger rubrics.

Third, when we collaborate with our colleagues about developing rubrics, we also enhance student learning. For example, at an institution with common intended outcomes for general education, rubrics addressing those outcomes (e.g., written and oral communication, problem solving) can be developed and used institution-wide. This practice sends a strong, coherent message to students about the type of quality that professors expect in student work.

Within an academic program, common rubrics focusing on discipline-specific qualities can be developed as well. Not only can these rubrics be used within individual courses, but they can also be used by program faculty when they judge student work as part of their assessment at the program level. For example, when a group of faculty members are reviewing student portfolios or evaluating student products from a capstone course, common rubrics provide an organizing framework for judging and discussing student achievement.

Finally, we can use rubrics to inform audiences off campus—parents of students, practitioners in the field—about our intended learning outcomes and standards. This is something that multiple-choice test answer keys can never do. Unfortunately, few people usually know what happens in our courses, and this may be one reason for the public's current distrust of higher education. When we take a learner-centered approach in our courses and programs, involving our students in worthwhile activities that matter in the adult world, and when we hold students to high standards of achievement, important audiences should know about it.

Reflections

As you create your own meaning from the ideas in this section, begin to think about . . .

- How would using rubrics change the culture of my courses?

- How would I go about developing standards for student work that reflect the values of my discipline or those of an educated citizenry?

Continued

Reflections (*continued*)

- What do I think about
    . . . having students review former students' work and identify standards of their own?
    . . . using rubrics as the basis for conversations with students?

    . . . having students review each other's work using rubrics?
    . . . sharing or developing rubrics with colleagues?
    . . . using rubrics to reveal my standards to off-campus audiences?

Judging with Rubrics

We can also use rubrics to judge the quality of student work at various stages of development. We mentioned in Chapter 2 that in learner-centered courses professors take on the roles of coach and facilitator, guiding students as they attempt to achieve course goals. Providing useful feedback that students can use to improve the quality of their work is an important part of the coach/facilitator role. Although we have typically judged student work only when it was completed, we can help students know if they are on the right track by talking with them in the early stages of a project or by scoring earlier drafts or partially completed projects. This, of course, is useful only if students come away with information about how to improve. Whether or not they get that information depends on the quality of the rubric. Guidelines for developing useful rubrics are discussed in a subsequent section.

When feedback is given during the development of a project, it might be referred to as intermediate feedback as opposed to final feedback. Intermediate feedback can take different forms, all of which are consistent with the principles of continuous improvement.

For example, in the early stages of development of a project, we can provide guidance by informally discussing students' progress with them. A key goal in these discussions is to keep students focused on using the rubric as a guide in developing their work. This is particularly important if students are unfamiliar with rubrics, as most will be. Because students have spent many years developing work habits tailored to the traditional learning environment, they probably won't understand the role of the rubric. Until they get their first grade based on a rubric, it will be difficult for them to see that it matters.

Our own experience is that the rubric must be referred to consistently in class. We must intentionally bring it to students' attention many times during the course of a particular assessment. For example, we might take a few minutes at the beginning of each class to review one of the characteristics that will be graded using the rubric (i.e., one of the rows of the rubric). The goals are to remind students that this characteristic is an important quality to develop in their work and to foster discussion leading to students' understanding of standards.

As mentioned in the previous section, when we provide examples of previous students' work, we also help clarify the different levels of achievement in the rubric. Examples serve as benchmarks or models for work that is unacceptable, acceptable, or excellent.

Another way to provide intermediate feedback is to rate students' work when it is almost completed but while there is still time to revise it. We advise that this be done only after students have made every effort to do the best they can. It is not good use of a professor's time if students make a quick first attempt at meeting requirements and then pass their work by the professor for a complete review.

In fact, one way to encourage students to take their work seriously is to require them to judge their own work using the rubric, handing in their ratings with their product. This practice sends a message to students that ownership of their own learning is respected and valued. It also helps them create a better final product.

Figure 6–5 is one example of a rating form that professors and students might use to record their evalutions of students' work. (Many other formats could be developed.) This sample form is intended to be used with the Engine Design Rubric (Figure 6–2), and on the top of the form, the rating scale from the rubric is listed. The first criterion, Engineering Skill Utilization, along with its three components (analysis, documentation, and assumptions) are also listed, along with descriptions of the most proficient performance for each component (taken from the rubric), a place to put the numerical rating, and a few lines for comments. (A real form would include all the criteria in the Engine Design Rubric, but in Figure 6–5, only Engineering Skill Utilization is shown.)

Using rubrics is clearly an example of how the professor's time is used differently in a learner-centered course than in a traditional course. Although we may be reluctant at first to devote time to scoring students' work before it is completed, the improvement in student learning that results should make the extra time worthwhile. Also, even though more time is spent evaluating student work during the project or course, evaluation at the end is more efficient. Because we become familiar with the work our students are doing during the project or course, each subsequent judging goes much faster than the previous one. In addition, by the end, the class as a whole should be producing higher quality work that is easier to evaluate and more pleasurable to read and review.

The ultimate use of the rubric is to generate a final score for the student's work. Using the numerical rating scale built into the rubric, we can rate each characteristic listed in the rubric and sum the ratings for a final score. Some characteristics may be more important than others, and these may be weighted

---

Use the following scale to rate how well the project achieves the following criteria.

4   Excellent

3   Good

2   Needs Improvement

1   Unacceptable

Criteria

Engineering Skill Utilization

Analysis: Engineering analysis is detailed and challenging and is used at every stage of the design process.

Rating: _____ Comments: _____

_____

_____

_____

Documentation: Documentation is thorough and complete.

Rating: _____ Comments: _____

_____

_____

_____

Assumptions: All assumptions are stated and justified.

Rating: _____ Comments: _____

_____

_____

_____

FIGURE 6–5   Sample Rating Form for Engine Design Project Rubric

more heavily than others. The total score can be added to the set of other scores the student has earned in the course for eventual computation of the student's final course grade.

As mentioned in the previous section, when rubrics are used to judge students' work and more than one individual is involved in the judgment, (i.e., when the course is team-taught or when there are graduate assistants), it is important that the raters work together to develop the same perspective when grading. This is because grades carry with them important consequences for students. When students receive different scores, it should be because they have reached different achievement levels, not because their work was judged by different people. A high score should indicate high quality work, not a more lenient judge.

Herman, Aschbacher, and Winters (1992) point out that consistent scoring is best achieved by developing a scoring guide that includes the following:

- fully explicated scoring criteria (i.e., a carefully developed rubric);
- examples or models illustrating each level of achievement (these can be taken from the professor's file of past students' work);
- an abbreviated, one-page version of the criteria to refer to during actual rating; and
- a sample form for recording scores (see Figure 6–5).

Herman *et al.* (1992) also advocate training sessions in which raters discuss the criteria in the rubric to ensure a common understanding of their meaning. Raters should practice rating students' work together, discussing their judgments and resolving differences following the rating of each piece of work. They can also practice recording and summing scores as intended. When an acceptable level of agreement in rating has been reached, training sessions can end and actual rating begin.

Reflections

As you create your own meaning from the ideas in this section, begin to think about . . .

- Do I judge student work only when it's completed or do I review and critique it as it is being developed?
- How would I go about discussing rubrics with students during class?
- What benefits do I see in having students judge their own work

with the rubric before turning it in for a grade?

- Am I confident that I apply the same criteria to all students' work when I grade or is there a possibility that my criteria shift as I work through the papers or projects? How would rubrics help?
- How would rubrics help standardize grading in multi-section courses?

DEVELOPING USEFUL RUBRICS

We suggest asking yourself the six questions in Figure 6–6 when attempting to develop useful rubrics. Answering these questions should allow you to create a rubric that can be used in a variety of situations to address a general ability or skill. The Oral Communication rubric in Figure 6–1 is an example of this type of rubric. When a rubric is being designed for a particular assessment that will introduce elements that are unique to the context created in the assessment task, additional questions should be asked, and we will discuss them subsequently.

Question	Action
1. What criteria or essential elements must be present in the student's work to ensure that it is high in quality?	Include these as rows in your rubric.
2. How many levels of achievement do I wish to illustrate for students?	Include these as columns in your rubric and label them.
3. For each criterion or essential element of quality, what is a clear description of performance at each achievement level?	Include descriptions in the appropriate cells of the rubric.
4. What are the consequences of performing at each level of quality?	Add descriptions of consequences to the commentaries in the rubric.
5. What rating scheme will I use in the rubric?	Add this to the rubric in a way that fits in with your grading philosophy.
6. When I use the rubric, what aspects work well and what aspects need improvement?	Revise the rubric accordingly.

FIGURE 6–6   Developing Useful Rubrics: Questions to Ask and Actions to Implement

Six Questions to Ask When Constructing a Rubric

1. *What criteria or essential elements must be present in the student's work to ensure that it is high in quality?* These should be the criteria that distinguish good work from poor work. Include these as rows in your rubric. Figure 6–7 illustrates this step using a subset of the criteria in Figure 6–3.

When answering this question, it is important to focus on components that contribute to quality (Johnson, 1996) and avoid simply identifying aspects that are easy to evaluate.

> *Wiggins suggests a rule of thumb for ensuring the quality of rubric criteria: If a student can achieve a high score on all the criteria and still not perform well at the task, you have the wrong criteria. For example, criteria for writing an analytical essay might focus on organization, mechanics, and accuracy. But if the finished piece doesn't have an impact on the reader through its novelty or insight, it hasn't really achieved its purpose (O'Neil, 1994, p. 5).*

It is not uncommon to see first attempts at rubrics that include superficial criteria such as whether the student formatted a paper correctly or stayed within length guidelines. These may be good requirements to have, but conforming to them doesn't ensure excellent work.

In order to identify the way high quality work or performance is defined in your discipline, you might consider talking with colleagues or practition-

	Levels of Achievement			
Criteria				
Understanding of Economic Principles				
Significance of Economic Problem				
Feasibility of Proposed Bill				

FIGURE 6–7   Determining the Criteria that Characterize Excellent Work

ers in the field or doing a literature search. The article in the Appendix at the end of this chapter (Aldridge, 1997) is a brief discussion of teamwork that appeared in an engineering journal. It simply and clearly defines and describes eight components that comprise effective teamwork, a learning outcome that is becoming increasingly important in the education of engineers and students in many other fields. This article would be an excellent place to start when developing a rubric on teamwork.

Another strategy is to review samples of excellent work produced by experts in the field or even by your own students (Herman, Aschbacher, & Winters, 1992). Note the characteristics that make them exemplary and use them as criteria in your rubric.

Example: In his rubric (Figure 6–2), Professor Van Gerpen challenges his students to make oral presentations that interest and inform audiences. These qualities are central to effective public speaking, and Van Gerpen does not shy away from evaluating them. He also evaluates the number of visual aids and the length of the presentation, but he does not rely on these easy-to-measure characteristics alone.

Teamwork is another important process that students will use to complete the task, and developing skills in this area is important to Van Gerpen. Even though teamwork is difficult to evaluate, Professor Van Gerpen identifies several aspects that, in his opinion, make a difference between effective and ineffective teamwork. As he continues to teach and evaluate teamwork skills, his criteria may change over time. Factors that will help him understand more clearly the key components of teamwork include conferring with colleagues and reading available literature like the article by Aldridge (1997) in the Appendix.

2. *How many levels of achievement do I wish to illustrate for students?* Include these as columns in your rubric and label them. Figure 6–8 illustrates this step.

Although column headings should generally describe a range of achievement varying from excellent to unacceptable, a variety of descriptors can be used. Terms could be selected from sets like the following:

- sophisticated, competent, partly competent, not yet competent (NSF Synthesis Engineering Education Coalition, 1997);
- exemplary, proficient, marginal, unacceptable;
- advanced, intermediate high, intermediate, novice (American Council of Teachers of Foreign Languages, 1986, p. 278);
- distinguished, proficient, intermediate, novice (Gotcher, 1997);
- accomplished, average, developing, beginning (College of Education, 1997).

Example: As mentioned previously, Figures 6–2 and 6–3 include four levels of achievement. Most professors find it easiest to use the format in Figure 6–1 and begin with three levels of achievement, representing excellent, acceptable, and unacceptable work. After using the rubric, one can expand these levels in order to make finer distinctions.

3. *For each criterion or essential element of quality, what is a clear description of performance at each achievement level?* Include descriptions in the appropriate cells of the rubric. (See Figure 6–9 in which two cells have been completed.)

	Levels of Achievement			
Criteria	Exemplary	Proficient	Acceptable	Unacceptable
Understanding of Economic Principles				
Significance of Economic Problem				
Feasibility of Proposed Bill				

FIGURE 6–8   Deciding on the Levels of Achievement to Use

	Levels of Achievement			
Criteria	Exemplary	Proficient	Acceptable	Unacceptable
Understanding of Economic Principles	Your bill contains information which conforms to the correct application of principles of economics. The reader can tell that you understand these principles and have made them the central part of your bill.			
Significance of Economic Problem	Your bill addresses a recognized economic problem which has macro application and would benefit the majority of the American people with its passage.			
Feasibility of Proposed Bill				

FIGURE 6–9   Developing Commentaries for Each Cell in the Rubric

When developing descriptions, avoid undefined terms (e.g., the student's work is "significant," "trivial," "shows considerable thought") or value-laden terms (e.g., the student's work is "excellent" or "poor") in the commentary sections of a rubric. Such undefined terms tell students where they stand with the person judging, but they give little guidance for getting better when needed. They also imply that there is a "right answer" that hasn't been revealed. Objective descriptions of characteristics of work are needed.

Also, try to determine the *qualitative* differences that characterize work or performance at the different levels of quality.

Too often, rubrics suggest only that poor work has "less" of the same types of qualities as better work. "It's ultimately lazy just to use comparative language; it stems from a failure to keep asking for the unique features of performances," says Grant Wiggins (O'Neil, 1994, p. 5).

Example: For the most part, the commentaries in Figures 6–1 through 6–3 include clear descriptions. For example, in the last section of Figure 6–2 (oral communication skills) Professor Van Gerpen successfully avoids describing the students' oral presentation in vague, undefined terms. Rather than telling students that their presentations are "effective," "somewhat effective," "somewhat ineffective," or "ineffective," he informs students about several specific characteristics of a good oral presentation. A good oral presentation is interesting and well organized. Visual aids are easy to read and understand, and they are used frequently. The presentation is not too long or too short. Engineering analysis is somewhat detailed but not to the point of insulting the audience. By giving students feedback on the dimensions of interest, organization, quality of visual aids, frequency of visual aids, length of presentation, and level of detail, Van Gerpen provides direction for improvement.

Another example, not shown in the figures, illustrates an attempt to avoid comparative language in favor of qualitative differences in levels of achievement. A graduate faculty representing several areas of education were developing a rubric on leadership and attempting to describe levels of achievement for the criterion "practicing the ethical standards of the chosen discipline." It was pointed out that comparative language such as "acts in a highly ethical manner," "acts in a somewhat ethical manner," and so on, would not reflect the professional demand to *always* act ethically. In a sense, in real life, there are only two meaningful levels of achievement—ethical and not ethical. After the professors discussed this issue at length, they were successful in developing the following *qualitative* descriptions of the criterion in a way that allowed them to differentiate among students while being true to the standards of the discipline.

Criterion: Practicing Ethical Standards of the Chosen Discipline

Exemplary: Acts congruently with and advocates for the ethical standards of chosen discipline.

Proficient: Acts congruently with the ethical standards of chosen discipline.

Marginal: Acts within the ethical standards of chosen discipline. Any violations are relatively minor.

Unacceptable: Violates ethical standards of chosen profession. Violations are serious.

Professor Van Gerpen achieves a qualitative scale in the following descriptions.

Criterion: Team Skills—Group Functioning

Excellent: The group functions well. Peer review indicates good distribution of effort. All members are challenged and feel their contributions are valued.

Good: The group functions fairly well. Some people in the group believe they are working harder (or less hard) than others, but everyone is contributing.

Needs Improvement: The group is still functioning, but each individual is doing his/her own work and ignoring the efforts of others. There are frequent episodes where one person's design will not fit with another's due to lack of communication.

Unacceptable: The group functions poorly. All work is the product of individual efforts.

Another example of qualitative differences in achievement is shown in Professor Calvin's rubric.

Criterion: Knowledge of Past Economic Decisions

Exemplary: Your bill reflects economic decisions which have worked in the past, is based on research involving comparisons of previous eras, and makes reference to actual events.

Proficient: Your bill reflects economic decisions which have worked in the past, but your examples are limited. More examples would make your bill easily understood by the reader.

Acceptable: Your bill makes little reference to precedents from the past. You need to add some to help the reader decide if the bill would work and should be passed into law.

Unacceptable: Your bill makes no reference to precedents from the past. The reader is left wondering if you know what past economic and political practice has been.

4. *What are the consequences of performing at each level of quality?* Add descriptions of consequences to the commentaries in the rubric.

Example: In the descriptions inserted in Figure 6–9, note that consequences are included. Students are informed that if they apply economic principles correctly, their expertise will be apparent to readers. If they choose to address a significant economic problem with macro application, they will have succeeded in pursuing legislation beneficial to the majority of the American people.

Also notice that in the oral communication rubric (Figure 6–1), students are reminded that when oral presentations are not well organized or communication aids are not professional, listeners get confused. If the speaker's understanding of content is superficial or inaccurate, listeners gain little information or may actually be misled. When language reveals bias, listeners will be offended. On the other hand, by deliberately attending to various elements of the rubric, students can design a presentation that helps listeners follow the reasoning, creates an atmosphere of comfort for all, and expands listeners' knowledge.

5. *What rating scheme will I use in the rubric?* Add this to the rubric in a way that fits in with your grading philosophy. You may wish to weight some criteria in the rubric more than others.

Example: Returning to Figure 6–3, notice that Professor Calvin uses a rating scale from 0–6 (Figure 6–3). She gives no credit for unacceptable work, but she allows herself a two-point range within each of the levels of acceptable, proficient, and exemplary. Each of the six characteristics in the rubric is evaluated using this scale, providing for total scores that can range from 0 to 36.

For each of the criteria in his rubric, Professor Van Gerpen gives scores of 4, 3, 2, and 1, corresponding to letter grades of A, B, C/D, and F, for work that is Excellent, is Good, Needs Improvement, or is Unacceptable in quality (Figure 6–2). If Professor Van Gerpen wished to weight some criteria more than others, he could redesign the rubric so that each section would have its own rating scale. For example, he could give twice as much weight to the criteria in the first three sections related to use of disciplinary content (Formulation of Design Problem, Engineering Skill Utilization, and Extension of Knowledge About Internal Combustion Engines) by using the scale 8, 6, 4, and 2 for these sections, while rating the rest of the criteria with the 4, 3, 2, 1 scale.

Another way to achieve differential weighting is shown in Figure 6–10 in which weighting factors are built into a redesign of the rating form shown in Figure 6–5. In this figure, stating and justifying assumptions is weighted twice as heavily as documentation, and engineering analysis is weighted two and a half times as heavily as documentation.

Use the following scale to rate how well the project achieves the following criteria.

4   Excellent

3   Good

2   Needs Improvement

1   Unacceptable

Criteria

Engineering Skill Utilization

Analysis: Engineering analysis is detailed and challenging and is used at every stage of the design process.

Rating: _____ x 2.5 = _____ Comments:_____

_____

_____
_____

Documentation: Documentation is thorough and complete.

Rating: _____ Comments: _____

_____

_____

_____

Assumptions: All assumptions are stated and justified.

Rating: _____ x 2 = _____ Comments: _____

_____

_____

_____

FIGURE 6–10   Incorporating Weighting Factors into Sample Rating Form for Engine Design Rubric

6. When I use the rubric, what aspects work well and what aspects need improvement? Revise the rubric accordingly.

One way to identify aspects of the rubric that need improvement is to use the rubric to evaluate a sample of student work. Does the rubric help you distinguish among the levels of quality in the sample? Do the criteria seem to be appropriate? Are there too many or too few levels of achievement specified? Are there any descriptions that are incomplete or unclear? Another approach to testing the rubric is to ask for a friendly review by a program advisory committee or an informal group of colleagues.

Example: After interviewing Vicki Spandel, a performance assessment trainer, O'Neil (1994) points out

The rubric Spandel uses to evaluate writing has been through 12 revisions. Originally, criteria for sentence fluency had teachers counting the number of complex and compound sentences in student work. "Hemingway wouldn't have gotten very far" with such criteria, Spandel points out. Now the criteria refer to such elements as variety of sentence beginnings and sentence length, and how the sentence plays to the ear. The criteria "are constantly being refined and reshaped just a little bit to more closely resemble what we actually see in student writers at work," Spandel says (p. 4).

Additional Questions to Consider

Frequently, rubrics are developed for use with specific assessments, as is illustrated in Figures 6–2 and 6–3. When this is done, the following additional questions, shown in Figure 6–11, should be asked.

1. *What content must students master in order to complete the task well?* Develop criteria that reflect knowledge and/or use of content and add them to the rubric.

Examine the intended learning outcomes you are assessing, as well as the specific assessment task you are assigning (e.g., performance, project, product, portfolio, paper, or exhibition). What do you intend students to know, understand, or be able to do?

Example: Professor Calvin's intended outcomes (1995) are as follows.

- Students will understand the relationship between economic concepts and informed political action and will use this knowledge in solving problems faced by active citizens in a democracy.

Question	Action
1. What content must students master in order to complete the task well?	Develop criteria that reflect knowledge and/or use of content and add them to the rubric.
2. Are there any important aspects of the task that are specific to the context in which the assessment is set?	Identify skills and abilities that are necessary in this context and add related criteria to the rubric.
3. In the task, is the *process* of achieving the outcome as important as the *outcome itself?*	Include and describe criteria that reflect important aspects of the process.

FIGURE 6–11   Additional Questions/Actions When Developing Rubrics for Specific Assignments

- Students will understand that economic and political actions affect society as a whole and that informed action requires a broad point of view rather than narrow self-interest.
- Students will analyze political and economic statements and actions carried out by leadership in various areas of the public and private sector and use this analysis to make informed choices (Calvin, 1995).

The task she assigns students is as follows:

> *Create a national economic program and present it to the class as a bill to be considered by Congress. In preparing the bill, compare and contrast economic programs during presidential administrations from Johnson through Clinton. Analyze the three branches of government as they have applied to national economic policies. Focus on the War on Poverty under Johnson, its modifications, and Clinton's "Contract with America" (Calvin, 1995).*

Content areas specified in Professor Calvin's outcomes and assessed in her task include economic principles, economic problems and their significance, and economic programs from Johnson through Clinton.

2. *Are there any important aspects of the task that are specific to the context in which the assessment is set?* Identify skills and abilities that are necessary in this context and add related criteria to the rubric.

Example: Although Professor Calvin's chief goal in her assessment is to have students reveal their knowledge of economic principles and programs, she adds a real-life element to the assessment by having them formulate their ideas in a bill to be considered by Congress. Thus, students' knowledge in the area of writing bills is also evaluated in the rubric.

3. *In the task, is the* process *of achieving the outcome as important as the* outcome itself? Include and describe criteria that reflect important aspects of the process.

Example: Because the ability to work in teams is an important goal of engineering curricula, Professor Van Gerpen decides to assess his students' ability to work as a team throughout the development of their project.

Reflections

As you create your own meaning from the ideas in this section, begin to think about . . .

- How could I make the procedure for developing rubrics work for me?

- What materials do I already have that could be used in preparing rubrics?
- What questions do I have about rubics?

QUESTIONS THAT EMERGE AFTER USING RUBRICS

Do all rubrics have to look alike?

The steps explained in the previous section result in well-developed rubrics that describe the defining characteristics of student work or performance at various levels of quality. This level of detail can be very helpful to students who are trying to understand what is desirable and undesirable about the work they have produced. For the novice, knowing the characteristics of work that is considered poor or unacceptable can be just as helpful as knowing the characteristics of work that is acceptable or exemplary.

As students become more familiar with the criteria used in judging their work, it may be possible to develop an abbreviated form of the rubric. The rating form in Figure 6–5 is, in effect, an abbreviated form of the rubric in Figure 6–2. In this shortened rubric, the characteristics of exemplary work are described, and students are judged on a Likert scale according to how well they have achieved this level. Of course, for students whose work does not correspond well with the description, there is little guidance about what the shortcomings are and how to correct them. The brief section for comments in Figure 6–5 might help in this regard because professors or peers could describe the type of improvements that are needed.

This abbreviated form could also be used in conjunction with a completely developed rubric. Both professors and students could have the completely developed rubric in their possession for reference, and the abbreviated form could be used for giving feedback more simply.

Do you even need rubrics in an advanced learner-centered culture?

After students have taken many courses in a learner-centered culture, they will undoubtedly begin to internalize the standards against which their work is evaluated. This is especially true when faculty in a program or at an institution work together to develop common learner outcomes and common definitions of desirable characteristics in student work or performance—in other words, when faculty use common rubrics across courses. In this type of environment, less reliance on written rubrics will probably develop as students progress through the program.

As discussed in Chapter 4, faculty at Alverno College have developed an institutional learning environment in which common learning outcomes and common assessment criteria are considered extremely important. At Alverno, *we find that students at the start need very explicit criteria. They are trying to figure out what they are supposed to do . . . While students see highly detailed directions as "picky," they see broader directions as vague."*

After a semester or two, students begin . . . to recognize that the criteria are related, that they come together to define an ability . . . that making inferences and supporting them with data are not complete steps in themselves, but are part of the ability to think critically . . .

At more advanced stages . . . students have begun to develop their own understanding of an ability, and specified criteria serve to supplement what learners have internalized . . . At this level, criteria can be stated holistically. For example, a student might be told that "thorough analysis" is a criterion for her performance. Both student and teacher understand that "thorough analysis" means applying a framework, identifying elements and relationships, supporting inferences with evidence, and so on (Loacker, Cromwell, & O'Brien, 1986, pp. 51–52).

Less reliance on external, formal rubrics in an advanced learner-centered culture is not a step back to a traditional teaching environment, however. In that environment, standards are private or unformulated, and students have to guess what they are. In an advanced learner-centered culture, standards are known and publicly shared to the point that they may not need to be written down.

Should the criteria in a rubric change as learners become more advanced in an area?

If rubrics are based on the criteria that distinguish expert and novice work in a discipline, then they should not change as students progress. However, students' understanding of criteria may develop over time, as discussed by Loacker *et al.* (1996) in the previous section, and this will lead them to use rubrics in increasingly sophisticated ways.

On the other hand, if professors have not yet identified the key criteria distinguishing expert and novice work in their disciplines, they will find that they need to change the criteria in their rubrics as their understanding of the distinguishing characteristics of work in their field increases. It is not unusual to start developing and using rubrics, only to find that some students get relatively high ratings on the criteria in the rubric, even though their work is not really outstanding. As discussed in an earlier section, this is an indication that the criteria in the rubric are based on rather superficial aspects of quality, rather than on the characteristics that distinguish truly good work from truly inadequate work.

Rubric Categories

Can rubrics be used to judge thinking processes and the affective component of learning, as well as skills and achievements?

Marzano, Pickering, and McTighe (1993) have developed several rubrics that address the five categories of lifelong learning outcomes (they use the term lifelong learning standards) discussed in Chapter 4: complex thinking, information processing, effective communication, cooperation/collaboration, and effective habits of mind. Their rubrics clearly show that criteria can be developed for aspects of learning dealing with how students think and feel about learning.

For example, Marzano *et al.* (1993) view problem solving as an attempt to reach a desired outcome when there are obstacles or constraints blocking the way. When we solve problems, we try out strategies or products that will help us overcome the barriers.

According to the authors, problem solving involves four components. The first is accurately identifying the obstacles or constraints in our way, and the second is identifying a variety of feasible methods for overcoming them. The third is trying out the methods, and the fourth is being able to evaluate them. Evaluation includes describing the methods accurately, justifying why they were tried in the order chosen, and explaining their effectiveness in overcoming the obstacles or constraints. Figure 6–12 presents a rubric for these components. Note that there are four levels of achievement, but the authors chose not to label them.

In the area of Habits of Mind, Marzano *et al.* (1993) identify 15 cognitive and affective components listed in Chapter 4 of this book. Learners who have developed effective habits of mind exhibit intellectual and emotional dispositions that support learning. Developing habits of mind is related to the topic of metacognition discussed in Chapters 7 and 8.

Figure 6–13 is a rubric comprised of three of Marzano *et al.*'s (1993) components of Habits of Mind. The first criterion shown addresses the degree to which a learner is aware of his or her own thinking. Learners who are aware of how they think are more able to improve the way they learn. The second addresses the degree to which the learner is open-minded and receptive to new knowledge or differing points of view. The third addresses the extent to which learners carefully consider situations and the need for more information before taking action.

Is it possible to drown in all the rubrics you might need to develop?

As we begin to develop rubrics for a variety of applications in a variety of courses, we may find that we need some way to organize and manage them. Each rubric will have some criteria that overlap with those in other rubrics,

Accurately identifies constraints or obstacles

4   Accurately and thoroughly describes the relevant constraints or obstacles. Addresses obstacles or constraints that are not immediately apparent.

3   Accurately identifies the most important constraints or obstacles.

2   Identifies some constraints or obstacles that are accurate along with some that are not accurate.

1   Omits the most significant constraints or obstacles.

Identifies viable and important alternatives for overcoming the constraints or obstacles.

4   Identifies creative but plausible solutions to the problem under consideration. The solutions address the central difficulties posed by the constraint or obstacle.

3   Proposes alternative solutions that appear plausible and that address the most important constraints or obstacles.

2   Presents alternative solutions for dealing with the obstacles or constraints, but the solutions do not all address the important difficulties.

1   Presents solutions that fail to address critical parts of the problem.

Selects and adequately tries out alternatives.

4   Engages in effective, valid, and exhaustive trials of the selected alternatives. Trials go beyond those required to solve the problem and show a commitment to an in-depth understanding of the problem.

3   Puts the selected alternatives to trials adequate to determine their utility.

2   Tries out the alternatives, but the trials are incomplete and important elements are omitted or ignored.

1   Does not satisfactorily test the selected solutions.

If other alternatives were tried, accurately articulates and supports the reasoning behind the order of their selection and the extent to which each overcame the obstacles or constraints.

4   Provides a clear, comprehensive summary of the reasoning that led to the selection of secondary solutions. The description includes a review of the decisions that produced the order of selection and how each alternative fared as a solution.

3   Describes the process that led to the ordering of secondary solutions. The description offers a clear, defensible rationale for the ordering of the alternatives and the final selection.

2   Describes the process that led to the ordering of secondary solutions. The description does not provide a clear rationale for the ordering of the alternatives, or the student does not address all the alternatives that were tried.

1   Describes an illogical method for determining the relative value of the alternatives. The student does not present a reasonable review of the strengths and weaknesses of the alternative solutions that were tried and abandoned.

(Source: McREL Institute)

FIGURE 6–12   Problem-Solving Rubric

Is aware of own thinking.

4 Consistently and accurately explains in detail the sequence of thoughts he or she uses when faced with a task or problem, and provides analyses of how an awareness of own thinking has enhanced his or her performance.

3 Consistently and accurately describes how he or she thinks through tasks or problems and how an awareness of own thinking enhances his or her performance.

2 Sporadically but accurately describes how he or she thinks through tasks or problems and how an awareness of own thinking enhances his or her performance.

1 Rarely, if ever, accurately describes how he or she thinks through tasks or problems or how an awareness of his or her thinking enhances performance.

Is open-minded.

4 Consistently seeks out different and opposing points of view and considers alternative views impartially and rationally.

3 Is consistently aware of points of view that differ from his or her own and always makes a concerted effort to consider alternative views.

2 Is at times aware of points of view that differ from his or her own and sporadically makes an effort to consider alternative views.

1 Rarely, if ever, is aware of points of view that differ from his or her own and seldom makes an effort to consider alternative views.

Restrains impulsivity.

4 Consistently and carefully considers situations to determine if more study is required before acting; when further study is required, engages in detailed investigation before acting.

3 Consistently considers situations to determine whether more study is required before acting; when further study is required, gathers sufficient information before acting.

2 Sporadically considers situations to determine whether more study is required before acting; when further study is required, sometimes gathers sufficient information before acting.

1 Rarely, if ever, considers situations to determine whether more study is required before acting; when further study is required, usually doesn't gather sufficient information before acting.

(Source: McREL Institute)

FIGURE 6–13   Habits of Mind Rubric

as well as criteria that are unique to the application. Thus, it may be helpful to develop a population of criterion descriptions from which one can pick and choose when developing a new rubric. Strategic Learning Technologies has developed a software package called The Rubricator to assist with this process, and information about it can be found on the World Wide Web (http://www.sltech.com/)

Reflections

As you create your own meaning from the ideas in this section, begin to think about . . .

- Which of the issues raised by these questions are the most significant for me?

- What other questions do I have about using rubrics that this chapter has not addressed?
- How can I modify my schedule so that I find time to develop rubrics?

ENHANCING THE PROCESS OF GIVING FEEDBACK TO STUDENTS

This book has stressed the importance of creating learner-centered environments in which we treat students with respect as people and as learners. Increased dialogue between us and our students contributes to developing a respectful learner-centered environment. Rather than "giving" feedback to students, we engage in feedback discussions with them. Through these discussions, we coach and facilitate, helping students to construct their own understanding of their disciplines.

One of the most important discussions we can have with a student is a dialogue about the student's progress in learning. Just as we need feedback to improve our teaching (Chapter 5), so students need continuous feedback to acquire the information they need to improve. Rubrics can form the basis for many important conversations with our students in which we discuss progress toward known criteria.

However, as Wiggins (1997, 1998) points out, feedback is too often associated with criticism, and conversations in which students feel that they are being evaluated rather than guided inhibit their ability to "hear" the message being sent. Figure 6–14 presents 12 guidelines for participating in effective feedback discussions (Cormier & Cormier, 1985; Johnson, 1972; McKeachie, 1976; Stewart, 1997; Trotzer, 1989; Wiggins, 1997, 1998). Although many derive from guidelines for counselors, they apply remarkably well to educational settings. Following these guidelines can help us carry on mutually satisfying conversations with students that lead to improved learning.

First and foremost, we should engage in feedback discussions with students, and our motivation should be to help, not hurt. A conversation in which we and our students share our perspectives about the student's progress and explore ways to improve is more satisfying and productive than one in which we give advice (Wiggins, 1997, 1998).

In addition, we should schedule feedback discussions in a timely manner, during as well as after assessment.

1. Engage in feedback discussions to help, not hurt.
2. Share information and explore alternatives. Don't give advice.
3. Schedule feedback discussions in a timely manner, during as well as after assessment.
4. Create a climate in which feedback is solicited rather than imposed.
5. Take into account the needs of the learner.
6. Share the amount of information the student can use. Avoid the temptation to share all the information you wish to send.
7. Focus on behaviors, not the person.
8. Focus on behaviors or characteristics you observe rather than those you infer.
9. Focus on specifics rather than on generalities.
10. Discuss behavior over which the student has control.
11. Ask questions that help students understand themselves as learners.
12. Be sure that you and the student have really understood each other. Paraphrase each other's ideas.

FIGURE 6–14   Guidelines for Effective Feedback Discussions

The chief finding from the Harvard Assessment Seminar about the most effective courses at Harvard, as judged by students and alums, was the importance of quick and detailed feedback . . . A second major finding was that an overwhelming majority of students were convinced that their best learning takes place when they have a chance to submit an early version, get detailed feedback and criticism, and then hand in a final version (Wiggins, 1997, p. 35).

When conversations with us are nonthreatening experiences in which students come away with insights about their learning and their progress, they are more likely to seek them out, making the feedback more useful.

Before a feedback discussion, we should review the student's current needs as a learner and plan to discuss only information the student can use at the time. After all, learners themselves must construct their own understanding of how they are doing and what they need to do next. According to Wiggins (1997, 1998), feedback is not the same as guidance; rather, feedback is conversation leading to a description of where students are relative to where they want to be. This means that, at times, we may have to avoid the temptation to share all the information and insights we have developed about students' progress.

During the discussion, the focus should be the student's work and behaviors rather than the student's personal characteristics. The behaviors should be those we observe rather than those we infer. It is helpful when feedback is specific—and thus more understandable—and if it is directed toward behavior that can be modified, behavior over which the learner has control. Following these guidelines minimizes any potential threat that students may perceive and allows them to become more fully engaged in the conversation.

Questioning is a powerful tool we can use to help students create their own understanding of their learning and progress. Questioning can also help us understand how and what students have learned. Figure 6–15 presents several types of questions that can be asked to help students consider not only issues related to the topic of their assignment (in this case, Business), but also issues related to completing the assignment (e.g., teamwork, use of the library, oral presentation of findings, and so forth).

Open-ended questions help us understand how students mentally organize information. They also prompt students to share their thoughts about, and reactions to, their work. Answers to diagnostic questions reveal whether or not, or to what extent, students have thought critically and insightfully about their work, and answers to information-seeking questions reveal students' knowledge of facts and concepts. Challenge questions require students to defend their arguments, and action questions and questions on priorities lead them to plan ahead. Prediction questions assist students in anticipating what will happen as a consequence of certain actions, and hypothetical questions help them understand what might have happened. Questions of extension help students look beyond their work to understand its implications. Questions of generalization prompt them to abstract some general principles about their discipline from their experiences or to develop a clearer understanding of themselves as learners.

Finally, it is important that we and our students really understand each other. Paraphrasing the other person's ideas helps ensure that we understood them. Summaries emphasize the most salient points of a discussion and bring it to closure.

Reflections

As you create your own meaning from the ideas in this section, begin to think about . . .

- How do I tend to give feedback to students?
- Which of the guidelines for effective feedback discussions in Figure 6–14 describe what I typically do?

- On which characteristics do I need to improve?
- How skillful am I in using the questioning techniques in Figure 6–15?
- How could I get better?

Open-ended questions	What are your reactions to the Microsoft case? What aspects of this problem were of greatest interest to you? Where should we begin? What are the most important environmental variables? In terms of your progress on this assignment, what are you particularly pleased about? What concerns do you have?
Diagnostic questions	What is your analysis of the problem? What conclusions did you draw from these data? Why do you think your team is having difficulty working together? Why were you so successful in developing this solution to the problem?
Information-seeking questions	What were interest rates at the time? What was the rate of inflation? What was the economic situation? How often did your team meet? What group problem-solving strategies did you use?
Challenge questions	Why do you believe that? What evidence supports your conclusion? What evidence is contrary to your argument?
Action questions	What needs to be done to implement this recommendation? Who needs to do what in order for it to work?
Questions on priorities	Given the limited resources, what step should be taken first? Second? Third? You mentioned that there are three aspects of your paper that you still need to work on. Which one will you address first? Why?
Prediction questions	How do you think employees would react to this action? What do you anticipate the board's response to be? How comfortable will you feel presenting your findings to the class?
Hypothetical questions	What would have happened if a strike had been called by the union? How do you think management might have reacted if there had not been a change in top leadership? How would your project be different if you had spent more time researching your topic in the library?
Questions of extension	What are the implications of your conclusions for the community in which this business is located? How would the business community react to your recommendations? If you succeed in developing your work so that it has all the "exemplary" qualities outlined in the rubric, what will that mean to you?
Questions of generalization	Based on your study of computer and telecommunications industries, what do you consider to be the major opportunities and threats? Based on the opportunities you have had to reflect on your learning, how do you assess your ability to complete a long-term project?

(Adapted from Christensen, 1991, p. 159)

FIGURE 6–15   Questioning Techniques to Support Useful Feedback Discussions

LOOKING AHEAD

Rubrics can be used with a variety of types of assessments. Chapter 7 discusses assessments that we can use to evaluate students' ability to think critically and solve real-world problems. Such assessments require that students master disciplinary content and demonstrate that they can *use* it by employing other important skills in the areas of inquiry, communication, and cooperation. The chapter presents characteristics of effective assessment tasks, as well as a step-by-step approach to developing them.

TRY SOMETHING NEW

1. Using the procedure described in this chapter, develop a rubric you can use in your courses.
2. Involve students in critiquing and contributing to the rubric you develop.
3. Identify a situation in which you can use the rubric to *educate* students about the qualities of excellent work. After using the rubric, list some ways that the rubric can be improved and revise it accordingly.
4. Identify a situation in which you can use the rubric to *judge* student work. After using the rubric, list some ways that the rubric can be improved and revise it accordingly.
5. Review the guidelines for effective feedback discussions, and plan how you will implement them in an upcoming meeting with a student. After meeting with the student, reflect on the guidelines you used successfully and identify those areas in which you need to improve.
6. Review the different types of questions in Figure 6–15 that can be used for various purposes. Plan to use questions to engage students in the learning process.

REFERENCES

Aldridge, M. D. (1997, December). Briefings: Team players. *ASEE Prism Magazine (American Society of Engineering Education)*, 9.

American Council of Teachers of Foreign Languages. (1986). *ACTFL proficiency guidelines*. Hastings-on-Hudson, NY: American Council of Teachers of Foreign Languages.

Calvin, L. (1995). *Unpublished economic bill writing project description and rubric*. Des Moines, IA: Urbandale High School.

Christensen, C. R. (1991). Every student teaches and every teacher learns: The reciprocal gift of discussion teaching. In C. R. Christensen, D. A. Garvin, & A. Sweet (Eds.), *Education for judgment: The artistry of discussion leadership* (pp. 99–119). Boston: Harvard Business School Press.

College of Education, University of Central Florida. (1997). *What is WebCamp? Guidelines for final project, Final project rubric*. http://www.itrc.ucf.edu/webcamp/rubrics.html

Cormier, W. H., & Cormier, L. S. (1985). *Interviewing strategies for helpers* (2nd ed.). Monterey, CA: Brooks/Cole Publishing Company.

Department of Educational Leadership and Policy Studies. (1998). *Unpublished formal oral communication rubric.* Ames, IA: Iowa State University.

Gotcher, L. (1997). *Assessment rubrics.* http://129.7.160.115/COURSE/INST_5931A/Rubric.html#User.

Herman, J. L., Aschbacher, P. R., & Winters, L. (1992). *A practical guide to alternative assessment.* Alexandria, VA: Association for Supervision and Curriculum Development.

Johnson, B. (1996). *The performance assessment handbook. Volume 2. Performances and exhibitions.* Princeton, NJ: Eye on Education.

Johnson, D. W. (1972). *Reaching out: Interpersonal effectiveness and self-actualization.* Englewood Cliffs, NJ: Prentice-Hall.

Loacker, G., Cromwell, C., & O'Brien, K. (1986). Assessment in higher education: To serve the learner. In Adelman, C. (Ed.), *Assessment in American higher education* (pp. 47–62). Washington, DC: U. S. Department of Education, Office of Educational Research and Improvement.

Marzano, R. J., Pickering, D., & McTighe, J. (1993). *Assessing student outcomes: Performance assessment using the dimensions of learning model.* Alexandria, VA: Association for Supervision and Curriculum Development.

McKeachie, W. (1976). Psychology in America's bicentennial year. *American Psychologist, 31,* 819–833.

NSF Synthesis Engineering Education Coalition. (1997). *Assessment tool: Design project report* (F. McMartin, Ed.). Berkeley, CA: College of Engineering, University of California, Berkeley.

O'Neil, J. (1994, August). Making assessment meaningful: Rubrics clarify expectations, yield better feedback. *ASCD Update, 36* (6), 1, 4–5.

Paulson, F., & Paulson, P. (1991, April). *The ins and outs of using portfolios to assess performance.* Paper presented at the joint annual meeting of the National Council on Measurement in Education and the National Association of Test Directors, Chicago, IL.

Shapiro, H. (1998). Unpublished course materials. Ames, IA: Department of Mechanical Engineering, Iowa State University.

Silberman, M. (1996). *Active learning: 101 strategies to teach any subject.* Needham Heights, MA: Allyn & Bacon.

Stewart, W. (1997). *An A-Z of counselling theory and practice* (2nd ed.). Cheltenham, UK: Stanley Thornes (Publishers) Ltd.

Strategic Learning Technologies. *The rubricator.* http://www.sltech.com/

Trotzer, J. (1989). *The counselor and the group.* Muncie, IN: Accelerated Development.

Van Gerpen, J. (1999). *Unpublished rubric for internal combustion engine design project.* Ames, IA: Department of Mechanical Engineering, Iowa State University.

Wiggins, G. (1989, May). A true test: Toward more authentic and equitable assessment. *Phi Delta Kappan,* 703–713.

Wiggins, G. (1997). Feedback: How learning occurs. In *Assessing Impact: Evidence and Action* (pp. 31–39). Washington, DC: American Association of Higher Education.

Wiggins, G. (1998). *Educative assessment: Designing assessments to inform and improve student performance.* San Francisco: Jossey-Bass.

APPENDIX

Team Players

M. Dayne Aldridge

Effective teamwork doesn't just happen naturally, says M. Dayne Aldridge, associate dean of engineering at Auburn University, who along with seven other Auburn faculty members recently developed a course on interdisciplinary teaming. The Auburn group encourages its students to practice the following behaviors associated with effective teamwork.

1. **Collective Decision Making.** Effective teams discuss decisions that impact the team, and they generally reach decisions by consensus. Ineffective teams make decisions by fiat when one team member strongly asserts a position and no one objects verbally, even though some disagree silently.

2. **Collaboration/Interchangeability.** On effective teams, members help one another with the team's work, even when the tasks are outside a member's area of disciplinary expertise (this is known as interchangeability). On ineffective teams, members tend to work independently and will not do a task if it appears to fall outside their area of expertise or functional role.

3. **Appreciation of Conflicts/Differences.** Effective teams expect conflicts and differences of opinion and openly address and resolve them, using them as a way to explore alternatives and improve decisions. On ineffective teams, members avoid conflict in an attempt to preserve surface agreement.

4. **Balance of Participation.** On effective teams, members balance the team's time demands with their other responsibilities. Team members accept and help compensate for circumstances that require a team member to temporarily reduce his or her efforts. On ineffective teams, one or two members do most of the work, resent it, but never confront members whose level of effort is low.

5. **Focus.** Effective teams focus on their key goals and objectives and pace themselves accordingly. When the team falls behind in a certain area, everyone pitches in to get back on schedule. Ineffective teams spend too much time on early tasks and find they have little time when deadlines approach. When progress is not being made in a given area, everyone notices, but no one offers to help out.

6. **Open Communication.** Members of effective teams let each other know what is happening that might affect the team's work. They inform the team leader when they will miss a meeting or be late, and they keep other members informed about their progress or lack of progress. Communication is open and spontaneous in team meetings.

7. **Mutual Support.** Members of effective teams support each other. They let others know that they appreciate their efforts and ideas and that they will

help them as needed. On ineffective teams, members work on their own and show little interest in others' work unless it directly impacts their own efforts.

   8. Team Spirit. Members of effective teams take pride in and feel loyalty for their teams. On ineffective teams, the team is just a place to work or, worse, an impediment to getting one's own goals accomplished by one's self.

(Aldridge, 1997)

▶ # 7

Assessing Students' Ability to Think Critically and Solve Problems

Familiarize students with ill-structured problems within your own discipline or areas of expertise. Do this even early in the educational experience. Such problems should not be viewed as the exclusive domain of seniors, senior seminars, or graduate courses. Students are usually attracted to a discipline because it promises a way of better understanding contemporary problems in a particular field, yet they are often asked to "cover the basics" for three or four years before they are permitted to wrestle with the compelling, unresolved issues of the day. Ill-structured problems should be viewed as essential aspects of undergraduate education (King & Kitchener, 1994, pp. 233, 236).

College students are wrestling with issues of certainty and uncertainty, and ... they are struggling to find methods for resolving perplexity when they must make and defend judgments. Students need to learn the skills that will allow them to make judgments in light of that uncertainty; how to think about the relationship between evidence and a point of view, how to evaluate evidence on different sides of issues, how to conceive of objectivity and impartiality, and how to construct judgments in the face of complexity and uncertainty. Moreover, students need to understand the relevance and importance of these skills for their own lives—as effective citizens, consumers, or parents (King & Kitchener, 1994, pp. 256–257).

Making Connections

As you begin to read the chapter, think about the ideas and experiences you've already had that are related to assessing critical thinking and problem solving . . .

- Are your students familiar with the current problems that experts in your discipline are trying to solve?

- How do you involve students in trying to solve them?
- How do you help students develop skills in critical thinking?

What else do you know about assessing critical thinking and problem solving?

What questions do you have about assessing critical thinking and problem solving?

In Chapter 2, we discussed the importance of helping students acquire the critical-thinking and problem-solving skills necessary for completing the complex tasks that adults face daily. Learner-centered teaching helps students develop these skills and use them as they expand their discipline-related knowledge. Learner-centered teaching focuses on intended learning outcomes that represent the important knowledge, skills, and abilities that are valued by professionals in their discipline and by the public at large (Chapter 4). Typically, in addition to critical-thinking and problem-solving skills, these learning outcomes also include related skills in the areas of communication, the ability to collaborate successfully with others, and the self-regulating skills that allow people to pursue and reach goals over a prolonged period of time (Marzano, Pickering, & McTighe, 1993).

ILL-DEFINED PROBLEMS

One way we can guide students toward the achievement of important outcomes is to involve them in addressing enduring or emerging issues and problems that are important enough to warrant serious human attention but whose solution either is not obvious or has not been found. Exploring solutions to this type of problem helps students learn to ask the right questions rather than simply focusing on getting the right answers. Real-world issues and problems are different from the typical problems that textbooks present at the end of a chapter.

Textbook problems—even those that invoke a supposed real-world context—are typically highly structured problems that have been carefully written so that students can solve them using strategies or algorithms. Through the process of solving them, students have the opportunity to rehearse the skills they have learned, and by checking the answer key, they get feedback about whether their approach led to the right answer. This type of problem can be very useful in helping students develop their skills to the extent that they become automatic or habitual.

On the other hand, by virtue of their contrived nature, textbook problems are not "messy," as real life often is. Thus, textbook problems are limited in their ability to provide opportunities to practice important aspects of problem solving that are essential for success after graduation. The ability to manage time and meet deadlines, reach long-term goals, minimize negative consequences, resolve value conflicts, prepare and deliver various types of reports—these are some of the components that are missing from highly structured textbook problems but are ever-present in real life. Furthermore, the problems facing adults in the "real world" are those that have no clear-cut right answer, and because of this, we say they are *ill-defined*.

Solving ill-defined problems requires judgment, planning, the use of strategies, and the implementation of previously learned skill repertoires. Addressing ill-defined problems helps develop inquiry skills as students become researchers, seeking out and evaluating new information in their discipline, integrating it with what is known, organizing it for presentation, and having the opportunity to talk about it with others. In order to prepare students for life beyond graduation, learner-centered teaching should focus on solving ill-defined problems that require the integration of many skills and abilities at once.

	Well-Structured Problems	Ill-Structured Problems
Definition	Can be described with a high degree of completeness	Cannot be described with a high degree of completeness
	Can be solved with a high degree of certainty	Cannot be resolved with a high degree of certainty
	Experts usually agree on the correct solution	Experts often disagree about the best solution, even when the problem can be considered solved
Examples	Converting a unit of measure between its English and metric equivalents	Determining what really happened at the Hue massacre in Vietnam
	Solving for x in an algebraic equation	Judging the adequacy of a theoretical proposition
	Calculating the trajectory of a rocket's flight	Predicting how to dispose of nuclear waste safely
Educational Goal	Learn to reason to correct solutions	Learn to construct and defend reasonable solutions

(King & Kitchener, 1994, p. 11)

FIGURE 7–1   A Comparison of Well- and Ill-Structured Problems

Figure 7–1 from King and Kitchener (1994) contrasts well-defined and ill-defined problems in terms of their distinguishing features, although King and Kitchener refer to them as *well-* and *ill-structured* problems. For each type of problem, examples are included, as well as an appropriate educational goal. As can be seen, well-defined problems (or well-structured problems, to use King and Kitchener's term) are those that experts agree have correct solutions. An appropriate educational goal for students working with well-defined problems is to learn *to reason to correct solutions*. On the other hand, experts disagree about the appropriate solution to an ill-defined problem, and they may even disagree about whether or not the problem can be solved. Thus, an appropriate educational goal for students when they address ill-defined problems is to learn *to construct and defend reasonable solutions*.

President Harry S. Truman has requested that you serve on a White House task force. The goal is to decide how to force the unconditional surrender of Japan, yet provide for a secure postwar world.

You are now a member of a committee of four and have reached the point at which you are trying to decide whether to drop the bomb. Identify the alternatives you are considering and the criteria you are using to make the decision. Explain the values that influenced the selection of the criteria and the weights you placed on each. Also explain how your decision has helped you better understand this statement: "War forces people to confront inherent conflicts of values."

As you work on your task, try to use a variety of sources of information—books, magazine articles, newspapers, and people who lived through the war. Keep a list of those sources and be prepared to describe how you determined which information was most relevant and which information was not very useful.

Before you begin your task, establish a clear goal and write it down. Then write down a plan for accomplishing your goal. When you are finished with the task, be prepared to describe the changes you had to make in your plan along the way.

While working on your task, you will be collaborating in small groups with some of your classmates. As you work together, you will find that you must change certain things you are doing to make your group work more effectively. Be aware of your behavior in the group. Keep track of those behaviors you had to change and what you did to change them.

Present your conclusions and findings in at least two of the following ways:

- a written report
- a letter to the President following the completion of the committee meeting
- an article written for *Time* magazine, complete with suggested photos and charts
- a videotape of a dramatization of the committee meeting
- an audiotape
- a newscast
- a mock interview

(Source: McREL Institute)

FIGURE 7–2   Assessment in History

Place yourself in the role of an international expert in the field of Biology. You recently were contacted by the editor of *Science*, the journal of the American Association for the Advancement of Science, to write a review article on a topic in your area of expertise. The purpose is inform readers about the current state of the art in your area.

The editor explains that you should summarize research findings on your topic. Discuss areas and issues about which researchers have reached consensus, as well as areas and issues about which they disagree. In addition, give readers an overview of likely future directions in the area. Your paper must be written in a manner that both interests your readers and maintains their interest, at the same time that it accurately informs them about your topic.

Select the topic for your paper and complete the following steps.

a) Conduct a library search for primary and secondary sources related to the topic, as well as utilize other search strategies such as the World Wide Web.
b) Read, interpret, analyze, and evaluate data and information from primary and secondary sources related to the topic.
c) Organize and articulate assessment of arguments developed from information sources in a clear, logical, and persuasive manner.
d) Prepare a written presentation of a review article according to accepted convention using approved word processing software and hardware.
e) Prepare and deliver an oral presentation of the review article and lead a thoughtful discussion of it, according to accepted convention.

(Paoletti, 1999)

FIGURE 7–3   Assessment in Biology

Figures 7–2 through 7–8 present assessment tasks that incorporate ill-defined problems for students to solve. In all cases, students must draw upon relevant knowledge, present a response, and support it. In many cases, students are asked to describe and/or evaluate the approach they took as they addressed the problem.

The tasks represent a variety of major disciplines. In the task in Figure 7–2, history students are asked to marshal evidence and take a position about whether or not President Truman should drop the atom bomb. Students in the biology example must present a review paper for an academic journal, educating readers about the current state of the art as well as future directions in a particular area (Figure 7–3). In the assessments in Figures 7–4 and 7–5, mathematics students use their knowledge of mathematics to develop and defend mathematical arguments. In subsequent assessments, chemistry students critique an assertion by presenting technical information in language the average person can understand (Figure 7–6), and psychology students apply theoretical and methodological knowledge to modify a behavior (Figure 7–7). Finally, in Figure 7–8, engineering students are asked to identify a current engineering problem and design an engine or engine component to solve it. (The rubric for this task was included and discussed in Chapter 6.)

We have worked through several axiom systems in class and discussed what it means for axiom systems to be consistent and independent. In this project, you will design your own axiom system.

a) Begin by presenting a model of your choice. Don't make this model too complicated. Write down everything you can observe from the model and try to determine the dependence among the statements. Choose four or five statements as axioms and list the others as theorems. Consider including at least one existential axiom. By being very careful to make sure all of the statements are valid in your model, you will guarantee the consistency of your system.

b) Try to prove that each axiom is independent of the others by finding an independence model for it. If you cannot find a model for a particular axiom, try to prove it as a consequence of the other axioms, thus showing it to be a dependent axiom. In this case move it to the list of theorems. Remember that each time you change the axioms your change may (will) have repercussions for your earlier arguments.

c) Prove the theorems. If you are unable to prove a theorem, try to prove that it is independent of the axioms by finding an appropriate model or find an additional hypothesis under which the theorem can be proven. If it is independent of your axioms, you may want to add it to the list of axioms.

Hand in your axiom system, making sure that you have four axioms and two or three theorems along with proofs of the theorems. Also turn in your consistency model and a model for each axiom to show that it is independent of the others. During the last week of class, you may volunteer to make a short presentation (about 10–15 minutes) to show off your axiom system to the other students in the class.

(Berard, 1992)

FIGURE 7–4   Assessment in Mathematics 1

Reflections

As you create your own meaning from the ideas in this section, begin to think about . . .

- What well-defined problems do I ask students to solve in my course?
- How does solving well-defined problems prepare students for work in my profession?
- What ill-defined problems do I ask students to solve in my course?
- How does solving ill-defined problems prepare my students for work in my profession?

Mathematics Department Outcomes

1. Analytic Thinking/Communication: Understands and uses the language, frameworks, and processes of mathematics in varied contexts.
2. Problem Solving: With confidence and creativity, integrates mathematical knowledge and problem-solving strategies to solve complex problems in diverse contexts.
3. Communication: Independently and consistently adapts communication strategies and approaches to effectively convey complex mathematical concepts and processes.
4. Problem Solving: Abstracts patterns from specific examples to design general solutions to mathematical problems.

Course Outcomes—Calculus 3

1. Reads, writes and communicates mathematics at an intermediate level.
2. Integrates and applies content knowledge and multivariable and vector calculus to solve a variety of problems.
3. Works both independently and collaboratively to understand and formulate problems, solve these problems using the tools and techniques of calculus, and communicate this both orally and in writing.
4. Expands skill at using technology as a tool for understanding mathematical ideas, and as an environment for problem solving.
5. Explores theoretical questions using conjecture and testing.
6. Abstracts and articulates general patterns, procedures, or formulas for observation of particular examples.

Assessment

Problem

Each work group uses a *Spirograph* toy to produce a Roulette, the path resulting from rolling a small wheel (with a pen on the edge) around the edge of a larger wheel until the path meets itself. The group applies knowledge of vector functions to find parametric equations describing the path, and tests these by graphing them with software. A challenging extension is to formulate general conclusions relating the size of the wheel to the curve's shape and length. The group produces a self-contained report on this activity.

Selected Criteria

1. Constructs parametric equations to model the curve satisfactorily.
2. Effectively tests results using graphing technology.
3. Produces a self-contained report on the process used to solve the problem and test for accuracy; the report satisfies mathematics writing criteria and offers a valid mathematical argument, based on algebra and geometry, in support of generalizations made about the relation of the path of the parameters a, b, and c.

(Unpublished, Alverno College Institute, 1999)

FIGURE 7–5   Assessment in Mathematics 2

Major Outcomes

1. Communicates effectively, using the language, concepts, and models of chemistry
2. Uses the methodology of chemistry to define and solve problems independently and collaboratively
3. Uses a wide variety of laboratory techniques with accuracy, precision, and safety
4. Finds, selects, and uses appropriate scientific information to support her work
5. Uses values and scientific information to make responsible decisions about the use of chemical materials and knowledge
6. Uses different strategies and models of chemistry to analyze and synthesize chemical data
7. Critiques the data, strategies, and models of chemistry
8. Applies her learning in an off-campus, professional setting

Course Outcomes—CH 221 Organic Chemistry (2nd semester course)

Your principal goal for this course is to be able to *do* organic chemistry. (This is broken down to several components in your syllabus.)

A second goal is the understanding of, and ability to use, laboratory experimentation as a means of investigating organic substances and their reactions. (This includes more specific abilities listed in your syllabus.)

Assessment of Course Outcomes

Stimulus

At a recent meeting of the Alverno Photography Club, one member, who was not feeling well, asked another for a specific brand of aspirin, whereupon, the vice president said, "All aspirin is alike." A lively discussion followed, and you, as a chemistry student, were asked to give a short speech at the next meeting, outlining a chemist's perspective on the vice president's remark.

Criteria

1. Level 3 of Alverno College-wide Speaking Criteria
2. Understanding of structural theory from chemical perspective
3. Understanding of the molecular structure of aspirin
4. Clear application of relevant distinctions between pure compounds and mixtures

(Alverno College Faculty, *Student-Assessment-as-Learning at Alverno College,* Alverno College Institute, 1994, p. 127)

FIGURE 7–6   Assessment in Chemistry

Major Outcomes

1. Analyzes behavior within a theoretical framework supported by appropriate methodology and data interpretation
2. Explains behavior through an integration of psychology and specialized areas of study in the liberal arts
3. Demonstrates an awareness of the contributions and limitation of psychology in the world
4. Acts in ways that reflect the tenets of psychology, including tolerance of ambiguity, sensitivity to ethics, appreciation of individual differences, respect for ongoing inquiry, and the assumption of the complexity of human behavior

Course Outcomes—PSY 101 General Psychology (1st semester course)

1. To observe and make appropriate inferences about human behavior through experience in observing behavior and in studying the major concepts, methods and theories of psychology
2. To use what psychology has learned about problem solving to (1) self assess your own problem solving style and (2) identify methods for researching questions pertinent to psychology
3. To apply the knowledge and abilities acquired in the course to issues confronted by individuals and groups in today's society

One Course Assessment

Stimulus

(Process over a 6–week period with feedback at various stages)

1. Choose a behavior (habit) you would like to increase or a behavior you would like to decrease.
2. Record and graph this behavior for approximately one week. Also record any antecedents and consequences of the target behavior.
3. Formulate an hypothesis as to why this behavior is maintained at its present rate.
4. Design a program either to increase a behavior (applying the principles of Reinforcement) *or* to decrease a behavior (applying either "controlling antecedents" and/or punishment and/or reinforcement of reduced behavior).
5. Implement your program for about two weeks. Record the rate of your behavior during this time.
6. In a report for the class (written or oral), summarize the results. Interpret them by applying the principles of operant conditioning. Evaluate what factors contributed to the success or failure of your program.

Criteria

1. Distinguishes between behavior and inferences about behavior
2. Demonstrates accurate application of the principles of operant conditioning (behavior modification) for the purpose of increasing target behaviors or decreasing target behaviors
3. Presents data and results accurately and clearly
4. Formulates acceptable hypothesis
5. Designs and implements a workable program
6. Makes accurate inferences re. effectiveness of program

(Alverno College Faculty, *Student-Assessment-as-Learning at Alverno College*, Alverno College Institute, 1994, p. 126)

FIGURE 7–7   Assessment in Psychology

Intended Learning Outcomes

Students will:

1) use their knowledge regarding the design, development, and application of engines in a new context.
2) utilize the engineering skills developed during their undergraduate program.
3) function effectively on a design team.
4) express their ideas effectively orally and in writing.
5) plan and monitor their progress so that the project is thoroughly completed in a timely manner.

Task

In this project, you will work with a team to design an engine or engine component to solve a problem. Your project may be one of two types:

(1) Detailed Design

In this type of project, you will develop very detailed information about a specific engine component:

- a dimensioned layout drawing that conveys all of the essential information about the component
- material selection and manufacturing process information
- fully documented stress and heat transfer calculations.

Example: The Design of a Carburetor for Aftermarket LP Gas Conversion of a Lawn Mower Engine

(2) System Level Design

In this project, you will design an engine or engine component in the context of a system and provide the following:

- problem definition
- a set of general specifications and requirements that could be used by someone at a later stage of development to guide a detailed design program
- market assessment
- feasibility
- a description of parameters needed to ensure market success.

Example: The Design of a V-6 Engine with a 120° Vee Angle for Low Profile Automotive Applications

Completing the Task

There are several steps to take in completing this project:

(1) Develop a one-page proposal that describes

- the type of project you have chosen (i.e., Detailed Design or System Level Design)

- the problem to be addressed
- the scope of the proposed project.

Submit the proposal to the professor by Friday, March 7.

(2) Plan your work schedule.

- Divide the task into parts.
- Identify the individual(s) responsible for each part.
- Prepare a time schedule for the rest of the semester showing when each part will be completed and who is responsible for working on it.

Submit your initial plan to the professor by Friday, March 14.

(3) Update your plan periodically.

The plan will be a living document. You will make many changes and adjustments in it throughout the semester. Keep a folder with your revisions and a log that records why you made modifications. Be prepared to reflect on the process you used to complete the project, discussing in your meetings with the professor what worked, what didn't work, and how you would do things differently next time.

(4) Meet regularly with your team throughout the semester, using brainstorming and group problem-solving techniques to guide your progress and decision making. Keep thorough documentation of these meetings and your progress.

(5) Meet with the professor one or two times per week for the rest of the semester to report progress and receive feedback. Using the rubric on the following pages, the professor will give you feedback on all aspects of your work, including the formulation of your design problem, your use of engineering skills, your ability to use and go beyond the material in ME 445 (Internal Combustion Engines), and teamwork. Use this rubric to assess your own progress as your project develops.

(6) Prepare and submit a final written report that includes a main text, technical appendices, and an appendix in which each member of the team summarizes what he or she learned from completing the project. The final version of the written report will be due May 7. The Written Communication section of the rubric should serve as your guide in developing the paper. Note that the following features are important elements of a report: organization, definition of terms, integration of writing styles, grammar, and appropriate use of appendices.

(7) Make a one-hour oral presentation to the class during the final weeks of the semester. (We will develop the schedule of presentations at a later date.) Your oral presentation should be planned as a team, but each individual in the group should present about 10–12 minutes of the team presentation. Be prepared to answer questions from the class. Other members of the class, including the professor, will critique your presentation using the Oral Communication section of the rubric. You should use this section as a guide in preparing the presentation.

(Van Gerpen, 1997)

FIGURE 7–8   Assessment in Engineering

BENEFITS OF ATTEMPTING TO SOLVE ILL-DEFINED PROBLEMS

When students attempt to solve ill-defined problems like those in Figures 7–2 through 7–8, they gain experience and insight that will help them address real-world problems. For example, at Southern Illinois University at Edwardsville, faculty design departmentally owned Senior Assignments to evaluate students' achievement in both general education and the major discipline (Eder, 1996). Successful completion of a Senior Assignment is required for graduation. Senior Assignments have included conducting research and presenting findings, developing and defending a senior thesis, and composing, displaying, directing, or performing creative work.

> *Students have responded to these challenges with vigor. For example, a biology student investigated the role of the chemical dopamine as a protector of the retina from the damaging effects of light. The resulting poster went to a national meeting. An art student undertook a photographic and historical survey of local homes used in the Underground Railroad. The project formed the basis for a finely illustrated book. Psychology students examined subtle forms of sexual harassment on campus and compared the findings with theoretical models. The results raised consciousness locally and will be presented at a regional meeting (p. 85).*

When students participate in assessments like these, they are likely to be more effective as professionals and as citizens.

Attempting to solve ill-defined problems also helps students advance in their understanding of the uncertain nature of knowledge. King and Kitchener (1994) have studied a characteristic they term reflective thinking or reflective judgment in more than 1,700 young adults and adults.

> *Reflective thinking is called for when there is awareness of a real problem or when there is uncertainty about a solution. Reflective judgments are based on the evaluation and integration of existing data and theory into a solution about the problem at hand, a solution that can be rationally defended as most plausible or reasonable, taking into account the sets of conditions under which the problem is being solved (p. 8).*

Reflective thinking develops over time. It is similar to most conceptions of critical thinking, but it also includes an epistemological dimension. As students become more reflective in their thinking, they must develop in their understanding of what can be known and how knowing occurs. In other words, according to the Reflective Judgment Model (King & Kitchener, 1994), becoming more effective at critical thinking and problem solving means becoming more sophisticated in understanding the uncertainty of knowledge.

King and Kitchener (1994) have developed several stages of intellectual development that extend from pre-reflective thinking through quasi-reflective thinking to reflective thinking. Some are described in Figure 7–9. For each of the stages shown, the typical view of knowledge at that stage is described. There is also a section entitled "concept of justification." This section illustrates how students' view of knowledge at that stage influences the way they justify their point of view on an issue.

For example, pre-reflective thinkers (Stage 1) believe that people can obtain certain knowledge through direct observation. They feel no need to justify their beliefs because "they know what they have seen" and presumably others would agree with them. On the other hand, those who are reflective thinkers (Stage 7) believe that knowledge is the product of reasonable inquiry, and it is evaluated and reevaluated as new evidence becomes available. Students at this level justify their arguments by the type, depth, and consistency of the reasoning that produced them. Different individuals can have different but reasonable positions on the same issue.

Although relatively few students exhibit the ability to think reflectively when they enter college, one clear goal of a college education is to help students advance on this dimension. Traditional courses in which students passively receive information from an authority—the professor—reinforce the limiting notion that knowledge is certain and true, precluding the need for effective reasoning. On the other hand, learner-centered courses provoke students' development as reflective, critical thinkers by giving them active roles in constructing and defending their own knowledge. The opportunity to solve ill-defined problems influences students' understanding of the uncertain nature of knowledge and of the benefits of carefully reasoned and well-documented positions on topics of uncertainty.

Reflections

As you create your own meaning from the ideas in this section, begin to think about . . .

- What do my students seem to believe about the nature of knowledge?

- How do I help them examine their beliefs about knowledge?
- How can I help them become reflective thinkers?

Pre-Reflective Thinking (Stages 1, 2, and 3)

Stage 1

View of knowledge: Knowledge is assumed to exist absolutely and concretely; it is not understood as an abstraction. It can be obtained with certainty by direct observation.

Concept of justification: Beliefs need no justification since there is assumed to be an absolute correspondence between what is believed to be true and what is true. Alternate beliefs are not perceived.

"I know what I have seen."

(King & Kitchener, 1994, p. 14)

Quasi-Reflective Thinking (Stages 4 and 5)

Stage 5

View of knowledge: Knowledge is contextual and subjective since it is filtered through a person's perceptions and criteria for judgment. Only interpretations of evidence, events, or issues may be known.

Concept of justification: Beliefs are justified within a particular context by means of the rules of inquiry for that context and by context-specific interpretations of evidence. Specific beliefs are assumed to be context specific or are balanced against other interpretations, which complicates (and sometimes delays) conclusions.

"People think differently and so they attack the problem differently. Other theories could be as true as my own, but based on different evidence."

(King & Kitchener, 1994, p. 15)

Reflective Thinking (Stages 6 and 7)

Stage 7

View of knowledge: Knowledge is the outcome of a process of reasonable inquiry in which solutions to ill-structured problems are constructed. The adequacy of those solutions is evaluated in terms of what is most reasonable or probable according to the current evidence, and it is reevaluated when relevant new evidence, perspectives, or tools of inquiry become available.

Concept of justification: Beliefs are justified probabilistically on the basis of a variety of interpretive considerations, such as the weight of the evidence, the explanatory value of the interpretations, the risk of erroneous conclusions, consequences of alternative judgments, and the interrelationships of these factors. Conclusions are defended as presenting the most complete, plausible, or compelling understanding of an issue on the basis of the available evidence.

"One can judge an argument by how well thought-out the positions are, what kinds of reasoning and evidence are used to support it, and how consistent the way one argues on this topic is as compared with other topics."

(King & Kitchener, 1994, p. 16)

FIGURE 7–9   Three of King & Kitchener's (1994) Stages in the Development of Reflective Thinking

Solving ill-defined problems also helps students shift paradigms in terms of their understanding of the teaching-learning process and their role within it. When students address problems that have obvious importance in their disciplines, they begin to realize that passively receiving information from the professor will not prepare them for life after graduation. They come to understand that they must take an active role in their learning.

ESSENTIAL COMPONENTS OF CRITICAL THINKING AND PROBLEM SOLVING

Kurfiss (1988) suggests that, from the perspective of cognitive psychologists, three types of knowledge interact in the process of thinking critically and solving ill-defined problems.

> . . . (1) declarative knowledge, *knowing the facts and concepts in the discipline;* (2) procedural knowledge, *knowing how to reason, inquire, and present knowledge in the discipline; and* (3) metacognition, *cognitive control strategies such as setting goals, determining when additional information is needed, and assessing the fruitfulness of a line of inquiry (p. iv).*

In order to help students learn to think critically and solve problems, all three types of knowledge must be addressed.

Declarative Knowledge

Acquiring declarative knowledge—mastering the facts and concepts of a discipline—seems simple enough. After all, helping students acquire declarative knowledge has been the focus of traditional teaching for many decades. On the other hand, students are notoriously ineffective at remembering facts and concepts, and they typically have difficulty knowing when to use the facts and concepts they can remember. Recall the problem of "inert knowledge" referred to in Chapter 2.

Why is it that learners have so much difficulty remembering the facts and concepts of a discipline or knowing when to use them, but experts in the discipline are so skilled at recalling and using such knowledge? Kurfiss (1988) points out that declarative knowledge is more accessible to experts because it is so well developed and organized in their memories.

As emphasized previously, all individuals construct their own meaning and make their own sense of new information. Because of this, the development and organization of knowledge takes place throughout life. When information is introduced, learners ". . . remember *what they understand*, not necessarily what is said" (Kurfiss, 1988, p. 26). Their understanding of concepts may not match the understanding of experts. Over time, understanding changes as new information becomes available, forcing individuals to modify and reorganize what they know.

Experts typically have had many years to organize and reorganize information about their discipline in memory. Because individuals within a discipline typically organize information in similar ways, they can communicate at high levels of abstraction about their shared knowledge.

Although college students may be exposed to a considerable amount of declarative knowledge in their courses, the information may not be organized in memory in such a way that they can use it effectively in particular situations. Thus,

> ... *assignments that help students organize and develop the knowledge they are acquiring are likely to increase the quality of thinking they can do about a subject.*

> ... *In lectures, presenting material in a chart, matrix, or hierarchical outline helps students build an organizing schema that will assist them later in recalling the information, but it is probably equally important to assign tasks that require the students to construct their own schemas, perhaps with the assistance of a peer (Kurfiss, 1988, p. 39).*

Assessments that evaluate and promote students' ability to solve ill-defined problems should require that students reveal and evaluate the *organization* of what they know.

Procedural Knowledge

"Declarative knowledge suffices to talk or read about a subject; procedural knowledge makes it possible to *do* something in the subject domain (Kurfiss, 1988, p. 40). This distinction may help us see that it is just as important for us to help students *use* existing knowledge as it is to help them acquire new knowledge.

Experts are facile at employing the procedural knowledge of their discipline—inquiry, reasoning, and communication skills. Unfortunately, however, their use of procedural knowledge may be so automatic that it is difficult for them to identify the skills involved and teach them to students.

Although inquiry and communication skills are addressed in both the general education and major discipline components of most college programs, reasoning is a less visible component that tends to be embedded in disciplinary instruction and takes different forms from discipline to discipline.

> *In art history, the task is to interpret works of art and describe their historical significance ... In economics, a typical task is to analyze the effects of*

changes in one segment of the economy on other segments . . . Other examples of domain specific procedural knowledge include historical analysis in political science, setting up proofs in mathematics, and decomposing software problems to write computer programs (Kurfiss, 1988, p. 40).

Thus, the challenge for professors preparing to teach and assess critical-thinking and problem-solving skills is to attempt to identify the characteristic ways that individuals think and reason in their field. This is a difficult task and it involves not only knowing the types of problems addressed in each discipline but also knowing how members of the discipline approach them.

Martinez discusses how people approach problems using strategies called heuristics. "A heuristic is a rule of thumb. It is a strategy that is powerful and general, but not absolutely guaranteed to work. Heuristics are crucial because they are *the* tools by which problems are solved" (p. 606). There are innumerable heuristics that individuals use to approach problems, but four common ones are as follows:

- means–end analysis: break your overall goal into subgoals whose achievement will get you closer to the overall goal
- working backwards: consider your overall goal and work backwards identifying the goal that would have to be reached just before it; do the same thing with the newly identified goal and continue this process
- successive approximation: develop a solution and refine and revise it over and over
- representing the problem externally: make a list, graph, diagram, and so on.

Heuristics are different from algorithms because "algorithms are straightforward procedures that are guaranteed to work every time" (Martinez, 1998, p. 606). What constitutes a heuristic for a beginner (perhaps someone learning to prepare an omelet) is an algorithm for an expert (an accomplished chef).

Thus problem solving involves an interaction of a person's experience and the demands of the task. Once we have mastered a skill, we are no longer engaged in problem solving when we apply it. For a task to require problem solving again, novel elements or new circumstances must be introduced or the level of challenge must be raised. Some problem solutions, however, can never be reduced to algorithms, and it is often those problems that constitute the most profound and rewarding of human activities (p. 606).

If we wish to teach our students to solve ill-defined problems, we need to identify heuristics that are commonly used in our fields and reveal them to students so that they may learn to use them. For example, engineers rely heavily on the use of diagrams and graphics in solving problems.

Kurfiss (1988) provides some assistance for individuals in the fields of mathematics, composition, reading comprehension, physics, art history, and political science (pp. 31–33). For example, she refers to the research of Schoenfeld (1985) and points out that in mathematics,

> *Expert problem solvers read the problem, analyze it, explore it if necessary in search of relevant information, plan, implement, and verify the solution. They monitor the effectiveness of their efforts continually . . .*

> *Novices exhibit similar processes, but the proportion of time they devote to each differs radically from the pattern observed for experts. Experts spend more time in analysis and planning, while novices tend to advance rapidly toward implementation. Novices pay attention to form rather than to meaning, in one case spending more time "copying over" a proof than they spent developing it . . . (Kurfiss, 1988, p. 31).*

Typically we think of novices as having less knowledge than experts in a given area. This example suggests that, when novices attempt to use the knowledge they have, they may employ different strategies than those used by experts. It also suggests that when novices use strategies similar to those of experts, they may do so in a different way.

As we begin to try to identify the reasoning approaches that characterize our disciplines, it might be helpful to think about some general reasoning strategies that people tend to employ (e.g., see Quellmalz & Hoskyn, 1997). Marzano, Pickering, and McTighe (1993) discuss the following 13 different reasoning strategies (p. 19, see also pp. 67–84).

- comparing
- classifying
- induction
- deduction
- error analysis
- constructing support
- abstracting

- analyzing perspectives
- decision making
- investigation
- experimental inquiry
- problem solving
- invention

We can review these strategies and identify those that are typically used in our fields. When we have a clearer idea of how individuals think and reason in our disciplines, we will be better able to help our students think like professionals.

For example, Marzano *et al.* (1993) illustrate how the assessment task in Figure 7–2 was developed around the reasoning processes listed above. A history teacher began with the learning outcome that students will understand "that war forces sensitive issues to surface and causes people to confront inherent conflicts of values and beliefs" (Marzano *et al.*, 1993, p. 27). To help students reach this outcome, the teacher considered the following tasks developed around the reasoning processes of comparison, error analysis, constructing support, decision making, investigation, and problem solving.

> *Comparison: Compare the public reaction during World War II to that during the Vietnam war.*
>
> *Error Analysis: Identify the errors in reasoning made by those responsible for interring Japanese Americans during World War II.*
>
> *Constructing Support: Refute or support the claim that the atomic bomb had to be dropped to end World War II.*
>
> *Decision Making: What other alternatives could the United States have used to end the war?*
>
> *Investigation: Why did Japan attack Pearl Harbor? Some say Roosevelt intentionally provoked the Japanese. Others disagree.*
>
> *Problem Solving: If you were the President of the United States during World War II, how would you force the unconditional surrender of Japan without using the atomic bomb and yet provide for a secure postwar world? (Marzano, Pickering, & McTighe, 1993, p. 27).*

The teacher finally selected the problem-solving example above and proceeded to fully develop the task in Figure 7–2. Other examples could have been chosen, depending upon the type of procedural knowledge the teacher wanted students to develop.

Metacognitive Knowledge

Using declarative knowledge effectively depends upon skills in procedural knowledge, but it also depends upon metacognitive knowledge. Both Quellmalz and Hoskyn (1997) and Martinez (1998) emphasize the importance of metacognition in problem solving. Martinez (1998) says,

> *One common feature of problem solving is the capacity to examine and control one's own thoughts. This self-monitoring is known as metacognition. Metacognition is essential for any extended activity, especially problem solving, because the problem solver needs to be aware of the current activity and of the overall goal, the strategies used to attain that goal, and the effectiveness of those strategies. The mind exercising metacognition asks itself, What am I doing? and How am I doing? These self-directed questions are assumed in*

the application of all heuristics. However, in practice, teachers cannot simply assume that students will engage in metacognition; it must be taught explicitly as an integral component of problem solving (p. 608).

Quellmalz and Hoskyn (1997) indicate that metacognitive strategies help problem solvers "deploy and monitor their reasoning strategies" (p. 106) during all phases of problem solution from the early beginning approaches to the final reflection on solutions. They are self-conscious and deliberate strategies that include the following:

1. *Planning* involves analysis of a problem, comparison of elements to previously encountered problems and identification of potentially suitable strategies for addressing the problem.
2. *Drafting and trying out* typically involve a series of attempts to apply strategies to solve a problem or fulfill an assignment.
3. *Monitoring and revising* are interim checks and adjustments to see if subgoals are being met and if attempted strategies are approaching a solution.
4. *Evaluation and reflection* involve looking back at the adequacy of a solution to a particular problem or task as well as self-appraisal of the efficiency and effectiveness of the strategies or approaches used (p. 107).

Although like most college professors, we may have spent little time teaching these metacognitive strategies to our students, it is clear that students must learn to use them if they are to become effective problem solvers. Thus, in learner-centered teaching and assessment, we need to give increased attention to teaching metacognitive skills directly.

Reflections

As you create your own meaning from the ideas in this section, begin to think about . . .

- How much emphasis do I give in my teaching to declarative knowledge, to procedural knowledge, and to metacognition?
- How do members of my discipline think and reason; that is, what type of procedural knowledge is important in my field?
- How do I teach procedural knowledge to my students now? How could I do better?
- What aspects of metacognition do I teach now? What aspects should I teach?

USING ASSESSMENT TO DEVELOP CRITICAL-THINKING AND PROBLEM-SOLVING ABILITIES

When instruction focuses on critical thinking and problem solving, assessment techniques should also focus on critical thinking and problem solving. As pointed out in Chapter 1, traditional assessments like multiple-choice and true–false tests are limited in their ability to evaluate complex thinking. Their strength typically lies in their ability to evaluate knowledge of facts and understanding of concepts. In order to assess students' ability to use what they know to solve complex problems, as well as their ability to communicate, work together cooperatively, and so on, different types of assessment must be used.

Wiggins (1989) suggests that students at all levels of education deserve the opportunity to take "true tests" (p. 703), those that

- require the performance of exemplary tasks,
- replicate the challenges and standards of performance faced by typical professionals in the field, and
- are responsive to individual students, asking for human judgment and dialogue.

Wiggins' (1989) view of a true test is clearly compatible with the hallmarks of learner-centered teaching set forth in Chapter 2. A true test, as Wiggins describes it, gets students actively involved in learning. They must make judgments, interact with others, and do something worth doing so that others can observe and evaluate it. A true test provides students with opportunities to apply their knowledge and skills to enduring and emerging issues and problems—ill-defined problems—and it requires the integration of discipline-based knowledge and general skills.

Wiggins (1989, 1993a, 1993b) also highlights the need to intertwine teaching and assessment. He points out that true tests are not just opportunities to evaluate student learning; they are also central learning experiences for students in and of themselves in that students extend their learning during the process of completing the "tests."

True tests are also central experiences in instruction in that they help us teach more effectively. When we ask students to address enduring and emerging issues and problems that replicate the challenges faced by professionals in our disciplines, we have an opportunity to set high standards for student achievement and, at the same time, monitor whether or not they have been achieved. True tests reveal student achievement to us while at the same time revealing the challenges and standards of our disciplines to students. The rubrics discussed in Chapter 6 can be key tools in this regard.

In Chapter 4, we discussed five categories of learning outcomes that Marzano, Pickering, and McTighe (1993) propose are important in developing the skills and abilities to support lifelong learning. They can be loosely paraphrased as follows.

- inquiry—gathering, evaluating, and effectively using information
- communication—expressing ideas clearly and effectively for diverse audiences and purposes
- collaboration/cooperation—using interpersonal skills effectively to support group work and goals
- complex thinking—using a variety of reasoning strategies to address issues and problems
- habits of mind—demonstrating self-regulation skills, as well as critical thinking and creative thinking

True tests provide the opportunity to evaluate and promote student achievement in all of these areas.

Reflections

As you create your own meaning from the ideas in this section, begin to think about . . .

- What types of assessments do I use to evaluate student learning?

- Which of them have the qualities of a true test?
- In what ways are my assessments learning experiences for students?

EFFECTIVE ASSESSMENT FORMATS

The assessment formats listed in Figure 7–10 can be designed to have many, if not all, of the qualities of a true test. They can evaluate several desired outcomes simultaneously, and they are examples of ways to assess critical thinking and problem solving as discussed above. True tests should be used in all courses, even in the freshman year. Engaging students in their learning early in their undergraduate program is critically important to retention and success in an undergraduate program (see Chapter 1). Furthermore, true tests are ideal for capstone courses in which senior students are expected to integrate information gained in their program.

- Paper/Thesis. Students develop an argument and support it with information or data they have gathered. They present their ideas in writing that is organized and coherent. These assessments develop students' inquiry skills and their ability to process large amounts of information.

Paper/Thesis	Clinical Evaluation
Project	Oral Exam
Development of a Product	Interview
Performance	Comprehensive Exam
Exhibition	Portfolio
Case Study/Critical Incident	

FIGURE 7–10   Effective Assessment Formats

- Project. Students complete an assignment over a prolonged period of time. To be successful, they must set goals, plan, use resources, organize, make judgments, and craft a written and/or visual presentation of material. The project may require working with others, as well as an oral presentation of results.
- Development of a product. This type of assessment is a project whose focus is on the development of a tangible product. The product itself, as well as the process and quality of reasoning that led to it, is evaluated.
- Performance. Students prepare and present a performance of a valued activity.
- Exhibition. An exhibition is a project, product, or performance that is presented to judges and defended or debated with them.
- Case study/Critical incident. Students are given a realistic example of an application in their field. They respond with an analysis or professional response, using information and skills they have acquired.
- Clinical evaluation. Students perform a professional service in a real-life setting.
- Oral exam. Students answer spontaneous questions put to them by experts. They must think on their feet; draw upon relevant facts, theories, and/or perspectives; and speak in a coherent, organized fashion when presenting their ideas.
- Interview. An interview is similar to an oral exam, but the forum in which it is carried out may not be as public or involve as many questioners as an oral exam.
- Comprehensive exam. Students complete a time-limited essay test that requires them to organize and present central ideas, facts, and concepts in response to questions.
- Portfolio. In response to a goal developed by the professor or by professor and student(s) together, students gather examples of their work to include in a portfolio. They write about aspects of their learning and achievement and include their written reflections in the portfolio. Professors and individual students talk together about portfolio contents, gaining greater insight into the student's progress. (Using portfolios in assessment is the topic of Chapter 8.)

Reflections

As you create your own meaning from the ideas in this section, begin to think about . . .

- Which of the assessment formats listed above do I use in my courses?

- What have I found to be their advantages and disadvantages?
- Which assessment formats should I integrate into my courses?

CHARACTERISTICS OF AN EXEMPLARY ASSESSMENT TASK

An exemplary assessment task is one that involves college students in addressing enduring and emerging issues and problems that are ill-defined and of current relevance in their disciplines. An exemplary task evaluates student learning at the same time that it promotes it. Aspects of students' declarative, procedural, and metacognitive knowledge are assessed. In the completion of an exemplary assessment task, students become more sophisticated in their thinking and problem-solving abilities. They develop a clearer notion of the uncertain nature of knowledge.

What makes an assessment task exemplary? The characteristics in Figure 7–11 are important in ensuring that an assessment will help professors and students reach their goal of improved student learning.

Valid	yields useful information to guide learning
Coherent	is structured so that activities lead to desired performance or product
Authentic	addresses ill-defined problems/issues that are enduring or emerging
Rigorous	requires use of declarative, procedural, and metacognitive knowledge
Engaging	provokes student interest and persistence
Challenging	provokes, as well as evaluates, student learning
Respectful	allows students to reveal their uniqueness as learners
Responsive	provides feedback to students leading to improvement

FIGURE 7–11   Eight Characteristics of an Exemplary Assessment Task

Valid

A valid assessment task is one that yields useful information to guide learning. In order to do this, it must match important intended learning outcomes (Herman, Aschbacher, & Winters, 1992)—those of the professor, the department, and the institution. A valid task must ask for a demonstration of the actual achievements faculty want students to do well. Usually, this means that the task should be structured to provide measures of several learning outcomes at once.

Coherent

A coherent task is structured so that the activities students engage in lead to the desired performance or product (Association for Supervision and Curriculum Development, 1996). Ensuring coherence may be difficult for professors who are developing assessment tasks for the first time. A common pitfall may be to generate interesting activities for students, only to realize later that the activities don't really help students achieve the intended learning outcomes. For example, assigning students to work in teams without requiring that they use and document their use of team skills (Aldridge, 1997) may not lead to improved cooperation and collaboration skills. Students may simply divide up the requirements of the task into separate parts and work independently.

Authentic

An authentic task addresses important recurring issues or enduring problems. It replicates the challenges adults face in their daily lives or representative challenges within a discipline (Wiggins, 1989). It appears credible to important constituencies, and it is ill-defined; that is, the problems addressed have no "right" answer.

Rigorous

A rigorous task is structured so that students must understand content (declarative knowledge) to be successful. They must also show that they can use the content effectively (procedural knowledge), and they must explain and demonstrate the inquiry process they followed to complete the task. This makes it possible to assess their reasoning directly rather than as an undifferentiated component of their overall response (Quellmalz & Hoskyn, 1997). A rigorous task emphasizes "purposeful, sustained reasoning, rather than demonstration of discrete, isolated skills" (p. 110). Finally, a rigorous task also assesses students' "meta-cognitive strategies for planning, revision, and self-evaluation" (p. 110).

Engaging

An engaging task is one that is meaningful and intrinsically interesting to students. When their work is interesting, students are provoked to become involved and to persevere thoughtfully to completion (Wiggins, 1989, 1993b). They are motivated to learn, and they find learning satisfying. This satisfaction leads them to become more interested in and committed to their discipline.

Challenging

Because an exemplary assessment task is an ill-defined challenge similar to those adults face in their personal and professional lives, it allows students to learn while they are being assessed. In the absence of right answers, students must inquire, reason, develop hypotheses, make mistakes, try something else, and so forth. Problem solution inevitably involves learning. Even the application of what is already known involves learning because the application is typically in a new and perhaps unfamiliar setting.

An exemplary task also promotes learning by pointing students toward more sophisticated and effective ways of knowing (Wiggins, 1989). In this way, it helps develop their understanding of the uncertain nature of knowledge (King & Kitchener, 1994). Furthermore, because several learning outcomes are assessed simultaneously, an exemplary task lends itself to an interdisciplinary approach in which students have the opportunity to make connections among different domains of knowledge.

Respectful

An exemplary assessment task is respectful to students because it acknowledges the uniqueness of each learner. An ill-defined problem allows for multiple interpretations or solutions, rather than only one right answer (Quellmalz & Hoskyn, 1997). A task that requires students to develop their own approach to problem solution accommodates different learning styles, allowing students to learn in a manner that matches their preferred style.

An exemplary task is respectful to learners because it requires them to use their language abilities, the distinguishing feature of humans (Wiggins, 1989, 1993a, 1993b). Students must explain their answers and demonstrate the processes used to achieve them. They have opportunities to discuss and defend their ideas.

Finally, a respectful task is fair and free of bias. Care must be taken to structure the task so that it does not favor students of a particular group or background.

Responsive

An exemplary assessment task is responsive in that it provides students with feedback that guides improvement. It includes explicit criteria for judging in the form of rubrics that are available to students and that may have been developed in part by students. Opportunities are provided for discussing with the professor and other students how well student work meets the criteria.

An exemplary assessment task also provides for student self-assessment. Students use the criteria in the rubric to critique their work, progressively developing and shaping their response so that it meets the criteria. Requiring that students demonstrate metacognitive knowledge enhances the development of students' knowledge of themselves as learners.

Reflections

As you create your own meaning from the ideas in this section, begin to think about . . .

- Which of the characteristics of exemplary assessment tasks are

present in the assessment tasks that I use in my courses?

- How could I enhance my assessments to reflect these characteristics more clearly?

DEVELOPING AN EFFECTIVE ASSESSMENT TASK

Figure 7–12 presents nine questions we should answer as we develop an effective assessment task. The following discussion addresses each question in turn.

1. *What declarative knowledge do I expect students to draw upon in this task?*

When answering this question, as well as questions 2 and 3, we should examine our intended learning outcomes. If you return to the assessment tasks in Figures 7–5 through 7–8, you will notice that the first item in each figure is a list of intended learning outcomes which identify the body of knowledge that students should understand and utilize in completing the task.

For example, the engineering assessment (Figure 7–8) requires that students use their knowledge of internal combustion engines to design an engine or engine component. They must also present information that supports their design and the use of the product it represents. Developing support materials will reveal students' mental organization of their declarative knowledge regarding engines.

1. What declarative knowledge do I expect students to draw upon in this task?
2. What procedural knowledge do I expect students to use?
3. What metacognitive knowledge do I expect students to develop and reveal?
4. In what real-life settings do individuals use the knowledge I identified and what ill-defined problems do they typically address?
5. For each ill-defined problem, what task(s) could I sketch out for students to complete?
6. Which task best exemplifies the characteristics in Figure 7–11?
7. Which assessment format in Figure 7–10 will work best for this task?
8. How can I improve the task to more clearly reflect the characteristics in Figure 7–11?
9. What criteria should my students and I use in shaping and critiquing student work?

FIGURE 7–12   Questions to Ask When Developing an Effective Assessment Task

2. *What procedural knowledge do I expect students to use?*

Once again, we should turn to our intended learning outcomes to answer this question. In the assessments in Figures 7–2 through 7–8, several types of procedural knowledge are identified. For example, in the engineering assessment, many of the reasoning strategies identified by Marzano *et al.* (1993) will undoubtedly be used to complete the project. Students must reflect on and summarize the reasoning strategies they use so that they can discuss them with the professor. Other aspects of procedural knowledge that are clearly present are inquiry skills, engineering skills, teamwork skills, and oral and written communication.

3. *What metacognitive knowledge do I expect students to develop and reveal?*

Our desired use of metacognitive knowledge should be outlined in our intended learning outcomes. In several of the assessments used as illustrations in this chapter (Figures 7–2 through 7–8), students are asked to plan, monitor, and/or evaluate their work.

For example, in the history assessment (Figure 7–2), students are asked to write down a goal, a plan for reaching the goal, and a summary of modifications they made as they executed their plan. They are also asked to monitor their effectiveness as a team and to make modifications as needed. In the second mathematics example (Figure 7–5), students are required to test the equations they develop and write a summary report on the process they used to develop and test their solution.

The engineering project in Figure 7–8 has been constructed so that students must employ and use all four of Quellmalz and Hoskyn's (1994) metacognitive strategies. The requirement that students plan, draft and try out, monitor and revise, and evaluate and reflect is built into the task description. A component could easily be incorporated into each of the other sample assessments in which students would reflect upon and critique their work or the process they used to complete it.

4. *In what real-life settings do individuals use the knowledge I identified and what ill-defined problems do they typically address?*

In the sample assessments, several settings in which individuals use their knowledge to solve problems is identified. The history example (Figure 7–2) illustrates how a leader can use historical information to inform a decision that influences the course of national and international events. The biology example (Figure 7–3) refers to an academic setting in which experts synthesize information and interpret the field for others. The chemistry example (Figure 7–6) illustrates how scientists with good communication skills can help people use scientific information to improve their health. In all of these assessments, the task for students to complete is embedded in a real-life scenario.

In the engineering example (Figure 7–8), students apply their knowledge by designing a product that could be used in an industrial setting, providing all the documentation that would be needed to support its use. This is a typical real-life application for mechanical engineers, although a scenario was not included in the task description.

5. *For each ill-defined problem, what task(s) could I sketch out for students to complete?*

Identifying meaningful assessment tasks for students is a critically important activity during which it may be helpful to have the advice of colleagues. It is important for us and our colleagues to agree not only on intended learning outcomes in a program but also on appropriate ways to measure them. When we discuss topics like the measurement of outcomes in our program routinely, assessment in the program benefits. As discussed in Chapter 3, when gathering data to assess program effectiveness, we can rely on using data from course-embedded assessments that we or our colleagues have developed with the assistance of others.

6. *Which task best exemplifies the characteristics in Figure 7–11?*

After brainstorming about or sketching out several possible tasks, we should answer this question to help ensure that the data we collect about student learning are as useful and informative as possible. Selecting tasks that are valid, coherent, authentic, rigorous, engaging, challenging, respectful, and responsive also helps ensure that we are evaluating our students in a manner that will prepare them to be competent and effective in the future.

7. *Which assessment format in Figure 7–10 will work best for this task?*

We must ask ourselves whether the task we have developed or selected can best be completed through a writing assignment like a paper or through a more "hands on" approach like a project or a performance. Should there be an element in which students function like practitioners in a "real-life" setting as in a case study or a clinical evaluation? Is it important that the student dialogue with us or with others (as in an oral exam, in an interview, or when using a portfolio in assessment)? Questions like these will help us carefully consider the features of the different assessment formats in Figure 7–10.

In the engineering example (Figure 7–8), the professor decided to have students complete his assessment as a project with a presentation to the class at the end of the term. Students were also expected to keep logs of the reasoning and planning processes they used throughout the semester so that they could discuss them with the professor. The final presentation is similar to the oral exam assessment format, and the use of written logs followed by discussion is similar to the format of portfolio assessment.

In the chemistry example (Figure 7–6), the professor asked students to make an informal presentation of scientific information to peers in a club, whereas in the biology example (Figure 7–3), students were asked to write a formal review paper. In the history example (Figure 7–2), the professor gave students seven formats for presenting their work and asked them to employ at least two of them.

8. *How can I improve the task to more clearly reflect the characteristics in Figure 7–11?*

Once the task and the assessment format have been selected, we should finalize the requirements of the assessment and the directions that will be given to students. Revisiting the characteristics in Figure 7–11 will provide guidance for making additional improvements so that the assessment yields data that accurately evaluate student learning and provide guidance for improvement.

9. *What criteria should my students and I use in shaping and critiquing student work?*

Chapter 6 discussed a process for developing or selecting criteria and presenting them in the form of rubrics that can be used to both promote and evaluate learning. When professors and students have clearly identified criteria for critiquing and evaluating student work, learning is enhanced.

LOOKING AHEAD

One new idea introduced in this chapter is the important notion of metacognition, the ability of individuals to reflect upon and monitor their thinking and learning. An important tool for developing students' metacognitive abilities is the portfolio. Chapter 8 discusses the use of portfolios both in assessing individual student learning and in program assessment.

TRY SOMETHING NEW

1. Make a list of all the problems you ask students to solve in your courses. Identify those that are well-defined and those that are ill-defined. Evaluate what your students are learning from each type.
2. Using the questions in Figure 7–12, develop an assessment task you could use in one of your courses. Share it with colleagues and seek their reactions.
3. Review your course requirements. Revise them to ensure that students have the opportunity to complete true tests.

REFERENCES

Aldridge, M. D. (1997, December). Briefings: Team players. *ASEE Prism Magazine (American Society of Engineering Education)*, 9.

Alverno College Faculty. (1994). *Student assessment-as-learning at Alverno College* (3rd ed.). Milwaukee, WI: Alverno College Institute.

Alverno College Faculty. (1999). Unpublished mathematics assessment. Milwaukee, WI: Alverno College Institute.

Association for Supervision and Curriculum Development. (1996). *Developing performance assessments*. Alexandria, VA: Association for Supervision and Curriculum Development.

Berard, A. D., Jr. (1992). The use of small axiom systems to teach reasoning to first-year students. *Primus, II* (3), 265–277.

Eder, D. J. (1996). The departmentally owned senior assignment as an assessment mechanism. In T. W. Banta, J. P. Lund, K. E. Black, & F. W. Oblander (Eds.), *Assessment in practice: Putting principles to work on college campuses* (pp. 82–86). San Francisco: Jossey-Bass.

Herman, J., Aschbacher, P. R., & Winters, L. (1992). *A practical guide to alternative assessment*. Alexandria, VA: Association for Supervision and Curriculum Development.

King, P. M., & Kitchener, K. S. (1994). *Developing reflective judgment: Understanding and promoting intellectual growth and critical thinking in adolescents and adults*. San Francisco, Jossey–Bass.

Kurfiss, J. G. (1988). *Critical thinking: Theory, research, practice, and possibilities*. (ASHE-ERIC Higher Education Report No. 2). College Station, TX: Association for the Study of Higher Education.

Martinez, M. E. (1998, April). What is problem solving? *Phi Delta Kappan, 79*, 605–609.

Marzano, R. J., Pickering, D., & McTighe, J. (1993). *Assessing student outcomes: Performance assessment using the dimensions of learning model*. Alexandria, VA: Association for Supervision and Curriculum Development.

Paoletti, R. (1999). *Unpublished Sophomore–Junior Diagnostic Project in Biology*. Wilkes-Barre, PA: King's College, Department of Biology.

Quellmalz, E., & Hoskyn, J. (1997). Classroom assessment of reasoning strategies. In
    G. Phye (Ed.), *Handbook of classroom assessment* (pp. 103–130). San Diego, CA: Aca-
    demic Press.
Schoenfeld, A. H. (1985). *Mathematical problem solving.* New York: Academic Press.
Van Gerpen, J. (1997). *Unpublished internal combustion engine design project.* Ames, IA:
    Department of Mechanical Engineering, Iowa State University.
Wiggins, G. (1989, May). A true test: Toward more authentic and equitable assess-
    ment. *Phi Delta Kappan*, 703–713.
Wiggins, G. (1993a). *Assessing student performance: Exploring the limits and purpose of
    testing.* San Francisco: Jossey-Bass.
Wiggins, G. (1993b, November). Assessment: Authenticity, context, and validity. *Phi
    Delta Kappan*, 200–214.

▶ 8

Using Portfolios to Promote, Support, and Evaluate Learning

In short, it is the purpose of portfolio assessment to help the learners become integral and conscious participants in their learning processes, by having them recognize both individual responsibility and ownership within that process, and by having them become interactive partners with the teacher in shaping that learning process. Likewise, portfolios provide teachers with the possibility of examining the learning process (and performance outcomes) from the point of view of the learner (what is actually occurring) rather than from some distanced point of view that is reflected in course objectives and syllabi (what is supposed to occur or what we sometimes pretend is actually occurring) (Courts & McInerney, 1993, pp. 85–86).

Self-examination outside the realm of academia is not new to students; they undoubtedly give much critical thought to their looks and the clothes they wear, the way they dance or play a sport. But sustained reflection on their learning processes is generally unfamiliar. Students have little experience examining their academic work in any systematic way and even less experience describing it in writing (MacGregor, 1993a, p. 36).

Learning succeeds to the degree that it gradually assists the learner to take control of his or her own learning process (Eaton & Pougiales, 1993, p. 55).

Perhaps more than any other assessment technique, portfolios provide a detailed mosaic of student learning as it develops over time (Black, 1993, p. 146).

Making Connections

As you begin to read the chapter, think about the ideas and experiences you've already had that are related to using portfolios in assessment . . .

- What experiences, if any, have you had using portfolios in assessment and what have you learned from them?
- What do you know about the different ways in which your students learn?

- How have you tried to involve your students as active partners in learning?
- In what ways do you encourage students to reflect about their learning?

What else do you know about using portfolios in assessment?
What questions do you have about using portfolios in assessment?

Most people are familiar with the portfolios developed by artists who gather their best or most representative work in a folder and share it with prospective employers or clients. Documenting learning in this way places the focus on actual achievements that are viewed directly, rather than on proxies of achievement like cumulative GPAs or test scores that are only indirect indicators of learning. The focus is also on what students *can do* with their knowledge and skills and not simply on whether knowledge has been acquired. Thus, portfolios of student work are compatible with a learner-centered approach to teaching in which students use what they know to complete important tasks.

However, a portfolio that is a collection of student work is not an assessment tool—it is just a folder. In order for a portfolio to be useful in assessment, someone must reflect and make judgments about its contents. When portfolios are used in program assessment, a group of faculty review and evaluate samples of students' work that have been collected in the portfolios. When portfolios are used in course assessment, the professor and individual students review and discuss work that the student has collected. Written reflections in which students evaluate their own learning are central components when portfolios are used in courses; they may also be included when portfolios are used for program assessment.

Using portfolios to reflect about and judge student learning can take place in any field, although the arts and humanities are probably most likely to come to mind first. Portfolios can be useful in the sciences and mathematical disciplines (e.g., Slater, 1995, 1996), as well as in the humanities (e.g., Castiglione, 1996; Horning, 1997; Mincey, 1996; O'Brien, Bressler, Ennis, & Michael, 1996). Portfolios can assist students and faculty in professional fields (e.g., Ducharmes & Ducharmes, 1996; Bolender, 1996; Box & Dean, 1996; Freidus, 1996; Olds & Miller, 1997; Smith & Crowther, 1996), as well as in the liberal arts (e.g., Lind, 1995; Katz & Gangon, 1998b). Portfolios can also be used to assess general education programs (e.g., Forrest, 1990; Katz & Gangon, 1998a; Magruder & Young, 1996; Wehlburg, 1998).

Reflections

As you create your own meaning from the ideas in this section, begin to think about . . .

- How could portfolios be used in my department for program assessment?
- How would using portfolios in my courses change the learning environment?

- How typical is it in my discipline to encourage students to reflect about their learning?
- Why would it be important for students in my discipline to reflect about their learning?

TYPES OF PORTFOLIOS

Broadly speaking, there are two types of portfolios: the all-inclusive portfolio and the selection portfolio.

The All-Inclusive Portfolio

The all-inclusive portfolio is a collection of all the work a student has produced in a course or program, and it provides a complete record of student achievement for faculty members and the student to review. Included in the portfolio are assignments as varied as papers, projects, homework, lab reports, problems solved, or even videotapes of presentations or performances. Courts and McInerney (1993) suggest another element for the all-inclusive portfolio: students should include a written explanation of the importance of each entry in the portfolio. Doing so will help them think about and critique their own work, leading to improved metacognitive knowledge.

The all-inclusive portfolio might thus be considered a day-to-day record of progress. As such, it allows us, along with our students, to identify areas of a course or program in which students demonstrated strengths and engagement and those in which they performed poorly or were less involved.

When used in program assessment, the all-inclusive portfolio allows a viewer to determine how much and what kind of work of a specific type is required in a program. For example, when reviewing portfolios, we can determine the quantity and type of writing required in a program, and we can identify courses that emphasize writing and those that do not. Reviewing portfolios also permits us to judge how well students perform or how quickly they improve (Courts & McInerney, 1993).

Perhaps offsetting the benefits of an all-inclusive portfolio are the logistical problems associated with storing and reviewing these comprehensive records. A great deal of space may be needed for storing all-inclusive portfolios, and a great deal of time is needed for reviewing them. When all-inclusive portfolios are used in program assessment, some of these difficulties can be resolved by relying on only a sample of students to maintain portfolios over time.

Another solution to the storage problem is provided by Pack (1998) who describes the electronic portfolios used at Winona State University. Although the Winona State portfolio is not an all-inclusive portfolio, it illustrates the fact that students can easily store large amounts of information on diskettes, Zip disks, CD-ROM disks, or the Internet. They can store a variety of types of information—text, graphics, animation, sound, and video—and they can organize it using multimedia software and an interactive electronic resume system. "A video of a recital, a photo essay, a page from a publication, and an audio-cassette of an interview all document accomplishments better than a written description of these events" (p. 25).

Furthermore, the electronic portfolio permits viewers to access the information in the manner they desire. The Winona State portfolios include a series of menus, submenus, and hyperlinks that can "take the user to more detailed information that documents, illustrates, or explains, then returns the user to the original page" (Pack, 1998, p. 25). This type of directed and personalized search of a large data base would not be possible with conventional paper portfolios.

The Selection Portfolio

In contrast to the all-inclusive portfolio through which we examine the entire body of a student's work, a selection portfolio is developed to achieve a particular goal. When the portfolio is developed for program assessment, the goal is identified by the faculty as a whole. When the portfolio is developed in a course, the professor alone or the professor and student(s) together develop the goal. In any case, students know the goal of the portfolio ahead of time, and they review their work and select pieces to include based on the goal.

For example, as shown in Figure 8–1, the possible goals of a portfolio include evaluating the achievement of intended outcomes, demonstrating the breadth with which learning outcomes have been achieved, illustrating the process associated with achieving a learning outcome, and understanding how one learns. A final possible goal is celebrating the fact that outcomes have been achieved. In this type of portfolio, students collect and review the assignments they enjoyed the most when learning.

Figure 8–1 also lists the types of required or supporting evidence that students may select for the other goals. Students should select their best work when the goal is to evaluate whether or to what degree intended outcomes have been achieved. They should select a variety of types of achievement when the goal is to demonstrate breadth in achieving outcomes. They should include multiple drafts of an assignment when the goal is to show improvement or to document the stages in the development of an assignment, as is the case with a "process" portfolio.

Johnson (1996) provides several examples of possible entries to include when the goal is either to show improvement or to document the stages in the development of a work.

- Clear documentation of solving a series of laboratory problems in any of the sciences. Students would have to keep running records or logs of their scientific method processes.
- Double-column mathematics problem solving—where students do their computation/ calculation/ "figuring" on the left side of the page and later write a running commentary explaining their thought

Goal	Entries
To evaluate the achievement of intended learning outcomes	Best work exemplifying outcomes
To demonstrate the breadth with which learning outcomes have been achieved	Work representing a range of accomplishments
To illustrate the process associated with achieving a learning outcome	Multiple drafts or versions that represent a chronology of progress
To understand one's own learning	Written reflections about learning
To celebrate the achievement of learning outcomes	Favorite assignments most representative of achievement

FIGURE 8–1   Portfolio Goals and Related Entries

process. (Imagine a series of these focused on a certain kind of problem or problem-solving strategy.)

- The evolution of a speech or public debate . . . from early notes through outlines, research notes, and final draft.
- The "history" of any piece of artwork, from its original conception (with journals and/or sketches) to first, second, third attempts, and final product (pp. 36–37).

Note that written reflections are included in three of the four examples in the form of records or logs, running commentaries, or journals. Some form of written reflection is essential for the development of metacognitive skills. When reflections are available, entries allow a viewer to understand not only the degree of improvement students have achieved, but also the way in which they think about and approach their work.

Wolf (1992) has discovered that, in a portfolio that documents improvement or the development of a work,

> *students regularly return to earlier works to revise or make comparisons with later ones. Students use samples of their own work to reflect on the changing nature of their own standards. After comparing satisfying and unsatisfying pieces and choosing one, students are invited, at a later date, to reassess and then change or preserve their earlier choice. This process of selecting and shaping a representative collection of work yields an autobiographical understanding that includes knowledge of past change and the prospect of future development (p. 5).*

Through this type of portfolio, students develop greater understanding of themselves as learners.

Reflections

As you create your own meaning from the ideas in this section, begin to think about . . .

- How could my faculty colleagues and I use all-inclusive portfolios to evaluate our academic program?

- How could I use all-inclusive portfolios in my courses?
- How could my faculty colleagues and I use selection portfolios to evaluate our academic program?
- How could I use selection portfolios in my courses?

USING PORTFOLIOS IN ASSESSMENT

Before designing a portfolio system . . . , serious consideration must be given to why such a system should be implemented. What purpose or purposes will the portfolio system serve? Because there is a certain familiarity with the concept, as evidenced by the artist/photography example, it is all too easy to simply say, "Let's use portfolios." Such snap decisions can easily contribute to creating yet another requirement for students with no clear purpose in mind (Johnson, 1996, p. 31).

We may specify the purpose and parameters for using portfolios in assessment at the institutional level, the program level, or the course level, depending on the level at which they are used. There also may be times when we tailor the goals and parameters of a portfolio to students individually. In all of these cases, guidelines describing what to include in the portfolio are developed, and often, students themselves participate in developing those guidelines.

Generally speaking, there are two purposes for which portfolios might be used in assessment. The first is to *evaluate* learning in programs, and the second is to *promote* student learning and student ownership of learning. For both of these purposes, the intended learning outcomes of the institution or program are critical in providing direction for using portfolios. How will the use of portfolios help faculty better understand whether or not the learning outcomes of the program or course are being achieved? How will the use of portfolios help students reach one or more of the intended learning outcomes of a program or course?

Evaluating Learning

One way we can use portfolios is to assess the impact of a program. The program may be the entire college experience, the general education program, the experience in the major discipline, or more specific programmatic components like peer tutoring or writing across the curriculum (Courts & McInerney, 1993).

In program assessment, we can use portfolios of typical or exemplary student work to gather student achievement information. Reviewing the portfolios helps us improve teaching and curriculum in our academic programs. For example, a group of faculty colleagues could review a sample of actual student work collected in the portfolios developed by graduating seniors. They could discuss portfolio contents, focusing on whether or not there is evidence that the intended learning outcomes of the program have been achieved. Rubrics would be useful tools to use in judging the contents. At the conclusion of their work, the group could report their findings to the faculty as a whole. In this way, the faculty would come to understand what graduating seniors are able to do well and where they need improvement. Through discussion of findings, they could identify areas of the program that need to be changed. According to Lendley Black from Emporia State University,

> *once the faculty began looking at student course products in portfolios, its understanding of student learning increased tremendously. For example, our faculty had established the integration of knowledge as a component of its general education goals—one that was assumed to be fulfilled by our core curriculum courses. Almost from the beginning of our portfolio analysis, however, there was little evidence that this goal was being achieved. As a result of these findings, the content and teaching strategies of some key courses have been refined to increase the integrative learning within the program (Black, 1993, pp. 143–144).*

Similar benefits have been noted at Manhattanville College where a committee of eight faculty, elected for a three-year term, review student portfolios each spring (Myers, 1996).

When portfolios are used to evaluate learning in a program or course, faculty are typically the primary individuals reflecting and making judgments about the contents of the portfolios. This would not be unlike the process used by the prospective employers or clients of the artists discussed above. However, the purpose would not be to select an individual with the best portfolio, but rather to come to a deeper understanding of typical student achievement in the program.

At the Colorado School of Mines a portfolio assessment program was developed in the late 1980s in response to a legislative mandate for increased accountability in higher education (Olds & Miller, 1997). Comprehensive portfolios are maintained throughout the undergraduate program for a statistically based sample of students consisting of about 10% of each freshman class. Portfolio contents include entering test scores, GPAs, student satisfaction surveys, and samples of work from a variety of courses. Although portfolio students and their parents give written permission to participate, students themselves are not actively involved in data collection. Rather, the data are collected by faculty and administrators at the department level. Freshman and sophomore portfolios are maintained by a campus Assessment Committee. Junior and senior portfolios are maintained by the major department.

The Assessment Committee reviews freshman and sophomore portfolios each year, and department faculty review those of upper-division students. Numerous curricular changes have been made at the department level (e.g., increased writing assignments, greater emphasis on higher-order thinking questions on exams) and at the institutional level (e.g., redesign of the writing-across-the-curriculum program).

> *There are several strengths to the portfolio method [when used to assess programs]: it does not intrude on normal classroom procedures; it allows us to view multiple examples of a student's work over time; it is deeply analytical; feedback can be used for both formative and summative changes. In addition, we have seen a heightened awareness of assessment and the need for continuous improvement on our campus, some real change in courses and programs, faculty involvement in the process through our bottom-up approach, and a data-based decision-making process. The only major weakness we have seen lies in our underuse of the rich data we have collected (Olds & Miller, 1997, p. 466).*

Another variation on using portfolios for program assessment is discussed by Courts and McInerney (1993). They suggest that a portfolio contain six entries: an entry paper, papers written in at least four different courses, and an exit paper.

> *For programmatic assessment . . . , students might be expected to include in their portfolios, an entry paper, a description of how they approached solving a problem (mastering a complex concept, developing a skill . . .); a research paper (or critical/analytical paper); an out-of-class essay exam (or, perhaps . . . a creative paper); a paper explaining the most significant or complex aspect of the discipline they have been studying; and a self-reflective exit paper (p. 69).*

Entry papers, written when students declare their major, can be structured to reveal students' attitudes and expectations about a discipline, as well as their reasons for choosing it. As mentioned in Chapter 2, students studying or wishing to study in a particular discipline have already learned something about or something related to the field in previous years of schooling. Entry papers could focus on students' views of themselves in relation to the discipline—their views of themselves as mathematicians, scientists, historians, writers, and so on. In some disciplines, entries besides papers (e.g., photographs or videotapes) may also be profitably used.

When the target experience being assessed is a multi-year experience, advisors may take on a key role in assisting students with the development and examination of their portfolios (Funk & Bradley, 1994).

> *Students in the English Education Program at Fredonia, for example, meet periodically with their academic advisors to review their portfolios, reflect on*

*their own learning and changes in attitudes they are experiencing, and to
consider areas in which they need to improve before they begin their student
teaching (Courts & McInerney, 1993, p. 88).*

This changes the advising process from one of selecting courses and meeting
requirements to one of promoting and developing student learning.

The College of Agriculture at the University of Minnesota has developed
an advising portfolio for students and advisors to use in assessing student
achievement of 14 learner outcomes (Hayes, 1995). Early in their undergraduate career, students and advisors review the 14 learner outcomes and develop plans about how students will achieve them through course and
extracurricular experiences. Discussion of the plans and of students' progress
in implementing them continues throughout the four years, and the portfolio
is used to track students' experiences. During the senior year, students compile work or product samples for the portfolio as evidence of their achievements, and these become a helpful resource when they are interviewing for
jobs.

Several institutions use portfolios to assess their general education programs. Forrest (1990) suggests that the portfolio process will improve general
education programs to the extent that it "(1) provides realistic and convincing
evidence of student learning; (2) generates useful clues about how student
learning is occurring; and (3) involves a wide range of students, faculty, and
administrators in frequent, meaningful feedback" (p. 18). When developing a
portfolio program, we must first be clear about what our general education
program consists of (general education courses only, general education
courses plus selected out-of-class activities, or all elements of the college
experience), and we must agree on its goals, purposes, and intended outcomes
(Forrest, 1990). Decisions will have to be made about the type of portfolio (all-
inclusive or selection), the students who will participate (all or a sample), and
how and by whom the folders will be developed and maintained.

Forrest (1990) suggests starting the process with a small number of students and allowing aspects of the assessment program to emerge as we develop experience with the process. The initial emphasis should be on pieces
of work completed in general education courses (e.g., papers, presentations,
lab reports, essay and multiple-choice tests), as well as on students' written
self-evaluations of their progress toward reaching the goals of the general education program. However, as the portfolio process develops, "the kinds of
student work, the amount of work collected, and the timing of that collection
will change as purposes change" (p. 10). For example, as the program becomes more sophisticated, examples of out-of-class achievements (e.g., audio
tapes of interviews) may be included.

We should be careful to maintain a focus on using results to *improve*
teaching and learning, a focus that was emphasized as a principle of good

practice in assessment in Chapter 3. "At the heart of portfolio-assisted assessment for program evaluation are the faculty. It is they who must make the connections among goals, evidence, and program improvement" (Forrest, 1990, pp. 10–11).

We may find it helpful to elicit the assistance of individuals outside the university in judging the adequacy of student work (Forrest, 1990). Faculty from other campuses could be brought in as external examiners to review portfolios and give advice on the assessment process. Employers, legislators, or members of governing boards could also be asked to participate, providing us with increased understanding of the expectations of these important constituencies.

Another approach to assessing general education using portfolios is that at Stephens College (Wehlburg, 1998). At Stephens, the focus is on the general education program as a whole rather than on specific courses, and the portfolio is compiled by students in their senior year. Beginning in their freshman year, students save all their college work. As they approach their senior year, they begin the process of selecting work or descriptions of work that meet portfolio component guidelines. Guidelines are derived from the institution's mission statement.

A. Two works which show growth as a critical thinker (one work done early and one done later on)
B. A work that shows interdisciplinary thinking
C. A work that shows your knowledge of cross-cultural issues related to scholarship by and about women
D. A work that shows your knowledge of cross-cultural issues related to scholarship by ethnic minorities
E. A work that shows your skills in using the scientific method or science reasoning
F. A work that shows your skills in an aesthetic analysis
G. A work that you consider one of the most personally satisfying results of your experiences at Stephens College (this could be work from a class, an account of an experience, a work from a co-curricular activity, etc.)
H. The Writing Assessment Portfolio begun during your freshman year, and
I. A cover letter which describes the method that you used to put your portfolio together and what you learned through this process and the educational process at Stephens College (Wehlburg, 1998, p. 1).

Promoting and Supporting Learning Directly

Using portfolios for program assessment is an important strategy to use in learner-centered programs, but there is an even more important use for portfolios: to promote both student learning and student ownership of learning.

When we use portfolios for this purpose, student reflection and judgment about portfolio contents is central.

This is because, as discussed in Chapter 7, one characteristic of many effective learners is an awareness of themselves as learners. Their awareness is more than simply admitting to themselves and others that they have more to learn. It includes the ability to reflect on the intellectual processes they use in learning, an ability that results in an awareness of *how* they learn. Termed "metacognition," this ability

> *suggests a meta-level of consciousness of one's own thought processes. As such, it involves an almost simultaneous, conscious degree of self-awareness. "This is how I approach or think about a situation (problem, issue, concept)"; "this is how I might best approach this particular concept in order to more fully understand it"; "this is how I am thinking about this issue and it is or is not effective"; "these are other possible approaches I might take instead" (Courts & McInerney, 1993, p. 57).*

Metacognition implies that the learner has knowledge of the private intellectual approaches and strategies that he or she employs in learning, as well as some awareness of how other learners' approaches may differ. These perspectives allow students to critique and evaluate their own effectiveness as learners, providing feedback to themselves to guide improvement. When we use portfolios and invite students to engage in self-evaluation, the process helps develop students' metacognition.

In addition, interaction with others supports both learning and metacognition, and using portfolios effectively depends upon and fosters interaction between students and professors. Through portfolios, learners share with us and with their peers their understanding or skill, as well as their ideas about how they learn. In the process, they receive reactions and feedback that change the way they think and behave.

Along the way, professors also learn and grow. We develop a deeper understanding of the nature of our disciplines and of how our students learn. As learners ourselves, we are driven to construct new knowledge, to create meaning from our experiences as teachers.

This process of mutual learning flows more smoothly when we and our students share a common view of ourselves as active learners and when we view our respective roles in compatible ways. Baxter Magolda (1992) found that college students who viewed their role in learning as passively receiving certain and true information from the professor claimed to learn better when professors taught using a traditional lecture approach. Those who viewed knowledge as less certain and who felt that they had an active role to play in developing new understanding, or perhaps in learning independently, claimed to learn more when professors engaged students in active learning.

The implication is that, when we shift paradigms and move from teacher-centered to student-centered strategies and approaches, we must help our students shift paradigms as well. Students who expect us to lecture and impart information may not view other strategies as "real teaching." They may question or invest minimal energy in small or large group discussions or in applications like case analyses or experiments because they view these activities as fillers that take up time until real teaching begins. They may find the self-evaluation process to be "foreign and demanding" (MacGregor, 1993a, p. 63) because reflecting about their learning may challenge their beliefs about knowing and knowledge.

Paradoxically, however, the portfolio process itself may provide the support students need to develop a new paradigm about learning and to become reflective thinkers (see Chapter 2). Developing a portfolio not only involves students actively in their learning, it also provides for mutual discussion between student and teacher about the learning process itself.

Cambridge (1996) suggests that such discussion is enhanced when faculty develop course portfolios to document their own learning in a course and then share the portfolio with students. Course portfolios might contain information illustrating how the course fits within an institution and program (e.g., institutional and department or academic program missions and goals; professor-prepared course materials and descriptions of pedagogy with the professor's rationale), as well as evidence of student learning, the professor's reflections and self-assessments, and perhaps the reactions of peers in the discipline. Through the sharing of student and professor portfolios, we and our students can examine our joint views about the process of learning as it unfolds (Jons, 1996; Zidon, 1996). In this way, the assessment portfolio helps students shift paradigms and learn more effectively.

Courts and McInerney (1993) point out that "the possible uses of portfolios are, to some extent, determined by the time period over which they are created" (p. 86). When we use portfolios within semester courses, it may be difficult to experience the full benefits of portfolio use because we and our students are simultaneously involved in the process of creating the portfolios and reflecting upon the meaning of the work within them. A semester may simply not be long enough for us to benefit fully from the process.

When we use portfolios over a two- to four-year period, however, both we and our students can examine students' work and progress as they develop over many college experiences and over a significant period of time. In order for the use of portfolios to become established at the program level, however, it must undoubtedly occur in courses as well.

Since the longest journey obviously does begin with the first step, from a purely practical view, it is essential that individual teachers begin the portfolio process in their individual courses. Ultimately, however, the most important aspects of this particular journey will only occur insofar as the portfolios are required across many courses and over several years, providing a map of the journey that teachers and learners might reflect on and analyze as they move forward through the learning process (Courts & McInerney, 1993, p. 86).

The topic of changing the assessment culture on campus is discussed at greater length in Chapter 9.

Reflections

As you create your own meaning from the ideas in this section, begin to think about . . .

- Which institutional example of using portfolios to evaluate learning outcomes appeals to me the most? Why?
- How could I use portfolios *to promote student learning and student ownership of learning* in my courses?

- How do I help my students in their efforts to "make sense" of my courses? What types of interactions are most effective in this regard?
- How and when do I discuss metacognitive knowledge with my students?
- How many of my students share my view of the role of the teacher and the role of the student in learning?

USING SELECTION PORTFOLIOS TO PROMOTE AND SUPPORT LEARNING

Although we can use portfolios to address many different educational goals (Figure 8–1), effective use of selection portfolios to promote and support learning includes three stages:

- student involvement in the selection of entries,
- student preparation of written reflections about learning, and
- discussion of student reflections and the reflections of others (e.g., a professor, an advisor, or other significant persons in a student's life, such as peers, a mentor, or an employer).

All participants in the process may be referred to as "stakeholders," individuals who are interested and/or involved in the student's learning. Paulson and Paulson (1991) consider the student who assembles and therefore owns the portfolio to be the primary stakeholder in portfolio assessment. All other individuals are secondary stakeholders.

Student Selection of Entries

The first stage of reflection about learning begins when students review their work and select pieces that will be entered in their portfolios, according to the guidelines that have been developed. This is a highly personal process, one that provides students with the opportunity to make judgments and choices. It is a process that focuses on what is unique about each student (Diez & Moon, 1992), and it fosters the development of student ownership of their own learning (Shulman, Luechauer, & Shulman, 1996).

> . . . It has been our experience to find that when students see the contents of a portfolio to be directly tied to their own learning and growth, when the portfolios function as an important part of their discussions with their teachers and advisors, students take them very seriously (Courts & McInerney, 1993, p. 77).

At Winona State University, students develop their electronic portfolios by spending considerable time documenting the skills and knowledge they have achieved that will be useful in their chosen careers (Pack, 1998). They then select materials from courses, extra- or co-curricular activities, and work experiences to document their achievements.

Different departments use different approaches to help students prepare their electronic portfolios (Pack, 1998). Some use an informal process in which students are coached individually or in pairs by a faculty member. They learn what to include, how to structure their portfolio, and what type of documentation they will need. Other departments offer credit courses at the beginning and end of students' programs in which they first learn to organize their portfolios and then later create them. Still other departments focus on portfolio development in a capstone course.

> "Students who decide to use this powerful tool report that they are more aware of the knowledge and skills gained from their education than they were before creating the portfolio. They can better connect what they have learned from different courses and departments" (Pack, 1998, p. 26).

Student Reflection About Learning

Student reflection about learning continues into the second stage when students prepare written reflections or assessments of their progress. Although people typically think of writing as a tool to *document or record* what they think, feel, and know, experts in the field of writing tell us that writing is actually a tool that helps us to *develop* our thoughts, feelings, and knowledge (Britton, 1982; Russell, 1991). Writing is a useful and powerful strategy for shaping our learning and helping us reflect on it.

Figure 8–2 describes an assignment from the University of Washington in which a culminating reflective essay is prepared for an interdisciplinary course in writing and geography (MacGregor, 1993b). The assignment requires that students review all the work they have produced during the course, select representative pieces, and write a reflective essay explaining how they understand themselves in the context of the course and how the selected work reveals their understanding. In the directions, the professor encourages students to reflect upon themselves as learners, as writers, and as students of geography. She challenges them to look deeply and analytically into the meaning of the work they have produced. She informs them that their work will be judged not only on their knowledge of geography concepts and conventions, but also on the depth of the metacognitive and procedural knowledge they reveal. Through this assignment, the professor promotes as well as evaluates student learning.

The Challenges of Involving Students in Reflection

When we initiate the process of student self-evaluation, we may experience several challenges (MacGregor, 1993a). Students who view their role as passively receiving knowledge may be unfamiliar with the process of "looking inward at learning" (p. 36), and they may lack confidence in doing so. They may resist participating, and their reflections may seem vague and superficial, focusing more on the teacher and the course than on their own learning.

Honest self-evaluation in which students identify their weaknesses as well as strengths may also seem risky to students who feel that they will be penalized (Eaton & Pougiales, 1993). As will be discussed in a subsequent section, it is important that we avoid evaluating students' reflections and self-evaluations on their content. Rather, we should focus instead on the depth of insight and self-knowledge that students reveal. Figure 8–3 presents a rubric used at Alverno College to assist students in developing their ability to assess their own work. The rubric describes beginning, intermediate, and advanced levels of self-assessment in relation to four criteria: observing, interpreting/analyzing, judging, and planning. By using this type of rubric, we can help students track their progress in metacognition over time.

Assignment for the final essay to accompany the writing portfolio assignment, used in the Interdisciplinary Writing Program at the University of Washington

Planning Your Portfolio. Toward the end of the quarter you will create a portfolio of your work to represent you as a writer participating in the discipline of geography. *Everything* you write this quarter is eligible for inclusion in your portfolio. This includes the three major essays, journal entries, peer reviews, other in-class or overnight writing assignments, and additional journal entries you generate from your own questions and reflections on writing and/or concepts and issues in development geography.

Because the portfolio is intended to be consciously and carefully selective, you should choose from six to twelve pieces of your writing. You can include more, but be sure you can explain why more pieces need to be included and why other pieces don't represent you in the way these additional pieces do.

Then write a reflective essay which creates your portfolio by integrating the pieces in the collection into a whole. Explain what the collection as a whole means to you and how this portfolio reflects you as a writer. *You* are the subject of this essay: Give attention to yourself as a writer in general and to writing geography in particular. Discuss how you think your writing and thinking skills are related and how they may have developed or changed over the course of the quarter. Use your own writing as evidence for the arguments you want to make; discuss the meaning and value of each piece of writing selected and the relation of the pieces to one another.

Because this essay creates and explains your portfolio, it tells me how to read and evaluate your portfolio. So what you tell me the portfolio means and how seriously you take it will directly guide my evaluation and grading. (This is not the place for b.s., arguments you don't believe, or flattery.) In reviewing your portfolio I will look for the following:

- Consideration of how thinking, writing, and reading are related for you
- Evidence of critical analysis, both of your writing, that of others, and of geographic concepts
- A consideration of how disciplinary conventions shape writing in geography, hence thinking in geography
- Evidence of initiative and authority in your writing and your role as a participant in the discourse of development geography
- A consideration of how your writing has changed, including your understanding of your writing process, your particular style, problems, and successful strategies

---

(MacGregor, 1993b, p. 102)

FIGURE 8–2　**Sample Student Reflection Assignment**

Framework for Development of Self-Assessment
Alverno College Council for Student Assessment

Components	Levels		
	Beginning	Intermediate	Advanced
Observing	• Reports own behavior (actions, thoughts and feelings) in performance and/or in the process of producing a performance in relation to abilities	• Begins to apply disciplinary and/or ability frameworks to own performance • Communicates observations using disciplinary and/or ability language. • Stands back at critical points to reflect on performance	• Applies disciplinary, interdisciplinary, and/or ability frameworks to the observations of a performance • Maintains balance between professional distance and personal engagement
Interpreting/ Analyzing	• Identifies patterns of strengths and weaknesses in behavior • Organizes details in relation to an identified focus • Articulates relationships between peer and instructor feedback and self assessment • Articulates impact of emotions on her ability to plan for a performance and to perform	• Explains the significance of patterns of strengths and weaknesses • Makes sense out of own performance in relation to frameworks • Uses peer and other assessor feedback to develop a larger picture of performance	• Explains components of performance that make it unique and distinctive, and are part of a student's style or voice • Uses frameworks in a way that reflects, extends or recreates them • Synthesizes patterns of behaviors and processes over time and in varied contexts
Judging	• Makes connections between criteria and performances	• Makes sense of the set of criteria as a whole in relation to own judgment of the performance	• Uses criteria and knowledge of the integration of her actions, thoughts and feelings to self-monitor and to adjust ongoing actions or plans accordingly • Shows where intervention or modification has or should have taken place

Planning	• Identifies aspects to maintain for performance and/ or the process of producing a performance • Identifies aspects to develop further and suggests approaches for performance and/or the process of producing a performance	• Relates goals for improvement to progress thus far and to possibilities for future development • Uses peer and other assessor feedback in planning for future performances • Uses awareness of her emotional responses to plan for continuing development	• Uses multiple models of performance to set and continue to refine goals for future ongoing development

(Alverno College Faculty, *Self Assessment at Alverno College,* Alverno College Institute, 1999)

FIGURE 8–3   Self-Assessment Rubric

In order to be effective in this role, we must be willing to accept students where they are and adopt the role of coach or facilitator, guiding students to become more sophisticated learners and knowers (Chapter 2). Our feet must be firmly planted in the learner-centered paradigm in which we view students as partners in learning. Without this, the process will falter.

To illustrate, one of us knows a teacher who makes students change their self-assessments when students' opinions do not agree with his own. Although this teacher is using a learner-centered method—self-assessment—his need to be the chief information giver, to establish a "right answer," and to have the final word in evaluation reveals that his beliefs about teaching align more with the traditional paradigm than the learner-centered paradigm. Students experience few benefits from reflecting on their learning in such an environment.

According to MacGregor (1993a), students' ability to reflect upon and write about their learning may also be limited by their writing ability and by the lack of a framework to judge their learning. Furthermore, as students become more aware of the impact their educational experiences have had on them, they may experience strong emotional reactions and become confused about the appropriateness of disclosing them in an academic setting. Therefore, our assignments should

set boundaries for students as to what is appropriate. We need to make clear to students that we respect their privacy: Self-evaluation about learning in class should not be self-revelation in general. But we cannot predict the

meanings our students will make of the course material or the emotional up-
heavals that are bound to occur in their lives (p. 43).

Despite these difficulties, most students become proficient in self-reflection over time, particularly if writing about their learning is integrated throughout the course (MacGregor, 1993a). Initially, we can ask students to write brief reactions at the end of each class (see Chapter 5), and over time, they will develop their "observational power, writing fluency, and familiarity with the process" (MacGregor, 1993a, p. 45). This will prepare them for developing a portfolio in which, through writing, they become actively involved in developing and questioning their knowledge. This role of writing—writing to learn—is a key component of using portfolios to foster metacognition in students. As students write about their learning, they grow in understanding of what they value personally and professionally, what their work represents to them, what they have achieved, and how they have changed.

Characteristic Qualities of Student Reflections
Kusnic and Finley (1993) discuss six qualities that typically emerge in students' self-evaluations. The first is an *attitude of inquiry*. The authors point out that, when students become actively involved with course material, their critical thinking increases as they begin to more fully understand the assumptions and implications of the material they have studied.

A second theme that emerges from students' self-evaluations is *integration of learning*. They "begin to integrate what they have learned with learning from other courses, with their previous understanding of a topic, or with their own experience" (p. 10). Synthesizing their knowledge may lead to greater understanding of new material or it may promote unrest if new perspectives clash with those they have previously held. "The act of writing frequently helps to sort out the issues and to further this process of integration" (p. 10).

Meaning and relevance describe the third quality observed in students' reflections. As students begin to integrate what they have learned, their awareness of how it relates to other aspects of their lives increases. They begin to see applications of new learning or they may use it to explain previous experiences they have had. "Ideas take on meaning; meaning creates a sense of relevance; relevance creates the motivation to apply the ideas in one's life" (p. 10).

As students write about the meaning of learning, they begin to assume authority for what they know, and their writing takes on the fourth quality Kusnic and Finley (1993) have observed—*voice and authority*. The fact that their reflections have been asked for and that there are audiences with whom they discuss them validates students' right to speak and have a voice and gives them greater authority for their knowledge and opinions.

Assuming greater authority for what they know leads students to increased *self-directedness*. Their self-evaluations bring questions to light that they wish to pursue and explore. They become more aware of themselves as learners and of how to become better learners.

The final theme that typically emerges in students' self-evaluations is *learning as a transaction between self and world*. "When students claim authority over the content, process, and direction of their education, they begin to connect more actively with the world outside themselves" (Kusnic & Finley, 1993, p. 11). Their explorations lead to greater understanding of how external influences affect their own thoughts and feelings, and they begin to see themselves as individuals who can take effective action.

The Challenge of Responding to Student Reflections

By including student reflections as part of the assessment process, the learner-centered professor acknowledges that the learner is a whole person, a thinking and feeling person. When discipline-related learning takes place, it is in the context of a developing life in which thoughts, feelings, and actions are interrelated.

Becoming engaged with the emotional aspect of students' learning may initially be uncomfortable for some of us. However, it is a necessary component of the relationships that must develop between us and our students if using portfolios in assessment is to be successful. As Eaton and Pougiales (1993) report, "One faculty member confessed, 'I was unprepared for the self-disclosure I got in so many of my students' papers. I had to decide how to reassure, refer, or confront in my office—not on their papers'" (p. 60).

It may be helpful to repeat here a powerful statement that was quoted in Chapter 2. According to King and Kitchener (1994),

> When certain topics or educational strategies are emotionally challenging for particular students, this situation should be acknowledged. For example, learning about atrocities conducted in a war in which a student's own relatives fought may make her wonder if her grandfather had been involved in such reprehensible conduct; studying about campus violence has made some men wonder if they have committed a rape . . . . To expect students to write detached, objective analyses of situations for which they have unresolved or emerging personal issues is to deny that students are multifaceted individuals, not just "talking heads," and that emotionally powerful questions may serve as barriers to reflective thinking on particular issues (p. 246).

This quotation points out that, as students develop and change the way they think and reason, they may experience frustration, disturbance, and even fear (King & Kitchener, 1994). In these circumstances, we need to be available and show support by acknowledging frustrations, encouraging students to take risks and showing confidence in their abilities, allowing students to make mistakes without penalties, and recognizing their efforts (King & Kitchener, 1994). These types of behaviors are critical because using portfolios depends upon mutuality in discussions of student learning and development.

Discussion of Student Reflections and the Reflections of Others

This point leads to the third and final stage of reflection about learning: using portfolios as the basis of conversations about student learning. When portfolios are used in assessment, students, their professors or advisors, and perhaps other stakeholders *talk* about portfolio entries. In other words, stakeholders,

> *do not operate in isolation. They talk about what has been learned and why it is important. This communication among stakeholders is a most powerful contribution. It is the link between isolated activities in the classroom and the overall goals for an educational program (Paulson & Paulson, 1991, p. 3).*

Stakeholders discuss why the student chose specific entries, what they indicate, and what they mean in the context of a course, an academic program, or the student's life. They provide genuine feedback to help the student grow and develop as a learner. As Eaton and Pougiales (1993) emphasize, this requires "concentration and commitment" (p. 60). We must avoid generalities and simplistic affirmations. In order to improve, students need specific feedback that gives them direction for improvement.

Conversations in which we discuss what students are learning are highly personalized, and they can promote learning only in an atmosphere in which students feel comfortable and not threatened. For respect and trust to develop between us and our students, we must interact with students as equal partners in learning and "drive out fear" (Deming, 1986).

This may be more difficult than we anticipate. Radnor (1994) investigated the ability of arts education teachers in Great Britain to engage in innovative, creative assessment conversations with students. Teacher participants in the study were volunteers who were trained to open up "generously and imaginatively to the work of the pupil and the pupil's response to it" (p. 157). Results showed that, even after training, teachers were unable to participate in conversations with the desired creativity, openness, and spontaneity. Their behavior, and that of their students, was restricted by their underlying view of the teacher as expert and sole evaluator. Valid knowledge was considered to be that transmitted by the teacher to the student, allowing little room for meaningful student participation.

Reflections

As you create your own meaning from the ideas in this section, begin to think about . . .

- If I used the selection portfolio in my courses, what process would I develop for student selection of entries?
- How would I incorporate written reflections into the portfolio process?

- When and with whom would portfolio discussions take place?
- How would it change my courses to include the use of selection portfolios to promote student learning and student ownership of learning?
- How would students react to the idea of a selection portfolio?

PROMOTING LEARNING WITH PORTFOLIOS: PROFESSORS AND STUDENTS IN PARTNERSHIP

In many ways, using portfolios in assessment is an opportunity for collaboration between us and our students. First, the issue of intended learning outcomes must be addressed. Although a professor may have introduced portfolios into his or her course in order to address certain intended outcomes, conferring with students individually about their portfolios may bring to light some additional learning outcomes that the students themselves wish to pursue.

For example, a professor's intended outcome in using portfolios may be to enhance students' metacognitive knowledge. Discussing this with a particular student may lead to the revelation that preparing entries for the portfolio is intimidating to the student who perceives a need to improve in the area of writing. This may lead to the agreement that both metacognition and writing will be addressed when this student develops a portfolio.

Second, we can also collaborate with our students in deciding what evidence will be included in the portfolio. Typically the student will be the primary person developing and selecting the actual entries in the portfolio after coming to an agreement with the professor about what should be included in it. However, if we identify a piece of the student's work that seems relevant to the intended outcome of the assessment, we may wish to enter that in the portfolio as well.

Third, we should meet periodically with our students to review and discuss the work in the portfolio, and we may also wish to include other individuals in these discussions. We and our students together should decide on appropriate stakeholders to involve. For example, we might invite other faculty with particular expertise or staff members from support units on campus (e.g., Student Affairs, the library, etc.) whose knowledge and experience are relevant to the focus of the portfolio. Students may identify individuals whom they know and whose opinion they admire and respect—advisors, friends, employers, or family members.

Students may also wish to meet in small groups of peers to share and critique each others' portfolios (Courts & McInerney, 1993). Peer review helps students gain insight into the different ways in which students respond to course activities. In any of the various discussions that may take place about the portfolios, all participants—including the students themselves—will be involved in reviewing and judging student work. In this way, students will come to better understand their achievements and their progress as learners.

The rubrics discussed in Chapter 6 can also play an important role in portfolio use. Wolf (1992) emphasizes the importance of having public criteria and standards for high quality work when portfolios are used. He says that portfolio work

> *takes place in a* portfolio culture, *that is, a setting in which there is frequent, public discussion about what makes for good work and a clear sense that good work takes a long time to emerge. Students have access to the criteria that will be used to score their work, and those criteria are explained, even debated. Students also have access to samples of work that have been scored and commented on. The point is to provide students with a clear sense of the multidimensional nature of good work; that it involves much more than, for example, neatness, length, or correct grammar. They learn something about the value of qualities like the ability to pose an interesting problem, to learn from and comment on someone else's work, or to revise an earlier draft (p. 6).*

As students develop their work in a portfolio, rubrics describing excellent work should be referred to regularly for guidance. As mentioned in the previous section, rubrics reflecting progress in metacognition can also be helpful (see Figure 8–3). Rubrics should be an important basis of discussion between professor and student or among peers who are reviewing a portfolio. And finally, when other stakeholders are involved in reviewing a portfolio, they can share their perspectives not only about the student's achievements, but also about the criteria that have been developed by the professor (and perhaps the student) for judging achievement.

Reflections

As you create your own meaning from the ideas in this section, begin to think about . . .

- How open am I to using an assessment approach in which students help decide on the goals to be pursued and types of evidence to be gathered?
- How would I prepare for a discussion with a student about his or her portfolio? What would I do to make the conversation a mutual dialogue?
- How would my students react to the opportunity to review and judge each others' work?
- What would I need to do to make the process of peer review positive and constructive?

PROMOTING LEARNING WITH PORTFOLIOS: PROFESSORS AND OTHER STAKEHOLDERS IN PARTNERSHIP

As discussed in Chapter 2, in learner-centered teaching, we acknowledge that we too are learners. We dialogue with students rather than talk at them, and we are open to students' opinions about how to improve courses and programs. We support student ownership of learning, and we show respect for learners' efforts and achievements. Because discussion of portfolio entries is a central part of using portfolios in assessment, the success of the portfolio process depends upon our ability to make the transition to these new roles. In order for students to develop in understanding their own learning and reach new stages of intellectual maturity, true mutuality between us and our students must exist.

As mentioned in the previous section, when we converse with students about their learning, we may also wish to invite other individuals or "stakeholders" to participate. For example, at Rappahannock Community College, a Citizen's Advisory Committee reviews the portfolios of business technology students to assess the professional quality of their work (Smith & Crowther, 1996). Members of the committee prepare comments that are later shared with students.

The participation of other stakeholders intensifies the personal nature of learning, and it also builds on the fact that much knowledge is socially constructed. When we invite others to review and judge student work, it helps change our role from "expert" to "partner." Students benefit from the increased perspectives that are brought to the discussion. Through sharing and debating their ideas with others, students clarify, modify, and more deeply develop their understanding.

One issue that arises when many people review and critique a student's work is that of reliability. As discussed in Chapter 7, in traditional approaches to measurement, it is considered essential that consistency among judges be observed. Some degree of consistency or consensus is desirable if an important decision will be made based on the portfolio. For example, if graduation or entry into a major depends upon the quality of work in the portfolio, it would be wise to develop rubrics and train reviewers to use them so that all are using the same criteria and standards in judging students' work.

However, when the portfolio is used to promote learning through developing a deeper understanding of how and what students are learning, it may not be as important to be sure that all stakeholders are viewing the work from the same perspective. Stakeholders may have different opinions about the merits of the student's work, and their multiple perspectives may actually enhance the process.

Paulson and Paulson (1991) illustrate this point by referring to the televised movie reviews of Gene Siskel and Roger Ebert. When Siskel and Ebert worked together, they selected a popular movie and both reviewers rated and discussed it at the same time. Paulson and Paulson point out that the most interesting aspect of their reviews was their disagreements. Rather than assume that their different views must be resolved and that consensus must be reached, Siskel and Ebert spent their discussion time clarifying the reasons for their differences.

> Siskel and Ebert may disagree for several reasons. Occasionally their disagreements reveal different interpretations of the same criteria. For example, one criterion both use is empathy; do they care about the characters in a film. Disagreement does not signal the need for resolution. Rather, it provides information on how events can be viewed from multiple perspectives leading to differences in interpretation. They may attend to different information or weigh the same information differently. This suggests that when raters disagree on how to "score" something found in a student's portfolio, it may be more valuable to provide the student with a discussion of how and why the judges disagreed than to promote the illusion of a "united front" represented by a resolved score.

> Occasionally, Siskel and Ebert disagree because they use different criteria, a possibility related to the stakeholder dimension of portfolio assessment. In portfolio assessment, students gain a valuable opportunity to learn from examining the criteria held by different stakeholders and by developing ways to accommodate to those divergent values and priorities. One student, struggling with this issue, wrote in his portfolio, "I'm doing o.k. is what most people seem to think, but my mom says I'm doing it wrong. I don't know what to think." . . . This student's problem stems from the fact that the world out-

side the classroom applies different criteria from the world inside the classroom. Rather than working to develop common criteria to apply inside the classroom, our efforts might better be directed at helping students find ways to accommodate to the multiple criteria our pluralistic society routinely applies outside the classroom (pp. 5–6).

Thus, developing a portfolio not only helps students better understand themselves and their approach to learning, it can also help them view their achievements from the broader framework of the world outside the institution. It helps them draw their own conclusions based on feedback from a variety of perspectives.

Implied in this discussion is the fact that the processes of creating the portfolio and reflecting upon it are the most critical elements of using portfolios in assessment, not the products found inside the portfolio. Therefore, portfolios have a fundamentally different purpose from other assessments. They are used primarily to help students develop their metacognition and take ownership of their own learning. Although portfolios can be graded (discussed below), the chief purpose is not to rank order students from high to low in terms of their achievement. Rather, whether it is used at the institutional, academic program, course, or individual student level, "a portfolio communicates what is learned and why it is important" (Paulson & Paulson, 1991, p. 1).

Reflections

As you create your own meaning from the ideas in this section, begin to think about . . .

- What are my reactions to the idea of using portfolios in assessment to develop a relationship of greater mutuality with my students?

- How open am I to including other stakeholders in discussions of student learning in my courses?
- How would I go about including other stakeholders?

BENEFITS TO PROFESSORS OF USING PORTFOLIOS

Figure 8–4 presents several benefits that we may experience from using portfolios. One benefit is that the use of portfolios establishes faculty as the primary evaluators of our courses and programs, allowing us to retain control of our programs during a time when external accountability requirements may appear to threaten our autonomy. When portfolios are used for program

Through the use of portfolios in assessment, professors

- take ownership of the evaluation of their program
- learn how much and what type of work is required in a program
- gain direction for the improvement of instruction and curricular planning
- establish mutual relationships with individual students
- become more aware of individual students' strengths, weaknesses, and needs
- engage in substantive discussions with students that promote learning
- become more aware of the attitudes and values in changing student populations
- experience increased collegiality within and across disciplines
- become aware of research opportunities related to teaching and learning
- may experience increased institutional support for teaching

FIGURE 8–4   Benefits to Professors of Using Portfolios

assessment, they provide a rich data base of actual student work that we can review and evaluate for program effectiveness. Reviewing portfolios engages us in meaningful discussion with our colleagues, and perhaps students, about our work as teachers. It makes us more aware of how much and what type of work is required in other courses in our program (Courts & McInerney, 1993), and it leads to the development of improved courses and curricula.

Another benefit of using portfolios is that we are more likely to establish relationships that foster learning with individual students (Myers, 1996). This is because conversations about student learning are an essential element of portfolio use. More than any other form of assessment, the use of portfolios emphasizes and honors the uniqueness of each student, and this is particularly evident when portfolios are used within courses. One goal of using portfolios is to help individual students develop a deeper understanding of how they learn. Although we may have some common overall goals for using portfolios in a course, the goal of each student's portfolio can be tailor-made for that student.

Through our relationships with students, we become more aware of their individual strengths, weaknesses, and needs. We ascertain what *is* being learned, instead of focusing only on what *should be* learned. We learn more about how students think, feel, and learn. Our increased knowledge about student learning leads to insights about how to improve teaching.

Conversations with students about their learning also lead to insights about how to improve curriculum. When we understand how students respond to the curriculum, we learn what's working for them and what is not. For example, we may learn whether courses are sequenced in a way that makes sense to students or in a way that confuses them. We can gain a deeper sense than we otherwise would about whether students are making progress in achieving course, program, and/or institutional learning outcomes.

We also may become more aware of the attitudes and values that characterize our student population at a given point in time, and this awareness may help us develop educational programs that meet students' needs. Since 1966, Alexander Astin and colleagues have documented changes in the beliefs, attitudes, and experiences of college freshmen through the Cooperative Institutional Research Program (CIRP) (Sax, Astin, Korn, & Mahoney, 1998). Although results of the CIRP survey are summarized in the media each year and are sent to the administrative offices of participating institutions, they probably have had little effect on curriculum and instruction at those institutions. Furthermore, many of us may find it difficult to understand why they should.

However, Levine (1980) and Levine and Cureton (1998) suggest that, at any point in time, what we know about the perspectives, dispositions, and needs of the current generation of students should affect the way we develop and deliver curriculum. For example, Levine and Cureton characterize students in the 1990s as a transitional generation, much like the young people at the beginning of the Industrial Revolution, because the world in which they live is undergoing fundamental change.

> *Today, as our society once again is being transformed, it is necessary to develop a new curriculum, an educational program that will prepare our students to live simultaneously in two societies, one dying and the other being born. Our current students are a transitional generation, and they need a curriculum that prepares them to assume the enormous responsibilities of building a new world while living in an old and rapidly changing society* (p. 166).

After gathering data themselves, as well as interpreting a variety of national data bases including Astin's (Sax, et al., 1998), Levine and Cureton (1998) identify twenty characteristics of American college students in the '90s, and they suggest curricular emphases to help them prepare for life in the Information Age. For example, Levine and Cureton perceive these students to be frightened, desiring security, and in need of hope. Their education must help them develop a sense that they can succeed in fields that interest them. Because they have grown up in a time of prosperity, students in the '90s need to develop a commitment to taking responsibility for others. Because they are a diverse and divided group, having a local rather than global perspective, they need a curriculum that helps them appreciate differences. Because they are socially conscious but disenchanted with political and social institutions, they need to develop the sense that they can make a difference in society.

The work of Levine (1980) and Levine and Cureton (1998) provides us with a new perspective on developing curricula and improving our teaching. Perhaps when we experience the attitudes and values of our students first-hand through the use of portfolios, we will better understand the implications they can have for curriculum development and instruction.

Discussions about portfolios also increase collegiality among faculty within and between departments. This is a critically important benefit for us because, at many institutions, factors like the press for increased research and the institution of merit pay have created competition among us. Creating and maintaining a sense of teamwork is essential if the teaching mission of the institution is to be fulfilled effectively.

Using portfolios in assessment may also lead to career development for faculty (Forrest, 1990). We may find that joint or individual research projects on the topics of improving learning and teaching result from our involvement with portfolios. As a result of assessment findings, institutions may devote more resources to faculty development activities in the areas of improving teaching and learning. This will lead to improved faculty performance and satisfaction.

Reflections

As you create your own meaning from the ideas in this section, begin to think about . . .

- Which of the benefits of using portfolios would I value the most?

- Which of the benefits of using portfolios would be most helpful to faculty at my institution?
- Which of the benefits of using portfolios would be most helpful to faculty in my academic program?

BENEFITS TO STUDENTS OF USING PORTFOLIOS

Figure 8–5 lists several benefits to students when portfolios are used in assessment. As previously mentioned, when students participate in the selection, discussion, and evaluation of their work, they begin to develop a view of themselves as learners. They develop a deeper understanding of what they know and don't know. They connect their current learning experiences with those that have occurred in the past, and they begin to develop a sense that learning will continue in an ongoing fashion throughout their lives (Courts & McInerney, 1993). Through reflection and self-evaluation, students become aware of how they learn, and they develop insights into how they can improve their approach to learning (Eaton & Pougiales, 1993).

Students also become more aware of what they value, and they gain a deeper understanding of the role that other individuals or groups (e.g., learn-

Through the use of portfolios in assessment, students

- develop a view of themselves as learners
- understand more deeply what they have learned and not learned
- develop a sense of learning as ongoing through life
- develop a better understanding of how they learn
- develop a better understanding of what they value
- gain feedback for improvement from stakeholders who view their portfolios
- understand how their work is viewed by others
- develop a better understanding of the faculty's intended learning outcomes
- see relationships among courses
- see relationships among in- and out-of-class learning experiences
- become more aware of and invested in their own learning
- become conscious of the role writing plays in learning

FIGURE 8–5   Benefits to Students of Using Portfolios

ing communities) have played in their development. The perspectives of their professors or their peers, as well as those of other possible participants in portfolio review, help students understand what their own work is like and what it means.

As students' knowledge of themselves as learners increases, their learning is likely to improve as well. "Through building a portfolio, students have the opportunity to learn—to learn about a subject, to learn about learning, to learn to make choices and judgments, and to learn about themselves" (Paulson & Paulson, 1991, p. 1).

When developing portfolios, students develop a clearer understanding of the faculty's intended learning outcomes. They may also have an opportunity to step back and look across the many courses they have taken—for patterns, contradictions, confusions, or harmony. They may make connections between experiences they have had in class and those that have taken place outside of class, perhaps not even related to the college experience (Courts & McInerney, 1993).

Through the use of portfolios, students become more invested in their own learning. The process of selecting and judging their own work empowers them to take ownership of their future direction as learners. They become better able to observe their own progress and to use self-generated feedback to improve. Finally, developing a portfolio creates an opportunity for students to become conscious of the role that writing plays in learning (Courts & McInerney, 1993).

Reflections

As you create your own meaning from the ideas in this section, begin to think about . . .

- Which of the benefits discussed in this section do I think would be most valuable for students?

- If my faculty colleagues and I were to use portfolios in assessment, how could we maximize these benefits for students?

---

1. What is the primary purpose in using portfolios in assessment? Is it to evaluate student learning in a program or to promote and support individual student learning directly?
2. What intended learning outcomes will be evaluated?
3. Will an all-inclusive portfolio or a selection portfolio be used?
4. What will the role of faculty be when using portfolios?
5. What will the role of students be in the use of portfolios?
6. What types of portfolio entries are desired?
7. How will logistical questions be resolved?
   - For program assessments, will all students participate or will a sampling process be used?
   - What form will the portfolios take—folder, disk, on-line database, and so forth?
   - Who will compile the portfolios?
   - Who will maintain the portfolios—student, professor, advisor, committee, or others?
   - Are there privacy issues to be addressed?
   - How often will the portfolios be reviewed?
8. Who else will participate in the review, discussion, and evaluation of portfolio contents?
9. If appropriate, how will we disseminate findings from the portfolio evaluation process?

FIGURE 8–6   Questions to Ask When Using Portfolios in Assessment

QUESTIONS TO ASK WHEN PLANNING TO USE PORTFOLIOS IN ASSESSMENT

Figure 8–6 presents several questions to ask when developing a plan for using portfolios in assessment. These questions review the main points of this chapter. When using portfolios, it is important first and foremost to decide what the purpose of using portfolios will be. We can use portfolios either to evaluate student learning in a program or to promote and support student learning directly. In either case, we should link the process to our intended learning outcomes. In the case of evaluating learning, will we evaluate all or some of our outcomes? In the case of promoting and supporting learning, on which outcomes will we focus?

We should also be clear about the roles that faculty and students will play in using portfolios. It is possible to involve both in many different aspects of portfolio use: determining purpose, setting goals, selection of entries, reflection on entries, discussion of entries. For a given portfolio project, roles should be specified in advance.

We will have to resolve several logistical questions including sampling, compiling, maintaining, and so on. The type of entries that are appropriate for the portfolio also must be established. We should determine if anyone besides faculty and students will participate in the process, and in the case of program assessment, we should provide for dissemination of findings to interested parties.

LOOKING AHEAD

This chapter concludes the section of this book devoted to techniques for implementing a learner-centered perspective. In the next and final chapter, we discuss several issues associated with making the shift to a learner-centered paradigm.

TRY SOMETHING NEW

1. Identify any activities you use in your courses to help students reflect on their learning. Then develop one more activity that will extend students' metacognitive understanding beyond their current level. If this is a new area for you, you may wish to start with Angelo and Cross's *Classroom Assessment Techniques*. Select an activity from the book that promotes student reflection and implement it within the next month.
2. Using the questions in Figure 8–6, develop a plan to use portfolios in one of your courses.

3. Bring up the possibility of using portfolios to assess student learning in your program with some of your colleagues. Identify in advance three points about portfolios that you think are relevant to your program and share them in your discussion.

REFERENCES

Alverno College Faculty. (1999). *Self assessment at Alverno College*. Milwaukee, WI: Alverno College Institute.

Baxter Magolda, M. B. (1992). Students' epistemologies and academic experiences: Implications for pedagogy. *The Review of Higher Education, 15* (3), 265–287.

Black, L. (1993). Portfolio assessment. In T. W. Banta, & Associates (Eds.), *Making a difference: Outcomes of a decade of assessment in higher education* (pp. 139–150). San Francisco: Jossey–Bass.

Bolender, R. K. (1996). *The development of a portfolio assessment process for the Bachelor of Business Administration Program.* (ERIC Document Reproduction No. ED 406 914)

Box, J. A., & Dean, C. D. (1996). Professional portfolio process. In T. W. Banta, J. P. Lund, K. E. Black, & F. W. Oblander (Eds.), *Assessment in practice: Putting principles to work on college campuses* (pp. 113–115). San Francisco: Jossey–Bass.

Britton, J. (1982). Writing to learn and learning to write. In G. M. Pradl (Ed.), *Prospect and retrospect: Selected essays of James Britton* (pp. 94–111). Montclair, NJ: Boynton/Cook Publishers.

Cambridge, B. L. (1996). The paradigm shifts: Examining quality of teaching through assessment of student learning. *Innovative Higher Education, 20* (4), 287–297.

Castiglione, L. V. (1996). Portfolio assessment in art and education. *Arts Education Policy Review, 97* (4), 2–9.

Courts, P. L., & McInerney, K. H. (1993). *Assessment in higher education: Politics, pedagogy, and portfolios*. Westport, CT: Praeger.

Deming, W. E. (1986). *Out of the crisis*. Cambridge, MA: Massachusetts Institute of Technology Center for Advanced Engineering Study.

Diez, M. E., & Moon, C. J. (1992). *Will portfolio assessment make a difference?* Unpublished manuscript. Milwaukee, WI: Alverno College.

Ducharmes, E. M., & Ducharmes, M. K. (Eds.). (1996, March–April). Portfolios and reflection in teacher education (Theme issue). *Journal of Teacher Education, 47,* (2).

Eaton, M., & Pougiales, R. (1993). Work, reflection, and community: Conditions that support writing self-evaluations. In J. MacGregor (Ed.), *Student self-evaluation: Fostering reflective learning (Theme Issue). New Directions for Teaching and Learning 56,* 47–63.

Forrest, A. (1990). *Time will tell: Portfolio-assisted assessment of general education*. Washington, DC: American Association of Higher Education.

Freidus, H. (1996, April). *Reflection in teaching: Can it be taught?* Paper presented at the annual meeting of the American Educational Research Association, New York, NY. (ERIC Document Reproduction Service No. ED 397 016)

Funk, G. D., & Bradley, J. (1994). Student portfolios: A comprehensive approach to academic advisement. *NACADA Journal, 14* (1), 46–49.

Hayes, L. S. (1995). Student portfolios for academic and career advising. In J. P. Lunde, M. Baker, F. H. Buelow, & L. S. Hayes (Eds.), *Reshaping curricula*. Boston, MA: Anker.

Horning, A. S. (1997). Reflection and revision: Intimacy in college writing. *Composition Chronicle: Newsletter for Writing Teachers, 9* (9), 4–7.

Johnson, B. (1996). *The performance assessment handbook: Volume 1. Portfolios & Socratic seminars.* Princeton, NJ: Eye on Education.

Jons, C. G. (1996). The portfolio as a course assessment tool. In T. W. Banta, J. P. Lund, K. E. Black, & F. W. Oblander (Eds.), *Assessment in practice: Putting principles to work on college campuses* (pp. 285–288). San Francisco: Jossey–Bass.

Katz, A. M., & Gangon, B. A. (1998a, June). *Assessing your MA program: Suggestions for graduate students in the Department of Communicating Arts emphasizing Speech Communication.* Paper presented at the annual meeting of the AAHE Conference on Assessment & Quality, Cincinnati, OH.

Katz, A. M., & Gangon, B. A. (1998b, June). *Assessing your general education program: Portfolio suggestions for freshmen students at the University of Wisconsin-Superior.* Paper presented at the annual meeting of the AAHE Conference on Assessment & Quality, Cincinnati, OH.

King, P. M., & Kitchener, K. S. (1994). *Developing reflective judgment: Understanding and promoting intellectual growth and critical thinking in adolescents and adults.* San Francisco: Jossey–Bass.

Kusnic, E., & Finley, M. L. (1993). Student self-evaluation: An introduction and rationale. In J. MacGregor (Ed.), *Student self-evaluation: Fostering reflective learning (Theme Issue). New Directions for Teaching and Learning, 56*, 5–14.

Levine, A. (1980). *When dreams and heroes died: A portrait of today's college student.* San Francisco: Jossey–Bass.

Levine, A., & Cureton, J. S. (1998). *When hope and fear collide: A portrait of today's college student.* San Francisco: Jossey–Bass.

Lind, N. S. (1995, September). *Assessment and the political science major: The movement afoot.* Paper presented at the annual meeting of the American Political Science Association, Chicago, IL. (ERIC Document Reproduction Service No. ED 391 728)

MacGregor, J. (1993a). Learning self-evaluation: Challenges for students. In J. MacGregor (Ed.), *Student self-evaluation: Fostering reflective learning (Theme Issue). New Directions for Teaching and Learning, 56*, 35–46.

MacGregor, J. (Ed.). (1993b). *Student self-evaluation: Fostering reflective learning (Theme Issue). New Directions for Teaching and Learning, 56.* San Francisco: Jossey–Bass.

Magruder, W. J., & Young, C. C. (1996). Portfolios: Assessment of liberal arts goals. In T. W. Banta, J. P. Lund, K. E. Black, & F. W. Oblander (Eds.), *Assessment in practice: Putting principles to work on college campuses* (pp. 171–174). San Francisco: Jossey–Bass.

Mincey, K. (1996, March). *The impact of KERA writing portfolios on first-year college writers.* Paper presented at the annual meeting of the Conference on College Composition and Communication, Milwaukee, WI. (ERIC Document Reproduction Service No. ED 403 576)

Myers, C. R. (1996). The portfolio: A crucial link between student and faculty development. In T. W. Banta, J. P. Lund, K. E. Black, & F. W. Oblander (Eds.), *Assessment in practice: Putting principles to work on college campuses* (pp. 308–310). San Francisco: Jossey–Bass.

O'Brien, J. P., Bressler, S. L., Ennis, J. F., & Michael, M. (1996). The Sophomore–Junior Diagnostic Project, Case B: English. In T. W. Banta, J. P. Lund, K. E. Black, & F. W. Oblander (Eds.), *Assessment in practice: Putting principles to work on college campuses* (pp. 93–95). San Francisco: Jossey–Bass.

Olds, B. M., & Miller, R. L. (1997). Portfolio assessment: Measuring moving targets at an engineering school. *NCA Quarterly, 71* (4), 462–467.

Pack, D. H. (1998, May–June). WINGS: The Winona State University electronic portfolio project. *About Campus*, 24–26.

Paulson, F. L., & Paulson, B. R. (1991). *The ins and outs of using portfolios to assess performance.* Expanded version of a paper presented at a symposium conducted by the National Council on Measurement in Education and the National Association of Test Directors, Chicago, IL. (ERIC Document Reproduction Service No. ED 334 250)

Radnor, H. (1994). The problems of facilitating qualitative formative assessment in pupils. *British Journal of Educational Psychology, 64*, 145–160.

Russell, D. R. (1991). *Writing in the academic disciplines, 1870–1990: A curricular history.* Carbondale: Southern Illinois University Press.

Sax, L. J., Astin, A. W., Korn, W. S., & Mahoney, K. M. (1998). *The American freshman: National norms for Fall 1998.* Los Angeles: Higher Education Research Institute, UCLA.

Shulman, G. M., Luechauer, D. L., & Shulman, C. (1996). Assessment for learner empowerment: The metacognitive map. In T. W. Banta, J. P. Lund, K. E. Black, & F. W. Oblander (Eds.), *Assessment in practice: Putting principles to work on college campuses* (pp. 281–285). San Francisco: Jossey–Bass.

Slater, T. F., and others. (1995, April). *A qualitative and quantitative comparison of the impact of portfolio assessment procedures versus traditional assessment in a college physics course.* Paper presented at the annual meeting of the National Association for Research in Science Teaching, San Francisco, CA. (ERIC Document Reproduction Service No. ED 391 835)

Slater, T. F. (1996). Portfolio assessment strategies for grading first-year university physics students in the USA. *Physics Education, 31* (5), 329–333.

Smith, L. S., & Crowther, E. H. (1996) Portfolios: Useful tools for assessment in Business Technology. In T. W. Banta, J. P. Lund, K. E. Black, & F. W. Oblander (Eds.), *Assessment in practice: Putting principles to work on college campuses* (pp. 115–117). San Francisco: Jossey–Bass.

Wehlburg, C. M. (1998, June). *Portfolio assessment of general education: Foundations of learning.* Paper presented at the annual meeting of the AAHE Conference on Assessment & Quality, Cincinnati, OH.

Wolf, D. P. (1992). Assessment as an episode of learning. *Assessment Update, 4* (1), 5–6, 14.

Zidon, M. (1996). Portfolios in preservice teacher education: What the students say. *Action in Teacher Education, 18* (1), 59–70.

9

Shifting the Paradigm: Individual and Organizational Implications

Learning begins with questions we cannot answer; it ends with questions we can (Ackoff, 1993, p. ii.).

At the individual level, shifting to the Learning Paradigm means a new way of thinking. Learning to think in a new way is somewhat like learning a foreign language . . . One has not made the shift to the new Learning Paradigm unless one thinks within it rather than about it. In other words, the paradigm must be put into use. As such it becomes the context for thinking rather than the content. It becomes the generator of thoughts, but it is not that which is thought about.

At the organizational level, the shift . . . involves two related but distinct dimensions or shifts. First, the mission shifts from providing instruction (read, essentially, "lecturing") to producing student learning . . . . A second shift . . . is the shift to operating as a learning organization . . .

This is no ordinary change. This is a transformation . . . . An organization is not transformed unless its fundamental structures and processes are significantly altered (Barr, 1998, p. 19).

Making Connections

As you begin to read the chapter, think about the ideas that have been prompted by reading this book . . .

- How have the suggestions in the book conflicted with your beliefs?
- What are your assumptions about how learners learn?
- What are your assumptions about the best way to teach?
- How do you know if your teaching has been successful?
- How can you help your students improve what they learn and how they learn?

- What should your students be learning that will help them be successful in the information age?
- How do you view your relationship to the rest of your institution?
- What have you learned about assessment in higher education?
- How do assessment results help you understand what your students know and don't know, what they can do and can't do?

What else have you learned from this book?

What questions do you have as you consider implementing the techniques that appeal to you?

We began each chapter in this book with a Making Connections section that encouraged you to ask yourself what you already know about the topic of the chapter and what you would like to know about it. The many Reflections questions provided opportunities to think about the material that was presented, identifying ways in which it is compatible with or challenges your current thinking and practice as a teacher. The Try Something New sections provided concrete suggestions for exploring new ideas and techniques. Each chapter concluded by Looking Ahead to the ideas in the next chapter.

Now it's time to look ahead once more and ask new questions about the future. Robbins (1991) contends that it's not our life events that determine how we feel and act, but rather how we interpret them (the constructivist view once again). "The *meaning* I attach to an event will determine the *decisions* I make, the *actions* I take, and therefore my ultimate *destiny*" (p. 179). Robbins suggests that thinking is a process of asking and answering questions. When our minds ask questions, answers inevitably result. The interpretations we give to our lives result from the questions we ask. Robbins believes that people who are successful ask themselves better questions and therefore get better answers.

> *Businesses succeed when those who make the decisions that control their destiny ask the right questions about markets or strategies or product lines. Relationships flourish when people ask the right questions about where potential conflicts exist and how to support each other instead of tearing each other down . . .*

When the automobile was in its infancy, hundreds of people tinkered with building them, but Henry Ford asked, "How can I mass produce it?" Millions chafed under communism, but Lech Walesa asked, "How can I raise the standard of living for all working men and women?" (pp. 180–181).

As you conclude this book, you might be tempted to ask, "Why do I have to change?" or "Why can't higher education be the way it used to be?" Robbins (1991) calls questions like these disempowering questions because they lead to answers that discourage and depress us, limiting our horizons and our feelings of being able to make a difference.

On the other hand, we could ask empowering questions like the following: "What ideas and techniques in this book appeal to me?" "Why are they appealing?" "Which of them can I make my own?" "What one thing could I do differently this semester?" "How could my career change as a result of reading this book?" Empowering questions change our focus and make us aware of what we are capable of doing. When we answer them, we become more aware of resources available to help us change.

If reading this book led you to the conclusion that assessment can be an effective tool in enhancing student learning, you may wish to ask additional questions: "How will I have to change in order to implement the assessment techniques in this book?" "What is involved in making a paradigm shift?" "Is it enough for faculty members to reform their teaching individually or must the entire campus undergo transformation?" "How can the institution facilitate the process of shifting to a new paradigm?" "Am I ready to make a commitment to change?" We conclude this volume with a discussion of these questions.

ISSUES IN MAKING THE PARADIGM SHIFT

What is involved in making a paradigm shift? Kuh (1998) illuminated the difficulties of adopting new paradigms by telling the story of two groups of firefighters, one in Montana in 1949 and one in Colorado in 1994, who lost their lives because they persisted in typical professional behavior when raging forest fires ran out of control. Basically, the firefighters ignored the warning of their leaders and failed to drop their heavy tools and packs, and as a result, they died within sight of safe areas.

Kuh (1998) reviewed several explanations for the firefighters' behavior and pointed out parallels with faculty and staff in higher education who resist the move to a learner-centered approach. The firefighters had difficulty hearing amid the roaring wind and fire of their work setting (our professional lives are increasingly demanding and it's difficult to keep up with current issues in higher education); they were not given good reasons to change their approach and they didn't trust those who told them to change (we often don't trust or listen to administrators or leaders in higher education who alert us to emerging trends and the need for change); they felt that they could actually control the situation by holding onto their tools (we persist in the belief that teaching the way we've always taught will surely make a difference); and the tools defined their professional identity (what will we lose if we become learner-centered?).

> The prospect of not doing the things we know how to do is threatening because changing what we do means changing who we are. What would we do instead? Who would we become? Who are we without our tools? . . . The important point that should not be lost is that all professionals—including wildlands firefighters, dentists, accountants, faculty members, and student affairs staff—are loaded down with assumptions, expectations, customs, routines, and personal preferences that make it difficult to see and do things differently, to entertain alternative interpretations about what is going on around us, and to change what we do (pp. 18–19).

Making a paradigm shift involves a willingness to seek out and examine the assumptions that underlie our current teaching practice. It means taking risks and trying new approaches that are unfamiliar to us, becoming novices again and returning to a period of learning by trial and error. Making a paradigm shift means becoming a learner, asking better questions, and opening ourselves to new opportunities.

Reflections

As you create your own meaning from the ideas in this section, begin to think about . . .

- What "tools" will I have difficulty dropping as I make a paradigm shift?

- How willing am I to develop a new view of teaching and learning?
- How willing am I to ask new questions that will lead to different behaviors?

INDIVIDUAL VS. CAMPUS REFORM

Is it enough for faculty to reform their teaching individually or must the entire campus undergo transformation? It is certainly possible for us to modify our approach to teaching on an individual basis, even if those around us do not; however, we will undoubtedly experience difficulties. First, making the change may well be a somewhat lonely process, and it may create distance between us and our colleagues. Even in institutions in which there is widespread endorsement and support for reform, only some individuals take on the role of change agent and rapidly embrace the new concept (Muncey & McQuillan, 1993). Hutchings (1998) points out that to reform teaching and adopt a continuous improvement perspective in which assessment plays a critical role, "ya gotta wanna" (p. 2). The first step may simply come down to will and resolve, and we may find that many of us simply don't have that resolve, or at least we haven't asked the right questions to get us started (Robbins, 1991).

Second, when individual faculty members take on the challenge of being the lone reformers on their campuses, it may also cause confusion for students. As we have pointed out several times, students develop their own paradigms about teaching and learning during their years of formal schooling. To the extent that their experiences have taken place in a traditional teaching environment, they probably view their role as passive receivers of information. When we shift to a learner-centered paradigm, students must be educated about their new roles (Warren, 1997). Understanding and accepting new roles is more difficult for students if some of their courses are taught within a teacher-centered paradigm having one set of expectations for them, and others take place within a learner-centered paradigm having an entirely different set of expectations and roles.

A third difficulty of becoming lone reformers is that we may find ourselves working harder than we did before or harder than other faculty currently do. As Barr (1998) points out, this will occur not because learner-centered approaches inherently take more time, but rather because we "must work against institutional forces and structures designed to support traditional lecture courses" (p. 22). Barr gives the example of faculty who become involved with learning communities.

> *Learning community faculty find that they must, for example, expend energy "tricking" administrative computer systems that are programmed to schedule only one instructor in a classroom or course at a time. They must engage in extensive marketing because established processes, such as class schedule production and academic advising, are geared to traditional discipline courses. They must convince hesitant and skeptical students that learning community classes will meet graduation and transfer requirements. And finally, learning communities must be justified to the rest of the faculty and to the academic leadership as not costing any more than the traditional discipline classes, even though they demonstrably produce more learning and student satisfaction (pp. 22–23).*

If institutions were structured to encourage and foster a learner-centered approach, the extra work and effort would not be needed.

Barr (1998) argues, and Guskin (Marchese, 1998) agrees, that the institution itself must be transformed if a learner-centered paradigm is to prevail.

An organization is not transformed unless its fundamental structures and processes are significantly altered. This is necessary because organizational structure is the lever for individual and collective efforts and creates the conditions of culture. The correct structural change and corresponding cultural shift increases the organizational leverage applied to members' efforts and hence shifts overall organizational performance to a higher level (p. 19).

Thus, although it is possible for professors to shift paradigms alone, the process works best when the entire institutional culture supports and rewards it. In this type of setting all faculty and staff are potentially focused on changing to a learner-centered approach (Engelkemeyer & Brown, 1998; Kuh, 1998), and structures and processes facilitate the shift. Professors view themselves less as individuals and more as part of an entire system committed to change. A critical mass of individuals actively examining their assumptions and practices can provide mutual support for one another during an otherwise challenging time, as illustrated in the following story.

This is a story about a little wave, bobbing along in the ocean, having a grand old time. He's enjoying the wind and the fresh air—until he notices the other waves in front of him, crashing against the shore.

"This is terrible," the wave says. "Look what's going to happen to me!"

Then along comes another wave. It sees the first wave, looking grim, and it says to him, "Why do you look so sad?"

The first wave says, "You don't understand! We're all going to crash! All of us waves are going to be nothing! Isn't it terrible?"

The second wave says, "No, you don't understand. You're not a wave, you're part of the ocean" (Albom, 1997, pp. 179–180).

When we are able to interpret our lives in terms of partnership and teamwork with others, shifting paradigms may be less threatening. When we perceive institutions as systems with interdependent parts, we begin to see ourselves as part of the ocean rather than as independent waves.

Furthermore, the assessment process will be more widely adopted when an entire campus becomes a "culture of evidence." In this type of environment, decisions about teaching and the curriculum are based at all levels and in all settings on the type of verifiable information that we value as researchers. This means that there is widespread understanding of the basic assessment concept, and the concept is articulated clearly by administrators as well as faculty and staff. Promoting and assessing learning takes place in the administration, in Student Affairs, in the library, as well as in all academic programs.

Barr (1998) suggests that, for the organization to be transformed, several things must occur. The institution must be driven by its mission, and the mission of every institution should be to produce student learning and success. This means that all faculty and staff, individually and collectively, must take responsibility for student learning and their efforts should be judged by how much learning occurs. Assessment thus plays a key role because it becomes the means for judging institutional effectiveness.

Successful implementation of the learner-centered paradigm depends also on changing how colleges are funded—shifting from funding for seat time to funding for student learning, as well as focusing on changing the organizational structures that set limits on how we work (Barr, 1998). In addition, institutions must "develop a systematic institutional capacity to gather, evaluate, experiment with, conduct, and use research related to learning" (p. 25).

The reward system is also critical in supporting change. According to a study by the National Center on Postsecondary Teaching, Learning, and Assessment, researchers in higher education are rewarded more than teachers (Fairweather, 1993). Results showed that, for full-time tenure track faculty, the more time spent on teaching and instruction, the lower the salary; the more time spent in the classroom, the lower the salary; the more time spent doing research, the higher the salary; and the more publications one had, the higher the salary. Because rewards are effective in changing behavior, institutions must begin to reward teaching that leads to enhanced learning if the shift to a learner-centered paradigm is to succeed.

According to Kerr (1995), numerous examples exist of reward systems that reinforce undesirable behaviors while ignoring those that are desirable. For example, we hope for teamwork and collaboration, but we reward the best members. We hope for innovative thinking and risk taking, but we reward avoiding errors. We hope for the development of people skills, but we reward technical advancements. We hope for employee involvement and empowerment, but we keep a tight control over operations and resources. We hope for high achievement, but we reward another year of the same effort and work. In higher education, we hope for effective teaching and enhanced learning, but we reward research, particularly when hiring, promoting, and granting tenure.

Finally, in order to shift successfully to the learner-centered paradigm, we need leaders who are willing to lead our institutions through a process of transformation despite the disruption and conflict that will result (Barr, 1998). Leaders will have to be prepared to "dismantle" (p. 25) and restructure the institution, its processes, and its systems in order to move from the teacher-centered to the learner-centered paradigm.

> *The two paradigms are simply inconsistent. They are not points along the same continuum . . . [Avoiding the disruption associated with change] will merely be another expression of the dominant paradigm in which talk about change is regarded as change itself (p. 25).*

Reflections

As you create your own meaning from the ideas in this section, begin to think about . . .

- What factors in my environment support developing a new view of teaching and learning?

- How likely is it that I will have to shift paradigms alone?
- Do I see myself as an independent wave or as part of the ocean?

CREATING AN ASSESSMENT MINDSET

What can we do while waiting for the transformational leader to arrive? How can the institution facilitate the process of shifting to a new paradigm? For the benefit of those readers brave enough to take on the challenge of reform and for those fortunate enough to teach at a learner-centered institution, we offer some suggestions for creating an assessment mindset.

One suggestion is that administrators take the leadership to promote the concept of assessment. Administrators can continually teach and remind faculty about key concepts and procedures in learner-centered teaching and assessment. They can help faculty understand the connections between assessment and learning. They can lead faculty in discussing important issues that are central to effective learning. This means that they may need to learn more about current learning theory and assessment themselves. Learning about principles of continuous improvement will also be of benefit, not only for the learning process but also for the functioning of the institution itself. (A more extended discussion of administrator roles in assessment was included in Chapter 3.)

Another suggestion is that faculty and/or administrators seek to create effective faculty development programs targeted at the improvement of teaching. According to Licklider, Schnelker, and Fulton (1997), this means providing sustained support for faculty over time because research has clearly shown that single session interventions (e.g., workshops, short courses) have little effect on behavior.

Effective faculty development programs are based on adult learning theory and research in the area of staff development (Licklider, *et al.*, 1997). Adult learning theory provides several principles for designing effective faculty development programs. The first is that professors are self-directed learners who "will initiate efforts to improve, will make their own decisions about what they want to learn and how learning should occur, and will pursue learning apart from sponsored efforts" (Licklider, *et al.*, 1997, p. 122). This implies that faculty must play an active role in determining the goals and setting the agenda for the faculty development program in which they participate.

The chief role of the facilitator in an effective faculty development program is to create an environment in which self-directed learners can flourish (Licklider, *et al.*, 1997). This involves directing and pacing the program according to participant needs rather than according to a preordained agenda. Attending to participant needs implies that participants must be increasingly involved in making decisions about the program and that the program should emerge and be developed around their own experiences. Participants must participate actively rather than by listening to lectures. A final and critical role of the facilitator is to use the type of group leadership skills that create a safe environment marked by trust and honest communication.

A second principle that derives from adult learning theory is that professors seeking to change their teaching practice will benefit from an opportunity to reflect critically on what they know about teaching and how they have developed their knowledge about teaching (Brookfield, 1995; Duffy & Jones, 1995). Reflection will help them understand how they teach and why they teach the way they do. Palmer (1993) suggests, for example, that faculty identify metaphors and images that represent their own approach to teaching and that they identify great teachers who influenced their own decision to become professors.

Another component of faculty development that derives from adult learning theory is the importance of community in learning.

As Palmer (1993) notes, members of the professoriat belong to one of the few professions that do not engage in continuing conversations with colleagues. This "privatization of teaching" has had negative consequences for faculty, leading to isolation and dissatisfaction, and for institutions, making it difficult for academe to improve student learning (Licklider, et al., 1997, p. 123)

Gabelnick, MacGregor, Matthews, and Smith (1990) contend that faculty members react positively when they have opportunities to discuss their teaching with colleagues. Involvement in learning communities and team teaching can be quite rewarding, as evidenced in the following testimonial.

Meeting other faculty in a context of discussing teaching is exhilarating. I'm more enthused about teaching than I've been in years and it's all about rediscovering myself as a learner. Without knowing it, I'd divorced myself from expanding in my field and in my teaching. All the interesting parts of my life were outside the college. I was putting in time so I could be elsewhere. I've learned again something that I knew long ago as an undergraduate. I enjoy learning for its own sake. It makes you feel good and alive. Working with other faculty has been the key to this awakening (Gabelnick, et al., 1990, p. 82).

Faculty development programs should seek to create this type of awakening by including a variety of types of social interaction among participants. These could include large and small group discussions, role-play and simulations in which participants react and give feedback to each other, and cooperative groups or learning partners that meet both during and outside formal meetings in which members discuss, reflect, and solve teaching-related problems together.

One reflective tool that could form the basis of group reflections is the teacher learning audit (Brookfield, 1995). It can be completed on a course or annual basis, but the focus is on identifying skills, knowledge, and insights recently gained. Even when faculty teach two sections of the same course during the same term, their experiences and outcomes vary. Routinely completing the teacher learning audit helps a professor gain insights into why the learning that occurred in each section is unique. The teacher learning audit is flexible, but common questions would include those illustrated in Figure 9–1.

The teacher learning audit encourages professors to think of themselves as learners about teaching, something that is important if they are to remain engaged in their work. Self-reflection is important in giving professors an accurate sense of how they change and learn. Knowing this information can help professors decide how to use available resources for improvement.

The critical incident technique is another reflective tool that encourages professors to reflect on their practice in order to learn from their experiences

---

Instructions

Please think back over the past term/year in your life as a teacher and complete the following sentences as honestly as you can.

1. Compared with this time last term/year, I now know that . . .

2. Compared with this time last term/year, I am now able to . . .

3. Compared with this time last term/year, I could now teach a colleague how to . . .

4. The most important thing I have learned about my students in the past term/year is . . .

5. The most important thing I have learned about my teaching in the past term/year is . . .

6. The most important thing I have learned about myself in the past term/year is . . .

7. The assumptions I had about teaching and learning that have been most confirmed for me in the past term/year are that . . .

8. The assumptions I had about teaching and learning that have been most challenged for me in the past term/year are that . . .

As you read through the responses to these open-ended statements, you can start sorting them by asking yourself a series of questions:

How much of your learning is in an entirely new area?

How much of the learning is a refinement, rethinking, or adaptation of something you already know or can do?

Is the learning of no great significance or does some of it appear to be transformative?

How much of the learning confirms your existing practices and assumptions?

How much of the learning challenges your typical ways of thinking and teaching?

Continued

FIGURE 9–1   Sample Teacher Learning Audit

Try to think about how you learned whatever you have identified. What triggered each of your learnings—a crisis, a directive from some external source, a personal feeling of dissatisfaction with your present practice, a desire to experiment for the fun of it, your identification of a gap to be filled or a discrepancy to be resolved, a chance event, or some other cause?

What methods did you use—trial-and-error experimentation, personal reflection, observation of colleagues, private individual study, or something else? Did you learn through your involvement with a group team effort, or in a self-directed way? Was conversation with others important, or did you learn through print or visual media (for example, videocassettes)? To what extent was your learning serendipitous and to what extent was it planned?

(Brookfield, 1995, pp. 75–76)

FIGURE 9–1   (*Continued*)

(Brookfield, 1995). Although it can be used by individuals alone, it is particularly useful in starting a conversation with other faculty members for the purpose of gaining self-knowledge. Whether used individually or used in discussion groups, questions are asked that cause teachers to reflect on their practices and attitudes about their work. Examples of questions are:

- *Reflect on the past week (month, semester). Choose an incident that made you say to yourself, "This is what makes my life as a teacher so difficult." Write some notes about the incident including details of when, where, who, and what.*
- *Reflect on the past week (month, semester). Select an incident that made you say to yourself, "This is what teaching is all about." Write some notes about the incident so that you understand why this event was so significant.*

When faculty discuss their responses with each other, they discover common themes to pursue and examine. They also learn that their own experiences are not completely unique.

The critical incident approach helps professors to both celebrate their work and make needed changes for improvement. Small wins and the unexpected pleasures that intrinsically reward people in the field of teaching should be recognized, but opportunities to improve should not be overlooked (Brookfield, 1995). When the focus is on improvement alone, it is easy to focus only on the negative and to overlook the positive aspects of teaching.

Reflections

As you create your own meaning from the ideas in this section, begin to think about . . .

- What institution-wide support do my colleagues and I have for our assessment efforts?
- How do administrators support us in our assessment efforts?

- Which of the self-reflection techniques appeal the most to me?
- What would be the best way for me to practice the art of self-reflection?
- How would I feel about being part of a group of colleagues that reflected about teaching together?

MAKING A COMMITMENT TO CHANGE

Are you ready to make a commitment to change? This final question of the book is one that only you can answer. We will simply point out that nothing different will happen in your teaching unless you are willing to change. For some readers, change will take place in an environment of support and collegiality. Although challenging, the experience of transformation will be shared with others and approved by your institution. For others, transformation will be a relatively solitary process, and those readers may need to seek support off-campus, perhaps by attending professional meetings devoted to assessment such as the annual Assessment Conference sponsored by the American Association of Higher Education.

In either case, you might take comfort in the continual reminder of one of our colleagues that "assessment is a journey, not a destination" (T. Polito, personal communication, 1998). The most important decision is to begin the trip and not turn back. Like most journeys, even those that are most carefully planned, this one will offer unexpected companions at different points along the way. Surprising and unplanned opportunities will crop up when you least expect them. Your students will travel with you, and a learner-centered approach to assessment should result in greater appreciation for them as people and as learners. In addition, students will appreciate you more as a teacher because of their engagement and increased ownership of the learning process.

We hope you will take this book along on your journey and use it flexibly as a travel guide—it's not meant to sit on a shelf. We wish you Bon Voyage, and we offer you our best wishes as you continue to explore the meaning of learning and teaching in your life.

TRY SOMETHING NEW

1. Complete the Teacher Learning Audit or the Critical Incident Questionnaire described in this chapter and evaluate what you learn from doing so.
2. Find out if there is a group of faculty members on campus who meet regularly to dialogue about teaching practices and experiences. If so, attend one of their meetings to see if this reflection format is helpful to you.
3. If you find out that there is no group that meets to discuss teaching on your campus, consider how you could start one.
4. Think about what you would like to do as a result of reading this book. Make a list of three things you will do in the next month and prioritize them in terms of their importance to you.

REFERENCES

Ackoff, R. L. (1993). *Ackoff's fables*. New York: John Wiley & Sons.

Albom, M. (1997). *Tuesdays with Morrie*. New York: Doubleday.

Barr, R. B. (1998, September–October). Obstacles to implementing the learning paradigm—What it takes to overcome them. *About Campus*, 18–25.

Brookfield, S. (1995). *Becoming a critically reflective teacher*. San Francisco: Jossey–Bass.

Duffy, D. K., & Jones, J. W. (1995). *Teaching within the rhythms of the semester*. San Francisco: Jossey–Bass.

Engelkemeyer, S. W., & Brown, S. C. (1998, October). Powerful partnerships: A shared responsibility for learning. *AAHE Bulletin*, 10–12.

Fairweather, J. (1993). *Teaching, research, and faculty rewards: A summary of the research findings of the faculty profile project*. University Park, PA: National Center on Postsecondary Teaching, Learning, and Assessment.

Gabelnick, F., MacGregor, J., Matthews, R. S., & Smith, B. L. (1990). Learning communities: Creating connections among students, faculty, and disciplines. *New Directions for Teaching and Learning, 41*. San Francisco: Jossey–Bass.

Hutchings, P. (1998, July–August). Pursuing improvement. *About Campus*, 2–5.

Kerr, S. (1995). On the folly of rewarding A, while hoping for B. *Academy of Management Executives, 9* (1), 7–14.

Kuh, G. D. (1998, July–August). Lessons from the mountains. *About Campus*, 16–21.

Licklider, B. L., Schnelker, D. L., & Fulton, C. (1997). Revisioning faculty development for changing times: The foundation and framework. *Journal of Staff, Program, and Organizational Development, 15* (3), 121–133.

Marchese, T. (1998, September). Restructure?! You bet! *AAHE Bulletin*, 3–6.

Muncey, D. E., & McQuillan, P. J. (1993). Preliminary findings from a five-year study of the Coalition of Essential Schools. *Phi Delta Kappan, 74* (6), 486–489.

Palmer, P. (1993). Good talk about good teaching: Improving teaching through conversation and community. *Change, 6*, 8–14.

Robbins, A. (1991). *Awaken the giant from within*. New York: Simon & Schuster.

Warren, R. G. (1997, March–April). Engaging students in active learning. *About Campus*, 16–20.

Index